IN PRAISE OF WH[A...]

IN PRAISE OF WHAT
PERSISTS

Also by Stephen Berg

POETRY

THE DAUGHTERS

NOTHING IN THE WORD

GRIEF

WITH AKHMATOVA AT THE BLACK GATES

TRANSLATIONS

SUNSTONE BY OCTAVIO PAZ

CLOUDED SKY BY MIKLÓS RADNÓTI
(translated with Steven Polgar and S. J. Marks)

OEDIPUS THE KING
(translated with Diskin Clay)

ANTHOLOGIES

NAKED POETRY AND NEW NAKED POETRY
(with Robert Mezey)

ABOUT WOMEN
(with S. J. Marks)

In Praise of
What Persists

Stephen Berg, Editor

HARPER COLOPHON BOOKS
Harper & Row, Publishers
New York, Cambridge, Philadelphia, San Francisco,
London, Mexico City, São Paulo, Sydney

A hardcover edition of this book is published by Harper & Row, Publishers, Inc.

Copyright acknowlegments appear on page 290.

IN PRAISE OF WHAT PERSISTS. Copyright © 1983 by Stephen Berg. All rights reserved. Printed in the United States of America. No part of this book may be used or reproduced in any manner whatsoever without written permission except in the case of brief quotations embodied in critical articles and reviews. For information address Harper & Row, Publishers, Inc., 10 East 53rd Street, New York, N.Y. 10022. Published simultaneously in Canada by Fitzhenry & Whiteside Limited, Toronto.

First HARPER COLOPHON edition published 1984.

Library of Congress Cataloging in Publication Data
Main entry under title:

In praise of what persists.

1. Authors, America—20th century—Biography—Addresses, essays, lectures. 2. American literature—20th century—History and criticism—Addresses, essays, lectures. I Berg, Stephen.
PS129.I5 1983   811'.54'09 [B]   81-47651
ISBN 0-06-091123-9

84 85 86 87 88 10 9 8 7 6 5 4 3 2 1

Contents

Introduction vii

MAX APPLE   A Love Affair with the Lingo 1

DAVID BRADLEY   The Faith 9

WESLEY BROWN   You Talk Like You Got Books in Your Jaws 19

HAYDEN CARRUTH   The Formal Idea of Jazz 24

RAYMOND CARVER   Fires 33

ROBERT COLES   The Bible and the Puritans 45

ROBERT COOVER   The Last Quixote 56

GEORGE DENNISON   In Praise of What Persists 69

CAROLYN FORCHÉ   El Salvador: An Aide-Mémoire 93

TESS GALLAGHER   My Father's Love Letters 109

JOHN GARDNER   Cartoons 125

JOHN HAWKES   Dark Landscapes 135

EDWARD HOAGLAND   On Becoming a Writer 148

RICHARD HUGO   The Anxious Fields of Play 157

LEONARD MICHAELS   The Chinese Girl 177

CYNTHIA OZICK   The Lesson of the Master 181

GRACE PALEY   A Conversation with My Father 188

REYNOLDS PRICE   For Ernest Hemingway 194

DAVE SMITH   An Honest Tub 222

TED SOLOTAROFF   A Few Good Voices in Your Head 239

GILBERT SORRENTINO   Genetic Coding 252

GERALD STERN   Some Secrets 256

C. K. WILLIAMS   Beginnings 267

PAUL ZWEIG   A Voice Speaking to No One 281

v

Introduction

The question of literary influence is at the center of critical thinking these days. One approach, much in vogue, is Harold Bloom's
concept of "anxiety": the impact of one writer on another is such
that the latter experiences it as an impingement on his autonomy.
To free himself, he unconsciously misreads the work of the mentor
or father figure so as to hide its influence from himself and his
readers, while continuing to draw on it as a source of creative
energy. Heady stuff! Though this variation of Oedipal rivalry is a
departure from the standard notion of literary indebtedness as a
more or less accurate and conscious appropriation of ideas, tech-
niques, tone of voice, and so forth, it is still no less academic in its
import. It quarantines the writer in the literary scholar's world of
books. Even when brilliantly expressed, Bloom's thesis strikes me
as only a small part of an unfinishable truth; at other times it seems
only another example of how critics deal with their own anxiety
about being original, of how much they need, unconsciously, to
displace their writer's performance by an ingenious interpretation
of it.

Well, then, why not ask a range of fiction writers, poets, and
essayists to write about what *they* believe has influenced their
work? That would not only reveal each writer's own special way
of seeing influence; it would provide an adventure for readers
whose interest in a writer's work is also an interest in the writer
—how he wrote a particular story, novel, poem, critical piece;
why he writes the way he does; what experiences have made him
the writer that he is. And, as literary criticism, it might break
fresh ground at the source and give readers a sense of the variety, the personal unfixed truths, the connections at the heart of a
poet's or novelist's work, and point up the vanity of generalizing

too far beyond the evidence of the writer's own testimony.

A writer's acknowledgment of his or her influences is part and parcel of the generosity and clarity of the act of writing itself. Hence most writers are remarkably forthright in declaring their literary ancestors and typically have fresh and acute things to say about their work. They also know that the creative act is one of the most mysterious of all human activities. There is, in fact, an aspect of creating that can only be accounted for by a notion such as inspiration. Writers and artists know better than anyone that the phenomenon of inspiration is essentially impossible to explain, and that no amount of critical theorizing or introspection will account for the mysterious sources and transformations of their imagination.

Nevertheless, whenever I read something that moves me I want to know in the simplest sense how the author wrote it, why it turned out as it did, where it came from. I want the author to tell me. Only the person who created what I love will do. We look for the author's inspiration because his work inspires us. But the author himself can only do what we, as grateful readers, try to do. Again, they don't know any more than readers do about the inviolable core of their identity as poets, novelists, essayists. But they do know what influences silhouette, as it were, that mysterious core, and they know it better than anyone. They can reach back into their experience, reconstruct and connect events, faces, books, gestures, impasses and transcendences in a limited attempt to define the conditions which, they come to discover and believe, have formed their work.

As I hoped they would, the essays in *In Praise of What Persists* restate, expand, and illuminate the question of literary influence. These essays are notably varied, for the authors were encouraged to rethink the subject of influence in the light of their own experience and of their way of interpreting that experience. Indeed, it was usually only when the question was reopened in this manner that most of them agreed to contribute.

Grace Paley comes to the question through a conversation at his bedside with her dying father, whose old-fashioned humanity is both a distraction from and yet finally the ground of her own fiction. Gerald Stern yearns for the literary father he never had and tells us what it was like to go on writing poetry detached from any literary community at all. Leonard Michaels reveals the power his wife's dreams have to affect his work. Carolyn Forché reports on how her notions of poetry were altered by the terrifying, brutal nightmare of her two years in El Salvador. Robert Coles's involvement in the civil rights movement links up with his New England Protestant background to form the matrix of his vocation as a writer. In Dave Smith's case, it comes from his association with Virginia watermen, while for Richard Hugo it lies in his years of playing industrial-league softball in Seattle and being sexually inhibited. David Bradley describes the permanent impact of listening as a boy to the rhetoric of black sermons, those of his father and of other vivid, eloquent preachers. C. K. Williams discusses books but remembers Louis Kahn, the architect, as his first true influence. For Max Apple, growing up in a Yiddish-speaking household and being enamored of a famous ventriloquist's dummy catalyzed his use of the American language.

While it is true that older writers figure as powerful influences on the work of some of the contributors, their choices tend to be as unexpected and revealing as the non-literary discussions. Southerner Reynolds Price's thorough, passionate essay shows him to be the son of Hemingway rather than of Faulkner, while Robert Coover finds in the temperament and drifting inconsolable precisions and futilities of Samuel Beckett and Cervantes his true literary soil as an ontological satirist. And Cynthia Ozick analyzes her early trials as a writer trying to learn James's Lesson of the Master by imitating artistic greatness, and traces the pain of discovering, later in life, that:

The great voices of Art never mean *only* Art; they also mean Life. . . . The true Lesson of the Master, then, is, simply, never to venerate what is complete . . . but instead to seek to be young while young, primitive while primitive, ungainly when ungainly—to look for crudeness and rudeness, to husband one's own stupidity or ungenius. . . . Rapture and homage are not the way. Influence is perdition.

As these essays make clear, so large is the variety of influence (among even this limited cross section of today's best writers) that the mystery of the phenomenon remains and grows richer and more complex as each writer defines it in his own way. And so individual are these pieces that they recall Proust's observation that as a human being grows he becomes more and more unique, not more and more like his fellows, and it is only his ability to share himself with others through his work that saves him, and them, from being isolated by the differences that make them unique. For Proust, writing is the ultimate way of revealing oneself—whose benefit is to keep us all in the same world, our own *and* that of others. "Art is awareness of life." With that sentence he offers us the most generous definition of art we have.

Hence it is not surprising that so many of these essays associate influence with the acquisition of this awareness. Wesley Brown remembers a speech delivered by Fanny Lou Hamer which fed his sense of the power he could have in "being able to articulate the encounter between your own life and the rest of the world." John Hawkes reveals the durable spell of an island, with its stories of child-molesting and the sexual trysts of the "Princess," which has beckoned to him in novel after novel. Raymond Carver finds that what most made him persist as a writer were the pressures of parenting and of working "crap jobs," which forced him into writing stories. George Dennison's essay ranges freely over artistic, family, political, clinical, and dream experiences that have provided the "long-enduring memories" in which his acquisitions of consciousness and his values as a writer are deposited.

Dennison's essay, whose title, "In Praise of What Persists," I have taken for the collection as a whole, richly bears out Ezra Pound's point that

> nothing matters but the quality
> of the affection—
> in the end—that has carved the trace in the mind.

One after another of these essays demonstrates that if there is a single quality essential to locating and articulating artistic indebtedness, it is fidelity of feeling. Emotion—the action of the soul, the dangerous-to-reveal, dangerous-to-hide "substratum of our being," in T. S. Eliot's phrase, is what guides, corroborates, and anneals these self-revelations and nourishes their sense of communion. "A writer's job is to pour out his heart," writes Edward Hoagland at the end of his essay, in which he has been doing just that in describing his ties to three very different models: Steinbeck, Bellow, and his father. Or there is Tess Gallagher's full-hearted exposition of her family life, centering as it does around her father's love letters to her mother, which continue to provide the "blind, persistent hopefulness that carries me again and again into poems." Hayden Carruth's essay on the influence of jazz music on his poetry comes to rest on his testimony that the improvisations of John Coltrane, Miles Davis, Jo Jones, et al., lie behind the central conviction of his own art, that "Freedom and discipline concur / only in ecstasy." Ted Solotaroff describes how his passion for the task of criticism has flowed continually from "the good voice in his head" of Isaac Rosenfeld. Paul Zweig traces his quest for a personal voice from the pinched sonorities of his father's recitation of poetry, to the full range of emotion in "the rumbling grandmotherly voice" of his Indian guru. And Gilbert Sorrentino explores his mixed Irish and Italian heritage to confirm his belief that "one's influences are deeper than the 'merely' literary; are, indeed, at the core of one's life."

Beyond all the literary information and insight in these essays, one reads this book and is enlightened by its honesty and inspired by its warmth. Those qualities make it a book of friendship— between writer and writer, between writer and reader: ". . . meaning by friendship the frank unreserve, as before another human being, of thoughts and sensations: the objectless and necessary sincerity of one's innermost life trying to re-act upon the profound sympathies of another existence." Thank Joseph Conrad for those faithful words. Throughout these pages you will find them exemplified again and again.

STEPHEN BERG

IN PRAISE OF WHAT PERSISTS

A Love Affair with the Lingo

MAX APPLE

"I live in the midst of Houston with my two children. As I approach the curve of middle age, I still want to play second base for the Detroit Tigers, write like Tolstoy, and enjoy the fruit of my labor."

I grew up in the heyday of ventriloquism. The dummy Jerry Mahoney was everyone's sweetheart. You could hardly go a day without hearing a joke about buttoning your lip or having a wooden head.

On the playground of my elementary school I practiced with all my might. I kept my lips close to the chain-link fence so that if they moved I would know it by the cold steel against them. My friends were doing the same. Two decades early, our playground was a herald of transcendental meditation. We were six years old, saying "om" to the fence, each of us hoping for our own dummy, a dummy who would supply all the punch lines, leaving us forever free to roam the playground practicing voice control.

Finally I got my dummy. An elderly cousin, moved by the seriousness of my tight-lipped practice, sent me an expensive one, a three-foot-high Jerry Mahoney in a cowboy outfit and an embossed half-face smile. But by the time my Jerry arrived he was too late; ventriloquism had already faded. The contestants on *The Original Amateur Hour* went back to thigh slapping and whistling through combs. My schoolmates, too, abandoned loneliness against the fence for kickball and pulling girls' hair. My dummy languished then as my wok and my food processor do now.

It took another twenty years for me to cast my voice again, this time into stories rather than dummies. It's a weak analogy, I know,

1

and yet fiction seems sometimes like my dummy, like that part of myself that should get all the best lines. I want to be the "straight man" so that the very difference between us will be a part of the tension that I crave in each sentence, in every utterance of those wooden lips redeemed from silence because I practiced.

Yet the voice from the silence, the otherness that fiction is, doesn't need any metaphoric explanations. It's true that I tried ventriloquism, but it was my fascination with the English language itself that made me a writer. Its coyness has carried me through many a plot, entertained me when nothing else could. If not for love of words, I couldn't have managed eighth grade sitting next to Wayne Bruining during lunch, listening to the details of his escapades as a hunter. These were not adventure stories of life in the wild; they were the drab minutiae of taxidermy. While I held an oily tuna sandwich, Wayne lectured on how to skin a squirrel. He brought pelts to school and supplied the entire class with rabbits' feet. As Wayne droned on, I wondered in all the words that were new to me if he hunted in fens, glades, moors, vales, and dales. Though his subject was gory, Wayne was a good teacher. I could probably skin a squirrel, based on my memory of his conversations. I imagine that Wayne is still at it somewhere deep in the Michigan woods, showing his own son how to position a dressed buck over the hood of the car and then wipe the knife clean on the outside of his trousers.

My grandmother had a word for Wayne and most of my other friends: *goyim.* It explained everything. The hunting, the hubcap stealing, the smoking, the fighting—all were universal gentile attributes. *Goy* was a flat, almost unemotional word, but it defined everything I was not. There was some difficulty. Grand Rapids, Michigan, in the 1950s was not an East European ghetto, although my grandma did her best to blur the distinctions. The First World War and poverty had moved her from her Lithuanian village, but even forty years in the wilderness of America did not make her learn English. She chose, above all, to avoid the language of the goyim. I told her about Wayne and everything else in Yiddish, which was the natural language of talking. I remember being surprised in kindergarten that everything happened in English. To us, English was the official language, useful perhaps for legal documents and high school graduation speeches, but not for everyday life.

My grandmother and I were quite a pair in the supermarket. Proud that I could read, I read all pertinent labels to her in loud Yiddish. The two of us could spend a long time in aisle four at the A & P over the differences between tomato paste and tomato sauce, while all around us gentiles roamed, loading their carts with what we knew were slabs of pork and shotgun shells. We wondered at them, these folks who could eat whatever they wanted and kill their own chickens. My grandma never learned English or strayed very far from her house, but she did glean from the gentiles a lust for technology. Our big nineteenth-century kitchen, which was also my playroom and her salon, was loaded with the latest. Before anyone else, we had an oven with a see-through door, a rotisserie, a Formica-topped dinette, and a frost-free refrigerator. The technology, though clearly "goyish," was never tainted. Sometimes I would come into the kitchen to find my grandmother admiring the simplest object, a cast-aluminum frying pan or a Corning Ware baking dish. Our kitchen needed only a wood-burning stove to become the kitchen in every Russian novel, yet in that old-fashioned place all the wonders of modern America blossomed. My grandmother never trusted the gentiles, but because of the way she savored kitchen gadgets, I know that at some time, probably before I was born, she gave up her fear of pogroms and settled down to take in, through translation and bargains, the available pleasures.

While she daydreamed in Yiddish and Americanized her domain, my grandfather worked in the American Bakery, among ovens that could bake two hundred loaves at once. He wore a white shirt, white trousers, a white apron, and a white cap. His hair was white and fine-textured. Puffs of flour emanated from him as he walked toward me. The high baking tables, the smell of the bread, the flour floating like mist, gave the bakery a kind of angelic feeling. In the front, two clerks sold the bread and customers talked in plain English. In the back, where the dough was rising, my grandpa yelled in Yiddish and Polish, urging his fellow bakers always to hurry. He went to the bakery long before dawn and would sometimes work twenty-four nonstop hours. He was already in his seventies. Twenty-four hours he considered part time. He did not bake what you might think; the American Bakery was true to its name. My grampa toiled over white bread, sticky air-filled white bread, and cookies shaped like Christmas trees, green at the

edges, blood red in the middle. He baked cakes for Polish wed-
dings and doughnuts by the millions. My grandmother preferred
store-bought baked goods. She accused him of pissing in the
dough. Their ghetto curses and old-world superstitions interrupted *I Love Lucy* and *The $64,000 Question.* He wished upon her
a great cholera, a boil in her entrails, a solipsism deeper than
despair.

My mother spent her energy running the household. My father earned our living as a scrap dealer. His work meant driving
long distances in order to buy, and then to load upon his short-
wheel-base Dodge, tons of steel shavings, aluminum borings, de-
fective machinery—anything that could eventually be melted back
to a more pristine condition. I rode with him when he didn't have
to go very far. I had a pair of leather mittens, my work gloves,
which I wore as I strutted among the barrels of refuse at the back
of factories. I touched the dirtied metals, I wanted to work as my
father did, using his strength to roll the barrels from the loading
dock to the truck. When he came home he washed his hands with
Boraxo, then drank a double shot of Seagram's Seven from a
long-stemmed shot glass. I imitated him with Coke or ginger ale.
He alone knew what I wanted and loved. My grandfather wanted
me to be a rabbinic scholar, my grandmother thought I should own
at least two stores, my sisters and my mother groomed me for a
career as a lawyer or "public speaker." My father knew that I
wanted to play second base for the Tigers and have a level swing
like Al Kaline. I probably love and write about sports so much as
a way of remembering him. I carry baseball with me always the way
he carried my mittens in the glove compartment of a half-dozen
trucks to remind him of his little boy who grew up to study the
secrets of literature but still does not forget to check the Tigers'
box score every morning of the season.

When I was not listening to the Tigers or playing baseball or
basketball myself, I was reading. A tunnel under Bridge Street
connected the Catholic school, next to the American Bakery, to the
west side branch of the public library. I don't know what use the
Catholic school made of the tunnel, but it was my lifeline. I would
have a snack at the bakery, then move through the tunnel to reap-
pear seconds later in that palatial library. In the high-ceilinged
reading room I sat at a mahogany table. Across the street, my

grampa in the heat of the ovens was yelling at Joe Post in Polish
and at Philip Allen in Yiddish; here the librarians whispered in
English and decorated me with ribbons like a war hero, just because I loved to read. The books all in order, the smiling ladies to
approve me, the smooth tables, even the maps on the wall seemed
perfect to me. The marble floors of that library were the stones of
heaven, my Harvard and my Yale, my refuge in the English language. What I learned from those boys' books was indeed American Literature. Wayne Bruining skinning squirrels was too close,
too ugly, too goyish. But in the aura of the reading room, *The Kid
from Tomkinsville* and *Huckleberry Finn* were my true buddies. I
wanted to bedeck them with ribbons the way the librarians decorated me, or better yet, take them through the tunnel for a quick
doughnut at the bakery.

When I came home from the library I sometimes told my
grandmother in Yiddish about the books. We wondered together
about space travel and the speed of light and life on other planets.
If there was life on other worlds, she thought it was only the souls
of the dead. She urged me to read less and think about someday
owning my own store.

I think it was in that library that I finally came to distinguish
the separateness of the Yiddish and English languages. I could
speak and think in both, but reading and writing was all English.
I specialized in reading and writing as if to solidify once and for
all the fact that the written language was mine.

My sisters found the language through speaking. They won "I
Speak for Democracy" contests; they were the Yankees and Dodg-
ers of debate tournaments. I could barely hit my weight in Little
League, but their speech trophies lined the windowsills like mold.
They stood in front of our gilded dining room mirror, speaking
earnestly and judging their looks at the same time. They used their
arms to gesture, they quoted *Time* magazine, their bosoms heaved.
My mother stopped her chores to swoon at her lovely daughters.
My grandma thought their padded bras were a clever way to keep
warm. Patrick Henry himself could not have outdone the rhetoric
in our dining room.

My sisters wanted it for me too, that state championship in
debate which seemed automatic just because we spoke English. I
resisted the temptation as a few years later I resisted law school.

I admired my sisters before the mirror and I, too, longed to understand *Time* magazine, but I didn't want to win anything with my
words. I just wanted to play with them. I was already in love.
Instead of debate, I took printing.

I, too, made words, but words laboriously made, words composed on a "stick," with "leads" and "slugs," words spelled out
letter by letter with precise spacing—words that had to be read,
not heard.

My hero was Ben Franklin. On his tombstone it said only:
"Ben Franklin Printer."

"Did he make a living?" my grandmother wanted to know.

"He made the country. He and George Washington and Alexander Hamilton, they made the whole country."

"Go on," she said. "You believe everything they tell you in
school."

I did believe everything I learned, but I listened to her too.
Her stories were sometimes about the very things I studied. She
had lived through the Russian Revolution. In a house in Odessa,
a shoemaker's daughter, she waited out the war until she could join
her baker husband, already sporting two-tone shoes and a gold
watch on the shores of Lake Michigan.

She had no political ideology; the Czar and the Communists
were equally barbarous in her eyes. Once, though, she did hide a
young Jew pursued by the Czar's police. It was my favorite story.
To me, that young Russian became Trotsky himself hiding for half
an hour among my grandmother's wedding aprons, feather beds,
long-sleeved dresses, and thick combs, the very objects I hid
among in our Michigan attic.

She didn't care about Trotsky or Ben Franklin, only about her
grandson, who she thought was making a mistake by becoming a
scribe rather than a merchant. Only once, shortly before she died,
did I convince my grandmother that being a scribe was not my
intention. "I make things up—I don't just copy them."

"I've been doing that all my life," she told me. "Everyone can
do that."

In a way she was right: making things up is not very difficult;
the difficulty is getting the sentences to sound exactly right.

I would still prefer to be the ventriloquist—to let the words
come from a smiling dummy across the room, but I'm not good

enough at buttoning my lip. An awkward hesitant clumsy sentence emerges. I nurse it, love it in all its distress. I see in it the hope of an entire narrative, the suggestion of the fullness of time. I write a second sentence and then I cross out that first one as if it never existed. This infidelity is rhythm, voice, finally style itself. It is a truth more profound to me than meaning, which is always elusive and perhaps belongs more to the reader.

Jacob wrestled with angels and I with sentences. There's a big difference, I know. Still, to me they are angels, this crowd of syllables. My great-uncle who came from the Russian army in 1909 straight to the American West told me he never had to really learn English. "I knew Russian," he said. "English was just like it." He bought horses, cattle, land. He lived ninety years and when he died he left me his floor safe, which sits now, all 980 pounds, alongside me in the room where I write. My eight-year-old daughter knows the combination, but there is nothing inside.

I don't know if that's a trope too—that safe that comforts me almost as if there were a way to be safe. There is no safety—not for my uncle, not for my sentences so quickly guillotined, not for me either. Yet I wish for the security of exact words, the security I knew as a four-year-old reciting the Gettysburg Address at patriotic assemblies in the Turner School auditorium.

I learned the Gettysburg Address from a book of great American documents that my father found in the scrap. It was a true found poem; Lincoln's cadences thrilled me long before I knew what they meant. Abe Lincoln was as anonymous to me as that Russian hiding in my grandmother's boudoir, but I could say his words, say them in English, in American, and as I said them the principal wept and teachers listened in awe to such a little boy reciting those glorious words. My parents coached me in Yiddish as they taught me to say "Four score and seven years ago," but I know that they wanted me to be an American, to recite the Gettysburg Address to prove beyond a doubt that I was an insider to this new lingo, to prove that our whole family understood, through my words, that somehow we had arrived, feather beds and all, to live next door to squirrel skinners.

Perhaps my grandmother was right. A store or two, or even a law office, makes a lot more sense than a love affair with words. At least in a business your goods and services are all there, all out in the open, and most of the time you even see your customers. To confront them and know what you're selling—those are pleasures the writer rarely knows. Believe me, reader, I would like to know you. Most of the time I am just like you, curled up on the sofa hoping not to be distracted, ready to enter someone else's fabric of words just as you are now in mine.

If I had you here I would serve tea, though not with the chunks of sugar my grandparents used—just plain old tea bags in water not quite hot enough. I would ask all about you and listen to everything. You might be surprised by how interested I am in you. After all, we are a couple waltzing down this page, my lead now, but yours when we meet.

Across the room from me, the safe is stuck half open. My son's tiny socks lie beside it, my daughter's lovely drawing of a horse, the sky, a cloud, and a flower. I wish I could tell you more, and I will perhaps in stories and novels: there I'll tell you more than I know. There I'll conjure lives far richer than mine, which is so pedestrian that it would make you seem heroic were you here beside me. Take comfort, though, in these sentences. They came all the way from Odessa at the very least and have been waiting a long time. To you they're entertainment; to me, breath.

The Faith

DAVID BRADLEY

David Bradley is the author of two novels, *South Street* (1975) and *The Chaneysville Incident* (1981). He has written nonfiction articles and reviews for the *Village Voice, Savvy, Signature,* the *Washington Post, Book World,* and the *New York Times Book Review.* He is currently associate professor of English at Temple University. His father, David Henry Bradley, was a minister in the African Methodist Episcopal Zion Church.

One evening not long ago I found myself sitting on a stage in front of a live audience, being asked questions about life and art. I was uncomfortable, as I always am in such circumstances. Still, things were going pretty well on this occasion, until the interviewer noted that my father had been a minister, and asked what influence religion, the church and the faith of my father, had had on my development as a writer. After a moment of confusion, I responded that since I had, at various times and with more than a modicum of accuracy, been labeled a heretic, a pagan, a heathen, and a moral degenerate, all things considered, the faith of my father had had very little to do with my writing. Which was, depending on how cynical you want to be, either a total lie or as close as I could get to the truthful answer—which would have been: "Practically everything."

The history of my relationship to religion cannot be stated so simply as "My father was a minister." In fact, I am descended from a long line of ministers. The first was my great-grandfather, a freedman named Peter Bradley, who, in the early part of the nineteenth century, was licensed to preach by the African Methodist Episcopal Zion Church, one of two denominations formed at that time by blacks who were tired of the discrimination they were forced to endure in the regular Methodist Church. Peter's son, Daniel Francis, followed in his father's footsteps and then went a step further, becoming a presiding elder with administrative and spiritual responsibility over a number of churches in western Pennsylvania and Ohio. Daniel Francis's son, David, followed his father's footsteps, and then added a step of his own: he was elected a general officer of the denomination (a rank just below that of bishop), with the dual responsibility of traveling the country to run conferences and workshops in Christian education and of publishing the church's quasi-academic journal, the *A. M. E. Zion Quarterly Review,* tasks he performed without interruption for nearly thirty years. Since David was my father, it would seem reasonable to expect that I would carry on the family tradition. That I did not was a fact that was viewed with great relief by all those who knew me —including David senior. Nevertheless, my apostasy had its origins in the church. For because of my father's editorial functions, I grew up in a publishing house.

My earliest memories of excitement, bustle, and tension center on the process of mailing the 1,400- or 1,500-copy press run of the *Quarterly Review.* The books came in sweet-smelling and crisp from the printer, were labeled, bundled, and shipped out again in big gray-green musty mailbags labeled with the names of far-off states, a process that was sheer heaven to a three- or four-year-old and sheer hell for everybody else, especially my mother, who did the bulk of the work and had to give up a chunk of her house to the process.

In fact, the work of publishing the *Review* took up the whole house most of the time; it was just that work usually went on at a less frenetic rate. While my father was away, my mother, who was the subscription and shipping department, spent some time cleaning the lists (a constant task, since ministers, the main subscribers, were regularly being moved around) and typing names and addresses onto labels. When my father returned home, the tempo picked up. He spent a good bit of time in the study, writing to other ministers and prominent lay people to solicit articles and publishable sermons, and editing those that had already arrived. At that same time, he would be writing a bit himself, composing the two or three editorials that graced each issue.

The *Review,* while it was called a quarterly, was not published every three months, but rather four times a year; my father took it to the printer when he was home long enough to get it ready, and when the printer had time to do the work. The date for that was sometimes fixed only a week or so in advance, and once it was set, the tempo became fairly furious; my father spent more and more time in the study, selecting cover art, editing the late-arriving articles, rewriting the press releases from the National Council of Churches that he used for filler. Then, on the date designated, with the copy in one hand, and my hand in the other, my father would go to the printer.

I looked forward to going to the printer with my father, in part because of the printer himself, a venerable gentleman named George, the perfect image of a chapelman all the way down to his ink-stained knuckles and honest-to-God green eyeshade. The chapel over which he presided was no mere print shop, but the printing plant of the local daily, a dark cavern with an ink-impregnated wood floor and air that smelled of hot metal and chemicals, crowded with weirdly shaped machines. On the left a bank of linotypes spewed hot type and spattered molten lead onto the floor. On the right were machines to do the tasks that at home I saw done by hand—address labels, tie bundles, stuff envelopes. At the back, dominating the entire scene, was the great press on which the paper was printed, a big, black, awkward-looking thing that towered to the ceiling and descended into the bowels of the earth. Once George invited my father to bring me down at night to see the press roll, a sight that proved to be so exciting I could not tell if all the shaking was due to the awesome turning of the rollers or to the weakness in my knees; but usually we went to the printer during the day, and the big press was simply a silent presence.

During the visits to the printer, my father and George would be closeted in the little cubbyhole that served as George's office, while I had the run of the chapel. It was on one of those occasions, I believe, that any chance I would follow in the family footsteps was lost. For on this one day, while George and my father muttered of ems and ens, one of the linotype operators paused in his work and invited me to write my name on a scrap of paper, and after I had done so, let me watch as he punched my name out in hot lead. I think that was the moment when my personal die was cast.

Of course, it might have had no lasting effect had not my father, at about the same time, inadvertently introduced me to the corrupting pleasure of having written a book.

A few years before I was born, my father abandoned his studies at New York University, where he had been working for a Ph.D. in history. Five years later, for no reason other than desire, he took up the writing of what would have been his dissertation: "A History of the A. M. E. Zion Church."

I do not remember what it was like being around him while he wrote—I was, after all, less than five. I recall his methodology, which was to write a fairly detailed outline in a flowing longhand on lined paper, which he would store in a big loose-leaf binder until he was ready to turn it into a messy typescript which a typist —often my mother—later rendered as clean copy. (For one reason or another, this is the method I now use to write nonfiction.) I believe there was a certain heightening of tension during the time he was sending the typescript off to publishers; I know that he eventually entered into a cooperative arrangement with a press in Tennessee, a measure which forced him to take out a second mortgage—something I know he felt guilty about, since years later he would explain that we were not in better financial shape because of the book, but something he did not really regret, since he did it again in order to publish the second volume.

At the time the first volume was published, I was only six, but already I was in love with books. I had my own card at the public library, and I had read everything they had that was suitable for a child my age, and a lot that was not. Moreover, I had reread much of it many times, and the characters and stories had become so familiar, that my imagination was no longer a participant in the process; as a result, I had taken to imagining the people behind the characters. I was not old enough for literary biographies (the biographies written for children at that time went heavy on Clara Barton and Thomas Alva Edison and the like, and concentrated on the time when they were children; I loathed the things). And so I made up my own, based on bits of story I had picked up here and there. I was fascinated with Herman Melville and Richard Henry Dana, Jr., both of whom my mother said had actually gone to sea. And I was captivated by Jack London, who, my father told me, had really gone hunting gold in the frozen Yukon.

But even though I was taken with these people, I felt removed from them; they were not real—not as real, anyway, as the characters about whom they wrote. For I could imagine myself standing before the mast or trekking the frozen tundra, but I simply could not imagine myself writing a book.

But then one day a big tractor-trailer pulled up in the driveway and began to unload cartons, and my father, normally not an impulsive or a demonstrative man, took the first carton and ripped it open and pulled out a book that had his name stamped on the front board in gold foil, and suddenly the men behind the books I'd read were as real to me as my father. And suddenly I began to see that slug of type, which I had kept safe, mounted and inked, imprinting my name on a book.

I have always been uncertain about the importance of some of the things that have happened to me, suspecting that if one thing had not pushed me in the direction of writing, then probably something else would have. But I know the importance of that moment. For time and time again, people have said to me that the writing of a book is an impossible task, even to comprehend. For me, though, it was not only comprehensible, it was visible. And so, by the age of six or seven, I had firmly turned away from the family tradition. Ironically enough, at about the same time I began to discover the majesty and beauty of the Christian worship service.

When I was four or five, my father had started taking me with him on some of his travels, usually in the summer, when his work took him mostly to the Southeast. The first place I went with him —and it became a regular trip—was Dinwiddie, Virginia, where, in an aging ramshackle three-story building, the church operated an "Institute"—a combination Christian education workshop, summer camp, and revival meeting.

The Institute ran for three weeks—a week each for children, teenagers (what the church called "young people"), and adults. The format for all was basically the same: a day of classes punctuated by morning and noon chapel services, an afternoon recreation period, and three meals of good plain food—corn bread, grits, chicken, pork, greens—and climaxed by evening worship. The morning and afternoon worship services were short and pretty plain affairs. The evening service was pageantry, if for no other reason than that it was the focal point of everybody's day. My father's involvement was primarily with the "young people," and so I spent more time at the Institute when they were there. Evening worship was important to them because it was the closest they could get to a dating situation, and they made the most of it. It was important to the ministers, who shared the various offices of the service on a rotating basis, competing eagerly for the choice assignments, preaching and praying. It was important to the people in the community, who used the evening worship as a kind of camp meeting. And it was important to me, because the Institute was not equipped with a radio or a TV, and worse, had a limited number of books. (I was so desperate for reading matter I practically memorized the begats.) For me, evening worship was a source of entertainment.

It began with the arrival of the audience, the scrubbed youths and their chaperones, followed closely by the people from the community: the older ladies in out-of-fashion but immaculate dresses and toilet water; the men, seeming all of an age, with big rough hands poking out of the cuffs of suit coats worn awkwardly; the younger girls, in light dresses, casting flirtatious glances at the young men at the Institute (who were usually from cities, and therefore seen as sophisticated) and sharp challenging looks at the Institute's young women (who were also usually from the city, and therefore seen as probably a little wild). They would all troop into the dilapidated auditorium, filling the rows of ragtag seating— trestle benches, tip-up seats from abandoned theaters, folding chairs mended with cardboard, even a couple of mismatched church pews—and wait impatiently for the ministers.

The ministers entered from the front, moving more or less in time to the sound that came from an off-key, beaten-up piano. They were not unfamiliar figures—they were around all day, teaching classes, arguing points of theology and church politics, and playing Chinese checkers beneath the trees. Now they were solemn and dignified in black suits and clerical collars, each intent on performing his role, no matter how minor, with as much style as he could muster.

Performance was the word, for the service was high drama, from the solemnly intoned ritual invocation, to the rolling hymns sung by a hundred people who needed no hymnals, in passionate voices that overpowered the doubtful leadership of the gap-toothed piano, to the hucksterish importunings over the collection plate, as a minister would announce the total and then proceed to cajole, shame, or bully the audience into bringing it higher. There was no applause, of course, but the performance of each minister was rewarded with responses from the worshipers; the preaching and praying being applauded with a spontaneous chorus of "Amen, amen," "Yes, yes, yes," and the ultimate accolade, "Preach on, preach on." Which they did, sometimes until midnight.

I was overwhelmed by the worship services, not because I was religious, but because there was something innately compelling about the form and pacing and order of it: the slow, solemn beginning, the rhythms of song and responsive reading, the spontaneous lyricism, the sense of wholeness and cohesion and abandon when a preacher really got going, the perfection of catharsis when the end of the service flowed swiftly and smoothly to the benediction.

I have often wondered why my initial emotional response did not manifest itself as some kind of visible expression of faith—why, while I sang the hymns and was moved by the pageantry, I never gave myself over to witnessing or even made a journey to the altar to accept Jesus as my savior. I believe this was due to the example of my father, who found emotional religious expression embarrassing, and took an intellectual approach to religion, to anything. In any case, my love of worship expressed itself in an analytical way —I began to see it as a critical paradigm. The order of service, with its variations in pacing and mood, its combination of poetic and prosaic elements, of mysticism and hucksterism, became, to me, the model of what a dramatic experience should be. This led to my development of a critical consciousness: I began to judge worship services as good, or not so good. More important, from the point of view of a writer, I saw enough services that were not so good to develop an editorial sense, a feeling for when the prayer was becoming repetitive, when the hymn was wrong, when the minister failed to create a sermon that expanded upon the text. But more important than even that, I learned that the analytical, critical approach, while a useful means, was not, for me, an end.

For I had on a very few occasions seen a preacher, sometimes not a usually good preacher, create, perhaps with the aid of divine inspiration, a service or a sermon that defied criticism. Once I saw it happen to my father.

The year was 1965. By that time, our summer travels had taken my father and me beyond Virginia into North and South Carolina. Nevertheless, the format of the Christian education conventions we attended was the same as that at the Dinwiddie Institute. In one place, that year, they asked my father to preach.

I was not overly excited by the prospect, since I had heard him preach two or three hundred times, and had always found his sermons to be rather dry, tending, as he tended, to focus on the head rather than the heart. The text was Isaiah 30:21: "And thine ears shall hear a word behind thee, saying, This *is* the way, walk ye in it," and as my father read it, I realized that I had heard the sermon he was beginning at least four times, liking it less each time. When he began to speak I expected the textual analysis and explication by definition that marked his style. But this night he abandoned that—something got hold of him. He followed the reading of the text with the telling of a tale.

He had, he said, been in high school, sitting in a classroom, when a man had come to the school asking for volunteers to go up to fight a forest fire that raged on a nearby mountain. My father and some others agreed to go, and were taken up by wagon, then went on foot a mile or two farther, to a point where they had been told to dig a firebreak. The fire, my father said, seemed a long way away; not sensing the danger, they allowed themselves to become absorbed in their task. When finally they looked up from it, they found that the fire had swept about them—they were surrounded by flames.

They reacted as one would have expected. My father told of his panic, how he had at first cried hysterically, then begun to curse, using words he had not realized he knew, had finally collapsed into desperate prayer, all, it seemed, to no avail. But then, when the smoke was at its thickest, when he was about to lose sight of his companions, when the very sound of their wailing was lost in the roaring of the flames, there came a voice calling to them to follow. They followed that voice, escaping with its guidance through what must have been the last gap in the fire. Afterward they asked who it had been who risked himself to save them, but no one could tell them who it was.

From the tale my father moved to the obvious but eloquent equation, exchanging that unknown savior for a known one, who called the same message, and who led all who followed him clear of the flames. And then, almost abruptly, and far sooner than anyone expected, he stopped. And he brought down the house.

That sermon shocked me. Because I knew my father, knew that he had hidden that story for forty years, had kept it out of previous versions of the same sermon because he was the kind of man who hated to admit weakness, or indecision, or helplessness. I knew that to relive that time on the mountainside had cost him greatly, and to admit his own helplessness had cost him even more. But I realized that the sermon had been something beyond that which was usual for him, and I believed, for no reason I could express, but nevertheless believed, that it was the paying of the price that had made the sermon possible. I believed that in confessing his own weakness he had found access to a hidden source of power inside, or perhaps outside, himself—in any case, a source of power that was magical, mystical.

Until that night I had not understood what it meant to write. I had known that the writer's goal was to reveal truths in words manipulated so effectively as to cause a movement in the minds and hearts of those who read them. But I had not understood that it would cost anything. I had believed that I could do those things while remaining secure and safe in myself—I had even believed that writing fiction was a way to conceal my true feelings and weaknesses. That night, I found out better. That night, I realized that no matter how good I became in the manipulation of symbols, I could never hope to move anyone without allowing myself to be moved, that I could reveal only slight truths unless I was willing to reveal the truths about myself. I did not enjoy the realization. For I was no fonder of self-revelation than my father, and though I knew I would love to do with written words what my father had done in speech, I was not sure I could pay the price. I was not sure I wanted to.

I do not know why my career as a writer did not end there. All I know is that, in fact, it began there. For out of that night came the only idea I have that could truly be called an aesthetic standard: expensiveness. When I ask myself, as all writers do, whether to write something this way or that way, whether to keep this bit, or throw it away, I ask myself, along with all the practical, technical, editorial questions, Does it cost? Is it possible that someone reading might discover something about me that I would rather not have him know? Is there something truly private here, something I would never admit face to face, unless, perhaps, I was drunk?

I would like to say that if the answer to those questions is No, I go back and dig down inside myself until I do find something it will cost me to say; the truth is I do not always do that. But I believe I should. And I believe that someday, when I am good enough, not as a manipulator of words and phrases but as a human being, I will. And I believe that each time I work, and make the effort, I get closer to that ideal.

I doubt that could be called a religious expression. That I act upon it is, however, a matter of faith. For I cannot prove that there is anything to be gained from writing with that sort of aesthetic in mind. I cannot show that my work will be read by more people, that my books will sell more copies, that I will make more money, get better reviews. I cannot truly say that the work is better—I believe it is, but I cannot prove it. Despite the fact that I cannot prove it, however, I believe this aesthetic of cost does make a difference in my writing and the reception of it. This belief is important. For without it I would not be able to pay the price of writing in the way that pleases me. I would write, but, by my standards, I would do it badly. Eventually I would give it up, or become a prostitute, in it only for the money. I need not fear this, because I do believe. The capacity for belief is something I acquired from being so much in contact with others who believed. This, perhaps, is the most important influence on me from the faith of my father.

You Talk Like You Got Books in Your Jaws

WESLEY BROWN

Wesley Brown's fiction has appeared in *Essence* magazine, *Pushcart Prize*, *Persea*, and *The American Rag*. He is the author of a novel, *Tragic Magic*, published by Random House, and has recently completed a second novel. He teaches creative writing and American literature at Rutgers University and lives in New York City.

The title of this essay, taken from one of the quips made by a character in Zora Neale Hurston's book of folklore, *Mules and Men*, is an example of what has always fascinated me about what happens to language in the mouths of black people. What is communicated is not merely a rich display of imagery but an evaluation of a particular kind of learning. The sentiment expressed is not anti-intellectual; rather it mocks the acquisition of knowledge that seeks only to glorify the person possessing it and not to communicate.

The talk that has made the strongest impression on me, as a writer, has been inventive in the arrangement and choice of words and insightful in its interpretation of the human predicament. The first examples were, of course, my parents and relatives. But as time went on, I began to identify barbershops and churches as places where conscious efforts were made to raise talking to a high art.

The preachers whose words have stayed with me over the years always understood the importance of the advice given in the James Young/Sy Oliver tune:

> When I was a kid about half past three,
> My daddy said, "Son, come here to me."
> He said, "Things may come and things may go.
> But this is one thing you ought to know—
> T'ain't what you do,
> It's the way that cha do it."

In other words, inflection and cadence are as important as the content of what is being said. So when I heard a preacher say, "When I'm wrong nobody forgets. When I'm right nobody remembers," his words were memorable, not for themselves alone but for the way they were spoken.

It was a similar conviction in the spoken word that drew me to Mississippi in the 1960s and was responsible for my involvement with the Student Non-Violent Coordinating Committee and the Mississippi Freedom Democratic Party. One of the enduring contributions made to this country by black Mississippians, such as Fanny Lou Hamer, was the high quality of what they had to say about the disparity between America's *high opinion* of itself and its *actions* toward its own people. I will never forget Fanny Lou Hamer's impassioned speech before the Credentials Committee at the Democratic National Convention in Atlantic City in 1964, when she said: "If the Freedom Democratic Party is not seated now, I question America." Listening to her give voice to how her decision to register to vote transformed her life had a profound effect on me. It convinced me of the power inherent in being able to articulate the encounter between your own life and the rest of the world. And while relying on your own experience of events may not give you control over them, it does ensure that you will not be, as readily, at the mercy of things you cannot immediately change. I believe this has had more to do with my becoming a writer than anything else.

Since that period of the early 1960s, black idiomatic expression continues to be a rendering of the spoken word that I listen for and trust. This verbal precision is often expressed in the blues. Bessie Smith's statement on the male prerogative that dominates in our society is still the best reading I've heard on the subject.

> Man sure do make me tired.
> Man sure do make me tired.

> Got a handful a gimme,
> and a mouthful a much obliged.

More recently, Bill Withers has written songs that carry the same authority of someone speaking with total commitment to what he or she is saying.

> You might be a sweet-toned
> sho-nuff high-class talker.
> You might be a stone expert at kissing.
> But it don't do too much good to be talking,
> Brother, when there ain't nobody listening.

It should be pointed out, as Albert Murray has in his book *Stomping the Blues,* that "the definitive element of a blues statement is not verbal. Words as such, however well chosen, are secondary to the music. . . . Blues singers almost always seem to be much more preoccupied with vocal subtleties than with rendering the lyrics as written." Granting this, however, does not in any way detract from the aptness and eloquence of the best blues lyrics.

Two of the most fully realized evocations in printed form of the celebration of words in the mouths of black people are Zora Neale Hurston's *Mules and Men* and John Langston Gwaltney's *Drylongso.* In *Mules and Men,* Hurston recounted her experiences in 1935 traveling through Florida, particularly to Eatonville, where she was born. What distinguishes this book from others on folklore is Hurston's attempt to present not merely a compilation of folk tales but a narrative portraying the black people of Eatonville as they worked, played, and quarreled. And this became the framework for telling their highly seasoned stories. In a conversation with a group of men, Hurston records one man's thoughts on why some are called into the service of wisdom and others are not.

There's a whole heap of . . . by-words like "Old coon for cunning, young coon for running" and "I can't dance but I know good moves." They all got a hidden meaning, just like in the Bible. Everybody can't understand what they mean. Most people is thin-brained. They's born with they feet under the moon. Some folks is born with they feet on the sun and they can seek out the inside meaning of words.

And then there are the words of a woman that have always represented, for me, the fierce determination among black people to
persist.

> I'm raggedy, but right; patchey but tight;
> stringy, but I will hang on.

Unlike *Mules and Men,* John Gwaltney's *Drylongso* does not
have a narrative but follows the conventional research approach of
an anthropologist. However, the separate statements of those
blacks who are the subject of Gwaltney's contemporary portrait of
black America do not require a story line. They provide a dramatic
reading of their lives without the need of literary devices. The
words of Ruth Shays testify to the great service she has done to
facking as opposed to *yakking.*

I think there is more talking around what black people are than there is
talking about what we are. I might not know how to use thirty-four words
where three would do, but that does not mean that I don't know what I'm
talking about. . . . The mind of a man and the mind of a woman is the
same. But this business of living makes women use their minds in ways
that men don't even have to think about. . . . It is life that makes all these
differences, not nature. . . . But if you don't know when you been spit on,
it does not matter too much what else you think you know.

Someone once said that the difference between a comic and
a comedian is that the former says funny things and the latter says
things funny. Richard Pryor clearly falls into the category of a
comedian and has created a series of characters worthy of any
novel. From the time I began seeing Pryor's first appearances on
the Ed Sullivan show, hearing his early record albums, going to see
him perform at the Bitter End club in New York City, I was impressed by how he never sensationalized or patronized the black
people who populated his comedic world. And it is Pryor's attention to the speech and body English of particular segments of black
America that place him high on the list of talkers of the first rank.
For example, check out his rendering of a portion of a preacher's
sermon:

You know, I first met God in 1929. I never will forget this. You see,
I-was-walk-kin-down-the-street. . . . I don't believe you heard me. I said,
I-was-walk-kin-down-the-street. I-was-not-runnin. I was waaahhhkin.

Eatin a tuna fish sandwich. And I heard this voice call unto me. And I knew it was the voice of God, for it came from without a dark alley way. As only the voice a God can come. However, my brothers and sisters, I did not venture down that dark alley way. For it might not have been the voice a God. But two or three niggers with a baseball bat. God only knows. And he wasn't talkin. And I wasn't walkin.

What I have learned from the special relationship black people have with the English language is that at its best, invention keeps pace with utterance. In a country that, as a matter of social policy, consistently tries to talk us out of an account of our own lives, there is no way to measure the importance of holding on to the language that is appropriate to experiences as they are lived and felt. As Jamake Highwater has said in his book *The Primal Mind:*

The world is made coherent by our description of it. Language permits us to express ourselves, but it also places limits on what we are able to say. What we call things largely determines how we evaluate them.

As a writer, I have been nourished by the good words and bad mouthing of relatives, friends, blues singers, preachers, and such people as Fanny Lou Hamer, Zora Neale Hurston, and Richard Pryor. Basic to all of them has been a determination to talk out of turn, no matter how exalted the source of official opinion. Like a woman did once in a Harlem restaurant known as Wilson's, when someone made the point that God didn't love ugly, and she said, "He ain't that excited about pretty neither!"

The Formal Idea of Jazz

HAYDEN CARRUTH

At present, Hayden Carruth is a professor at Syracuse University. For many years, however, he lived in northern Vermont, where much of his poetry was written. His most recent book is *Working Papers,* a selection of critical pieces, and his books of poetry include *From Snow and Rock, from Chaos* and *Brothers, I Loved You All.* A long poem, *The Sleeping Beauty,* was published in the fall of 1982 by Harper & Row.

Tracking influences has become an old game by now. We have had plenty of time to see its limitations and absurdities. If I say, for instance, that during the period when I first devoted myself seriously and searchingly to metrical composition, the poets whose works I read the most were Ben Jonson, William Yeats, and Ezra Pound, the statement is true but meaningless. The real question is not by whom I was influenced, but how. The crudest distinction would be between reactive and imitative, I suppose. Did I steal from the masters or reject them? The answer is undiscoverable, for which I am thankful. And even if one could find it, it would still need to be compounded incalculably with dozens of lesser influences, including those exerted on me by my own friends and contemporaries.

Then the further likelihood arises that the most important influences were not those impinging directly on my poems but those that came much earlier. Mother Goose, the songs of Shakespeare, *The Ingoldsby Legends,* Byron, Stephen Foster, the poets I read in school—Longfellow, Whittier, Tennyson—and scores of others, perhaps hundreds of others. They came to me when I wrote poems only as a kind of children's game. They entered the

24

inchoate sensibility of a struggling child in twisted ways that can never be unraveled. And again I am thankful.

A poem my father wrote for me when I was two years old was such a favorite of mine that he copied it out in a fair hand and framed it and hung it on the wall. The first line ran: "There was a little duck and he went quack, quack." I am ashamed to have forgotten the rest of it, ashamed that I do not know what happened to the framed manuscript.

A couple of years ago I read an article by a scholar who had found about a dozen "reduplicated" phrasings in *The Faerie Queene* and the works of Alexander Pope. The article was interesting and even slightly shocking; we think of Pope as remote from Spenser in every way, so that the two must fall into separate categories. Yet we know that Pope was a precocious child, that he read widely, that indeed by the time he was twelve years old he probably had read every poem accessible to him in English, to say nothing of French, Latin, Greek, etc. It would be folly to think that such a person, living in that time, could have avoided the Spenserian epic, or that the poem would not have left a deep impression, though who knows in what complex, conflicting, and hidden ways?

Complex and conflicting. That is almost as much as I can say about the literary influences on my own writing. What remains is that I was, during much of my life, pathologically uncentered in both style and personality, and that I freely took on the styles and personalities of others. Even at my present age, nearly sixty, I see no clearly identifiable center in the existence, poetic or other, of Hayden Carruth, that stranger. Not long ago I had occasion to study the works of Paul Goodman with care, and immediately I began to write poems in his peculiar and lovely syntax. Thirty years ago I might have been embarrassed by such anxious mimicry. Now I simply say that I am grateful to Paul for showing me a new means by which to express some of the troubles that have recently been on my mind.

And that is the end of it, provided we restrict ourselves to "literary" influences. What is more important, however, yet at the same time more difficult to discuss, is the influence on writing of the other arts; in my case particularly the influence of jazz. I have always insisted that the connections among the arts are nonformal, at best tenuous; and many people have complained about my editorial prejudice against mixed genres. The "art" of collage seems to me intrinsically self-contradictory. I dislike poems about paintings or pieces of music. Then what can I say about the influence of jazz on poetry? In fact there *is,* as we all empirically know, some functional analogy among the arts, and the problem is to define it, to discriminate precisely what can be transmitted from one artistic medium to another. I scarcely know how to attempt it.

An immediate difficulty arises from the fact that human beings are divided into two parts: a great majority that cannot experience jazz as music; a minority that can and does. Every member of the minority will know what I'm talking about. I don't know how many times—but over the years a great many—someone has come into my home, proclaimed his or her devoted enthusiasm for jazz: "Oh, I just love Billie Holiday," etc, and has asked me to put a record on the phonograph, only to begin, after the first eight bars, talking a blue streak that lasts till the record ends, by which time the topic of music has been long forgotten. It is infuriating. I am one who must have complete silence when music is playing; a small clash of cutlery from the next room, a dog barking somewhere down the road, can wipe out a vertical moment of sound (be it a solo piano or a full orchestra and chorus) and utterly destroy the passage in question. It was bad enough in the remote hills where I used to live. In the crude and graceless city where I live now, sirens never cease to wail, trucks to roar, plumbing to flush. But of all the sounds that destroy music, the human speaking voice is worst.

Some people can hear jazz, and others, by far the greater number, cannot. The worst poem Dr. Williams ever wrote was "Ole Bunk's Band" (I give the title from memory), in which he treats Bunk Johnson and the other old-time musicians playing with him as if they were some unintelligible anthropological specimens, people from another, distant culture making noises for the mere hell of it or out of animal exuberance. That they were artists like himself never crossed his mind. Delmore Schwartz, thirty years ago when he and I used to drink on Tuesday afternoons at a bar on Madison Avenue, could talk rings around me about baseball, although I was not unknowledgeable; but when it came to jazz, which he professed to love, he could not speak except in sociological terms: "this outpouring of racial misery," "phenomenon of human expression in industrial society," etc. I sighed (but only to myself).

This has nothing, incidentally, to do with being tone deaf. I know musicians trained in the European tradition who perform flawlessly and even imaginatively when they are reading a score by Mozart or Ravel but who cannot hear the musical qualities of jazz.

I do not say—and please note this well—that incalculably many social, historical, cultural, and other external values do not adhere to jazz. On the contrary, no art exists in a vacuum. But I do say that this is definably a question of adherence and not of intermixture. The music itself, the continuum of textured sounds and rhythms, is "pure." It cannot in itself contain or express any ideational substance, and even emotional substance—leaving aside titles, lyrics, and all other cultural adherents—can only be suggested through psychic analogy, a term I have just invented and do not care to try to amplify. Hence I conclude, equally unscientifically, that some people innately possess a sensory apparatus somehow capable of apprehending jazz as music, and that other people do not. Those in the former group will perfectly understand what I am writing here; they already know it in their own experience. To the rest, who may or may not be musically inclined but who lack the capacity to respond to the distinctive sensual qualities of jazz, what I have written so far will seem arbitrary and perhaps elitist, though that is not my intention at all, and what I shall attempt to write now will seem puzzling and inconsequential.

Nevertheless and in spite of the philosophical and verbal difficulties implicit in any attempt to discuss crossovers among the arts —difficulties so great that some aestheticians deny the possibility —I want to write something, if I can, about the influence of jazz as jazz upon my poetry as poetry, hoping thereby to illuminate the vexing enigma of influences in general.

I shan't attempt what so many who are more competent have tried and failed to do, namely, to define jazz at the same time completely and distinctly. Our vocabularies, even our technical ones and even, for that matter, our nonverbal systems of notation, are inadequate. Every characteristic of jazz to which the critics point can be found in other musics. The business about coming in ahead of or behind the beat, for instance, often only a hairsbreadth away from it: doubtless this accounts in part for the swinging quality of jazz. But the same manner of performance can be found in Gypsy music, flamenco, African, and Oriental music, and others; while some jazz musicians have attained the same propulsive force by playing almost nothing but eighth notes, each one squarely on the beat—Boyce Brown, the mad monk of Chicago in the late twenties and early thirties, being an extreme example, though in the early period of bop, Parker, Gillespie, Peterson, and many others were doing essentially the same thing. Moreover, it is undeniable that a swinging, propulsive quality is just as prominent in Bach, Scott Joplin, and the Rolling Stones as it is in jazz, although the former all composed and performed in standard, predictable, easily measurable and notatable rhythmic patterns.

It is the same with texture. Many inexperienced listeners used to think that raucous instrumental tone was the main ingredient of jazz, a belief upon which the entrepreneurs of pop culture—Clyde McCoy, the owners of the Cotton Club, Sophie Tucker, thousands of others—capitalized mightily. This belief has somewhat diminished, I think. But it is true without question that jazz instrumentalists have enlarged the textural capacities of their instruments beyond anything conceivable a century ago. What Coleman Hawkins, Lester Young, Ben Webster, Buddy Tate, Sonny Rollins, John Coltrane, and scores of others have done with the tenor saxophone could not have occurred in the wildest, most delightful fantasies of Antoine Sax, who invented the instrument (i.e., the "family" of instruments) less than a century before many of these musicians had become masterful stylists. But the real point is that textural expressiveness is part of *all* music; we cannot think of any music, or play it to ourselves inside our heads, without awareness of texture. Often people say that the themes of J. S. Bach are so pure that they can be played on any instrument without loss. But this is true only so long as one considers the music solely as a structure of tones; substitute a vibraphone for the harpsichord in the fifth Brandenburg concerto and see if the effect, the expressiveness, is not much altered. When it comes to Purcell, Boccherini, Berlioz, or Debussy, and when it comes to traditional Japanese or Arabic music, the case is plain. Instrumental textures, and for that matter vocal textures, are as various as can be, and throughout the world are regarded not as adjuncts to the particular music in question but as inseparable and integral parts of it.

Finally, the slur. Everyone knows that jazz performers commonly do not hit a note with true pitch but slide into it from below or above; the same when the note tails off. Slurs, glides, intentional muffs and clinkers, are conspicuous. Some musicians—Rex Stewart, Pee Wee Russell—have made false notes a deliberate part of their work. Granted, most musicians in the European tradition of the conservatories have regarded untrue pitch as anathema; yet a few knew the value of slurs—Paganini, Mahler, Ravel. And if we turn to other musics—the regional folk musics of Europe, the Chinese opera, and doubtless the shepherd's airs of Pan (for I believe the shawm, easy to slur, was likelier his instrument than the syrinx)—the point needs no further arguing.

I have dwelt on these qualities of jazz for one reason: to isolate them categorically and exclude them from further consideration. These along with other such properties are the essences of jazz, the musical values, without which there could be no jazz. They have deeply affected my writing, and I could search through my books to find examples that would illustrate such substantial analogies, passages of rhythmic, textural, and tonally modulative verbalisms—the extrinsic embodiments. But then so could someone else find these same things in his or her poetry, someone who knows nothing about jazz. How can I prove that my composition comes from jazz? I can't. I can only assert, as I do, that the verbal qualities of my poetry bear a close resemblance to the musical qualities of jazz, which have been powerful influences on me since the age of ten or eleven, and that I believe the best reader of my poetry will probably be a person who knows and loves jazz as I do. But maybe not. And in any event the question is indemonstrable.

What is more important to me than the essence of jazz is its formal idea. I must be careful here; the definition is difficult but necessary. But I do believe that the idea, in the Platonic sense, of jazz is spontaneous improvisation within a fixed and simple form, usually improvisation by more than one musician at a time, even if the ensemble comprises no more than a solo instrument and a rhythm section. (Though in fact good jazz of the kind that consists of successive solo improvisations—i.e., the mode that has been dominant for some decades—will be a linear evolution of themes and ideas involving all musicians of the ensemble, each in turn. It is as if the true ensemble improvisation of earlier jazz had been separated into its parts and performed consecutively. Thus the soloist improvises for and with his fellow musicians and selected other auditors, just as the poet writes for and with his fellow poets and selected other readers.) I do not mean to say that elements of convention and artifice are not operative in jazz; they obviously are; but the idea of spontaneous improvisation within a fixed, simple form has been present from the start (say, circa 1910) and has become only more and more dominant since then. This is common knowledge.

What happens, subjectively and spiritually, when a musician improvises freely? He transcends the objective world, including the objectively conditioned ego, and becomes a free, undetermined sensibility in communion with others equally free and undetermined. Long ago I wrote, in a poem about jazz, this couplet:

> Freedom and discipline concur
> only in ecstasy.

Taken from its context in the poem, this may seem an extravagant statement; yet it is my belief, it is my lifelong conviction. Freedom and discipline are both required, but they cannot be had separately, nor can they be had in the objective world that not only separates them but puts them into conflict. Hence my best poems have all been written in states of transcendent concentration and with great speed. Even my long poems break down into parts composed in this way. And all have been composed within the limits of a fixed and simple form, as fixed and simple as the chord changes of the traditional twelve-bar blues. Sometimes I have used the standard conventions of English prosody, at others I have (more musically) run my phrasings ad lib over a predetermined number of beats to the line, and occasionally I have used alliterative or syllabic meters. But always in my good writing, as I judge it, I have interfused thematic improvisation and metrical regularity, or as I prefer to say, metrical predictability. My less than good writing contains many attempts in which this interfusion failed for any of almost countless untraceable reasons, and also many so-called free form poems. Not one of the latter has ever satisfied me.

It goes without saying that style is another question. A percussionist may play like either Jo Jones or Max Roach. In general I prefer jazz that is stylistically reticent, probably because I am a man of my own generation and can't change that. The steady unostentatious beat of Jo Jones or Sid Catlett, with only an occasional rimshot or acciaccatura to accent or counteraccent the improvised melody, is my model, and I usually hope—but not always, because sometimes one wants technique to be the substance of one's poem —my use of regular measure and rhyme will be unnoticed by the reader. I suppose what I really hope is that these elements *will* be noticed, but then forgotten quickly in the onrush of other components, i.e., the overriding improvisation. In my best poems I think —though how can one know?—this is what happens.

And now I hear someone protesting: "But jazz is an urban phenomenon, or at least has been for the past forty years, and you are a poet of the rural scene." Yes. But the contradiction is apparent, not real. In fact I have heard as much jazz, one way or another, during my years in the hills of Vermont as I did thirty years ago when I lived in New York City. And if I haven't been able to perform with others, I have spent as much time as ever woodshedding (in my case sometimes literally) with my horn. The spontaneous act can occur anywhere, and discipline once learned does not depart. The textural, rhythmic, and tonally modulative qualities of jazz can apply as well to my love of natural beauty and my love of women, and to the moral, psychological, and metaphysical agonies arising from these loves, as they can apply to another poet's more urban and man-made experience.

(Further, for the past year and a half I have been living in an urban environment myself, and if I can write anymore at all I expect my poems will begin to reflect the change before long.)

Then, of course, a more fundamental reason for the pervasive influence of jazz in my writing, whatever my themes or feelings, comes to the surface. Freedom and discipline are the perennial and universal conditions for artistic creation; they are the two pillars on which all aesthetics stand. What I have written here is less a statement than a restatement, the primary elements of which can be found in critical attempts from all the times and places ever inhabited, so to speak, by human inquiry. But jazz gives us a new angle of vision, a new emphasis, and this is important too. The past sixty years of jazz have produced an eruption of both individual and communal genius that is truly astounding, and because of the nature of jazz this has placed the emphasis in creative intuition precisely where it should be, on the fusion of "tradition and the individual talent," on the concurrence of discipline and freedom, and on the mutuality of creative transcendence. I say, let us rejoice. We have little enough otherwise to please us.

Some years ago I wrote in a biographical note, which was published in an anthology, that if I'd had my choice I would have been a jazz musician. Some people have objected: "You are the opposite to that type, you are so quiet," etc. Well, there has been no shortage of reflective minds among jazz musicians, nor of any other type either. We should know from the histories of all the arts that genius is where it is, unpredictable. For myself, I know my sensibility was better attuned to jazz than to any other artistic mode; but the rest of my personality was unfit for it. Perhaps that accounts in part for the sorrow that appears to emanate from the center of my poems. The truth is, whether for good or ill and to the extent—is it any at all?—that we enjoy freedom of choice in this world, poetry for me was, and is, second best to jazz.*

---

*I have said nothing in this essay about the fact that jazz came from the black culture of North America or that its evolution to the present day has occurred almost entirely within the shared sensibility of black musicians. To my mind the relationship of white people, whether musicians or others, to jazz is highly problematic; also extremely difficult to define, analyze, and discuss. Hence, in spite of its importance, I have thought it not germane to the topic of this essay, though I hope eventually to say something about it elsewhere.

Fires

RAYMOND CARVER

"Born 1939 Clatskanie, Oregon. Presently living in Syracuse, New York, where I teach in the creative writing program at Syracuse University. I've published three books of poems, *Winter Insomnia, Near Klamanth,* and *At Night the Salmon Move.* Spring 1983 Capra Press will publish a collection of my essays, poetry, and short stories; and in September 1983, Knopf will bring out a new collection of short stories. Three books of short stories: *Will You Please Be Quiet, Please?, Furious Seasons,* and *What We Talk About When We Talk About Love.* I've received a Guggenheim Fellowship and a National Endowment for the Arts Award in Fiction, and in Poetry."

Influences are forces—circumstances, personalities, irresistible as the tide. I can't talk about books or writers who might have influenced me. That kind of influence, literary influence, is hard for me to pin down with any kind of certainty. It would be as inaccurate for me to say I've been influenced by everything I've read as for me to say I don't think I've been influenced by any writers. For instance, I've long been a fan of Ernest Hemingway's novels and short stories. Yet I think Lawrence Durrell's work is singular and unsurpassed in the language. Of course, I don't write like Durrell. He's certainly no "influence." On occasion it's been said that my writing is "like" Hemingway's writing. But I can't say his writing influenced mine. Hemingway is one of many writers whose work, like Durrell's, I first read and admired when I was in my twenties.

So I don't know about literary influences. But I do have some notions about other kinds of influences. The influences I know something about have pressed on me in ways that were often mysterious at first glance, sometimes stopping just short of the miraculous. But these influences have become clear to me as my

33

work has progressed. These influences were (and they still are) relentless. These were the influences that sent me in this direction, onto this spit of land instead of some other—that one over there on the far side of the lake, for example. But if the main influence on my life and writing has been a negative one, oppressive and often malevolent, as I believe is the case, what am I to make of this?

Let me begin by saying that I'm writing this at a place called Yaddo, which is just outside Saratoga Springs, New York. It's afternoon, Sunday, early August. Every so often, every twenty-five minutes or so, I can hear upwards of thirty thousand voices joined in a great outcry. This wonderful clamor comes from the Saratoga racecourse. A famous meet is in progress. I'm writing, but every twenty-five minutes I can hear the announcer's voice coming over the loudspeaker as he calls the positions of the horses. The roar of the crowd increases. It bursts over the trees, a great and truly thrilling sound, rising until the horses have crossed the finish line. When it's over, I feel spent, as if I too had participated. I can imagine holding pari-mutuel tickets on one of the horses who finished in the money, or even a horse who came close. If it's a photo finish at the wire, I can expect to hear another outburst a minute or two later, after the film has been developed and the official results posted.

For several days now, ever since arriving here and upon first hearing the announcer's voice over the loudspeaker, and the excited roar from the crowd, I've been writing a short story set in El Paso, a city where I lived for a while some time ago. The story has to do with some people who go to a horse race at a track outside El Paso. I don't want to say the story has been waiting to be written. It hasn't, and it would make it sound like something else to say that. But I needed something, in the case of this particular story, to push it out into the open. Then after I arrived here at Yaddo and first heard the crowd, and the announcer's voice over the loudspeaker, certain things came back to me from that other life in El Paso and suggested the story. I remembered that track I went to down there and some things that took place, that might have taken place, that *will* take place—in my story anyway—two thousand miles away from here.

So my story is under way, and there is that aspect of "influences." Of course, every writer is subject to this kind of influence. This is the most common kind of influence—*this* suggests that, *that* suggests something else. It's the kind of influence that is as common to us, and as natural, as rain water.

But before I go on to what I want to talk about, let me give one more example of influence akin to the first. Not so long ago in Syracuse, where I live, I was in the middle of writing a short story when my telephone rang. I answered it. On the other end of the line was the voice of a man who was obviously a black man, someone asking for a party named Nelson. It was a wrong number and I said so and hung up. I went back to my short story. But pretty soon I found myself writing a black character into my story, a somewhat sinister character whose name was Nelson. At that moment the story took a different turn. But happily it was, I see now, and somehow knew at the time, the right turn for the story. When I began to write that story, I could not have prepared for or predicted the necessity for the presence of Nelson in the story. But now, the story finished and about to appear in a national magazine, I see it is right and appropriate and, I believe, aesthetically correct, that Nelson be there, and be there with his sinister aspect. Also right for me is that this character found his way into my story with a coincidental rightness I had the good sense to trust.

I have a poor memory. By this I mean that much that has happened in my life I've forgotten—a blessing for sure—but I have these large periods of time I simply can't account for or bring back, towns and cities I've lived in, names of people, the people themselves. Large blanks. But I can remember some things. Little things—somebody saying something in a particular way; somebody's wild, or low, nervous laughter; a landscape; an expression of sadness or bewilderment on somebody's face; and I can remember some dramatic things—somebody picking up a knife and turning to me in anger; or else hearing my own voice threaten somebody else. Seeing somebody break down a door, or else fall down a flight of stairs. Some of those more dramatic kinds of memories I can recall when it's necessary. But I don't have the kind of memory that can bring entire conversations back to the present, complete with all the gestures and nuances of real speech; nor can I recall the furnishings of any room I've ever spent time in, not to mention my inability to remember the furnishings of an entire household. Or even very many specific things about a race track—except, let's see, a grandstand, betting windows, closed-circuit TV screens, masses of people. Hubbub. I make up the conversations in my stories. I put the furnishings and the physical things surrounding the people into the stories as I need those things. Perhaps this is why it's sometimes been said that my stories are unadorned, stripped down, even "minimalist." But maybe it's nothing more than a working marriage of necessity and convenience that has brought me to writing the kind of stories I do in the way that I do.

None of my stories really *happened,* of course—I'm not writing autobiography—but most of them bear a resemblance, however faint, to certain life occurrences or situations. But when I try to recall the physical surroundings or furnishings bearing on a story situation (what kind of flowers, if any, were present? Did they give off any odor? etc.), I'm often at a total loss. So I have to make it up as I go along—what the people in the story say to each other, as well as what they do then, after thus and so was said, and what happens to them next. I make up what they say to each other, though there may be, in the dialogue, some actual phrase, or sentence or two, that I once heard given in a particular context at some time or other. That sentence may even have been my starting point for the story.

When Henry Miller was in his forties and was writing *Tropic of Cancer,* a book, incidentally, that I like very much, he talks about trying to write in this borrowed room, where at any minute he may have to stop writing because the chair he is sitting on may be taken out from under him. Until fairly recently, this state of affairs persisted in my own life. For as long as I can remember, since I was a teenager, the imminent removal of the chair from under me was a constant concern. For years and years my wife and I met ourselves coming and going as we tried to keep a roof over our heads and put bread and milk on the table. We had no money, no visible, that is to say, marketable skills—nothing that we could do toward earning anything better than a get-by living. And we had no education, though we each wanted one very badly. Education, we believed, would open doors for us, help us get jobs so that we could make the kind of life we wanted for ourselves and our children. We had great dreams, my wife and I. We thought we could bow our necks, work very hard, and do all that we had set our hearts to do. But we were mistaken.

I have to say that the greatest single influence on my life, and on my writing, directly and indirectly, has been my two children. They were born before I was twenty, and from beginning to end of our habitation under the same roof—some nineteen years in all —there wasn't any area of my life where their heavy and often baleful influence didn't reach.

In one of her essays Flannery O'Connor says that not much needs to happen in a writer's life after the writer is twenty years old. Plenty of the stuff that makes fiction has already happened to the writer before that time. More than enough, she says. Enough things to last the writer the rest of his creative life. This is not true for me. Most of what now strikes me as story "material" presented itself to me after I was twenty. I really don't remember much about my life before I became a parent. I really don't feel that anything happened in my life until I was twenty and married and had the kids. Then things started to happen.

In the mid 1960s I was in a busy laundromat in Iowa City trying to do five or six loads of clothes—kids' clothes, for the most part, but some of our own clothing, of course, my wife's and mine. My wife was working as a waitress for the University Athletic Club that Saturday afternoon. I was doing chores and being responsible for the kids. They were with some other kids that afternoon, a birthday party maybe. Something. But right then I was doing the laundry. I'd already had sharp words with an old harridan over the number of washers I'd had to use. Now I was waiting for the next round with her, or someone else like her. I was nervously keeping an eye on the dryers that were in operation in the crowded laundromat. When and if one of the dryers ever stopped, I planned to rush over to it with my shopping basket of damp clothes. Understand, I'd been hanging around in the laundromat for thirty minutes or so with this basketful of clothes, waiting my chance. I'd already missed out on a couple of dryers—somebody'd gotten there first. I was getting frantic. As I say, I'm not sure where our kids were that afternoon. Maybe I had to pick them up from someplace, and it was getting late, and that contributed to my state of mind. I did know that even if I could get my clothes into a dryer it would still be another hour or more before the clothes would dry, and I could sack them up and go home with them, back to our apartment in married-student housing. Finally a dryer came to a stop. And I was right there when it did. The clothes inside quit tumbling and lay still. In thirty seconds or so, if no one showed up to claim them, I planned to get rid of the clothes and replace them with my own. That's the law of the laundromat. But at that minute a woman came over to the dryer and opened the door. I stood there waiting. This woman put her hand into the machine and took hold of some items of clothing. But they weren't dry enough, she decided. She closed the door and put two more dimes into the machine. In a daze I moved away with my shopping cart and went back to waiting. But I remember thinking at that moment, amid the feelings of helpless frustration that had me close to tears, that nothing—and, brother, I mean nothing—that ever happened to me on this earth could come anywhere close, could possibly be as important to me, could make as much difference, as the fact that I had two children. And that I would always have them and always find myself in this position of unrelieved responsibility and permanent distraction.

I'm talking about real *influence* now. I'm talking about the moon and the tide. But like that it came to me. Like a sharp breeze when the window is thrown open. Up to that point in my life I'd gone along thinking—what, exactly, I don't know, but that things would work out somehow—that everything in my life I'd hoped for or wanted to do was possible. But at that moment, in the laundromat, I realized that this simply was not true. I realized—what had I been thinking before?—that my life was a small-change thing for the most part, chaotic, and without much light showing through. At that moment I felt—I knew—that the life I was in was vastly different from the lives of the writers I most admired. I understood writers to be people who didn't spend their Saturdays at the laundromat and every waking hour subject to the needs and caprices of their children. Sure, sure, there've been plenty of writers who have had far more serious impediments to their work, including imprisonment, blindness, the threat of torture or of death in one form or another. But knowing this was no consolation. At that moment—I swear all this took place there in the laundromat—I could see nothing ahead but years more of this kind of responsibility and perplexity. Things would change some, but they were never really going to get better. I understood this, but could I live with it? At that moment I saw accommodations would have to be made. The sights would have to be lowered. I'd had, I realized later, an insight. But so what? What are insights? They don't help any. They just make things harder.

For years my wife and I had held to a belief that if we worked hard and tried to do the right things, the right things would happen. It's not such a bad thing to try and build a life on. Hard work, goals, good intentions, loyalty—we believed these were virtues and would someday be rewarded. We dreamed when we had the time for it. But eventually we realized that hard work and dreams were not enough. Somewhere, in Iowa City maybe, or shortly afterward, in Sacramento, the dreams began to go bust.

The time came and went when everything my wife and I held sacred, or considered worthy of respect, every spiritual value, crumbled away. Something terrible had happened to us. It was something that we had never seen occur in any other family. We couldn't fully comprehend what had happened. It was erosion, and we couldn't stop it. Somehow, when we weren't looking, the children had got into the driver's seat. As crazy as it sounds now, they held the reins, and the whip. We simply could not have anticipated anything like what was happening to us.

During these ferocious years of parenting, I usually didn't have the time, or the heart, to think about working on anything very lengthy. The circumstances of my life, the "grip and slog" of it, in D. H. Lawrence's phrase, did not permit it. The circumstances of my life with these children dictated something else. They said if I wanted to write anything, and finish it, and if ever I wanted to take satisfaction out of finished work, I was going to have to stick to stories and poems. The short things I could sit down and, with any luck, write quickly and have done with. Very early, long before Iowa City even, I'd understood that I would have a hard time writing a novel, given my anxious inability to focus on anything for a sustained period of time. Looking back on it now, I think I was slowly going nuts with frustration during those ravenous years. Anyway, these circumstances dictated, to the fullest possible extent, the forms my writing could take. God forbid, I'm not complaining now, just giving facts from a heavy and still bewildered heart.

If I'd been able to collect my thoughts and concentrate my energy on a novel, say, I was still in no position to wait for a payoff that, if it came at all, might be several years down the road. I couldn't see the road. I had to sit down and write something I could finish now, tonight, or at least tomorrow night, no later, after I got in from work and before I lost interest. In those days I always worked some crap job or another, and my wife did the same. She waitressed or else was a door-to-door saleswoman. Years later she taught high school. But that was years later. I worked sawmill jobs, janitor jobs, deliveryman jobs, service station jobs, stockroom boy jobs—name it, I did it. One summer, in Arcata, California, I picked tulips, I swear, during the daylight hours to support us; and at night after closing, cleaned the inside of a drive-in restaurant and swept up the parking lot. Once I even considered, for a few minutes anyway—the job application form there in front of me— becoming a bill collector!

In those days I figured if I could squeeze in an hour or two a day for myself, after job and family, that was more than good enough. That was heaven itself. And I felt happy to have that hour. But sometimes, one reason or another, I couldn't get the hour. Then I would look forward to Saturday, though sometimes things happened that knocked Saturday out as well. But there was Sunday to hope for. Sunday, maybe.

I couldn't see myself working on a novel in such a fashion, that is to say, no fashion at all. To write a novel, it seemed to me, a writer should be living in a world that makes sense, a world that the writer can believe in, draw a bead on, and then write about accurately. A world that will, for a time anyway, stay fixed in one place. Along with this there has to be a belief in the essential *correctness* of that world. A belief that the known world has reasons for existing, and is worth writing about—is not likely to go up in smoke in the process. This wasn't the case with the world I knew and was living in. My world was one that seemed to change gears and directions, along with its rules, every day. Time and again I reached the point where I couldn't see or plan any further ahead than the first of next month and gathering together enough money, by hook or by crook, to meet the rent and provide the children's school clothes. This is true.

I wanted to see tangible results for any so-called literary efforts of mine. No chits or promises, no time certificates, please. So I purposely, and by necessity, limited myself to writing things I knew I could finish in one sitting, two sittings at the most. I'm talking of a first draft now. I've always had patience for rewriting. But in those days I happily looked forward to the rewriting, as it took up time which I was glad to have taken up. In one regard I was in no hurry to finish the story or the poem I was working on, for finishing something meant I'd have to find the time, and the belief, to begin something else. So I had great patience with a piece of work after I'd done the initial writing. I'd keep something around the house for what seemed a very long time, fooling with it, changing this, adding that, cutting out something else.

This hit-and-miss way of writing lasted for nearly two decades. There were good times back there, of course; certain grown-up pleasures and satisfactions that only parents have access to. But I'd take poison before I'd go through that time again.

The circumstances of my life are much different now, but now I *choose* to write short stories and poems. Or at least I think I do. Maybe it's all a result of the old writing habits from those days. Maybe I still can't adjust to thinking in terms of having a great swatch of time in which to work on something—anything I want! —and not have to worry about having the chair yanked out from under me, or one of my kids smarting off about why supper isn't ready on demand. But I learned some things along the way. One of the things I learned is that I had to bend or else break. And I also learned that it is possible to bend and break at the same time.

I'll say something about two other individuals who exercised influence on my life. One of them, John Gardner, was teaching a beginning fiction-writing course at Chico State College when I signed up for the class in the fall of 1959. My wife and I and the children had just moved down from Yakima, Washington, to a place called Paradise, California, about ten miles up in the foothills outside Chico. We had the promise of low-rent housing and we thought it would be a great adventure to move to California. (In those days, and for a long while after, we were always up for an adventure.) Of course, I'd have to work to earn a living for us, but I also planned to enroll in college as a part-time student.

Gardner was just out of the University of Iowa with a Ph.D. and, I knew, several unpublished novels and short stories. I'd never met anyone who'd written a novel, published or otherwise. On the first day of class he marched us outside and had us sit on the lawn. There were six or seven of us, as I recall. He went around, asking us to name the authors we liked to read. I can't remember any names we mentioned, but they must not have been the right names. He announced that he didn't think any of us had what it took to become real writers—as far as he could see, none of us had the necessary *fire*. But he said he was going to do what he could for us, though it was obvious he didn't expect much to come of it. There was an implication, too, that we were about to set off on a trip, and we'd do well to hold onto our hats.

I remember at another class meeting he said he wasn't going to mention any of the big-circulation magazines except to sneer at them. He'd brought in a stack of "little" magazines, the literary quarterlies, and he told us to read the work in those magazines. He told us that this was where the best fiction in the country was being published, and all of the poetry. He said he was there to tell us which authors to read as well as teach us how to write. He was amazingly arrogant. He gave us a list of the little magazines he thought were worth something, and he went down the list with us and talked a little about each magazine. Of course, none of us had ever heard of these magazines. It was the first I'd known of their existence. I remember him saying during this time, it might have been during a conference, that writers were made as well as born. (Is this true? My God, I still don't know. I suppose every writer who teaches creative writing and who takes the job at all seriously has to believe this to some extent. There are apprentice musicians and composers and visual artists—so why *not* writers?) I was impressionable then, I suppose I still am, but I was terrifically impressed with everything he said and did. He'd take one of my early efforts at a story and go over it with me. I remember him as being very patient, wanting me to understand what he was trying to show me, telling me over and over how important it was to have the right words saying what I wanted them to say. Nothing vague or blurred, no smoked-glass prose. And he kept drumming at me the importance of using—I don't know how else to say it—common language, the language of normal discourse, the language we speak to each other in.

Recently we had dinner together in Ithaca, New York, and I reminded him then of some of the sessions we'd had up in his office. He answered that probably everything he'd told me was wrong. He said, "I've changed my mind about so many things." All I know is that the advice he was handing out in those days was just what I needed at that time. He was a wonderful teacher. It was a great thing to have happen to me at that period of my life, to have someone who took me seriously enough to sit down and go over a manuscript with me. I knew something crucial was happening to me, something that mattered. He helped me to see how important it was to say exactly what I wanted to say and nothing else; not to use "literary" words or "pseudopoetic" language. He'd try to explain to me the difference between saying something like, for example, "wing of a meadowlark" and "meadowlark's wing." There's a different sound and feel, yes? The word "ground" and the word "earth," for instance. Ground is ground, he'd say, it means *ground*, dirt, that kind of stuff. But if you say "earth," that's something else, that word has other ramifications. He taught me to use contractions in my writing. He helped to show me how to say what I wanted to say and to use the minimum number of words to do so. He made me see that absolutely everything was important in a short story. It was of consequence where the commas and periods went. For this, for that—for his giving me the key to his office so I would have a place to write on the weekends, for his putting up with my brashness and general nonsense—I'll always be grateful. He was an influence.

Ten years later I was still alive, still living with my children, still writing an occasional story or poem. I sent one of the occasional stories to *Esquire* and in so doing hoped to be able to forget about it for a while. But the story came back by return mail, along with a letter from Gordon Lish, at that time the fiction editor for the magazine. He said he was returning the story. He was not apologizing that he was returning it, not returning it "reluctantly"; he was just returning it. But he asked to see others. So I promptly sent him everything I had, and he just as promptly sent everything back. But again a friendly letter accompanied the work I'd sent to him.

At that time, the early 1970s, I was living in Palo Alto with my family. I was in my early thirties and I had my first white-collar job —I was an editor for a textbook publishing firm. We lived in a house that had an old garage out back. The previous tenants had built a playroom in the garage, and I'd go out to this garage every night I could manage after dinner and try to write something. If I couldn't write anything—and this was often the case—I'd just sit in there for a while by myself, thankful to be away from the fracas that always seemed to be raging inside the house. But I was writing a short story that I'd called "The Neighbors." I finally finished the story and sent it off to Lish. A letter came back almost immediately telling me how much he liked it, that he was changing the title to "Neighbors," that he was recommending to the magazine that the story be purchased. It was purchased, it did appear, and nothing, it seemed to me, would ever be the same. *Esquire* soon bought another story, and then another, and so on. James Dickey became poetry editor of the magazine during this time, and he began accepting my poems for publication. In one regard, things had never seemed better. But my kids were in full cry then, like the racetrack crowd I can hear at this moment, and they were eating me alive. My life soon took another veering, a sharp turn, and then it came to a dead stop off on a siding. I couldn't go anywhere, couldn't back up or go forward. It was during this period that Lish collected some of my stories and gave them to McGraw-Hill, who published them. For the time being, I was still off on the siding, unable to move in any direction. If there'd once been a fire, it'd gone out.

Influences. John Gardner and Gordon Lish. They hold irredeemable notes. But my children are it. Theirs is the main influence. They were the prime movers and shapers of my life and my writing. As you can see, I'm still under their influence, though the days are relatively clear now, and the silences are right.

The Bible and the Puritans

ROBERT COLES

"I am a child psychiatrist who has tried to understand how children grow up in various parts of America, under various social and economic circumstances. I have, more recently, been working in Northern Ireland, South Africa, and Latin America with a similar purpose in mind. I have, also, a strong interest in the work of such writers as William Carlos Williams, Walker Percy, Flannery O'Connor; and I use a number of novelists and poets in the teaching I do at Harvard University."

My first memories are of my mother reading out of Holy Scripture, from Isaiah or Jeremiah or Amos of the Old Testament, and in the New Testament, Saint Luke, a special favorite of hers, or Saint John, to whom she turned when a bit mystical (and she could be so!). She also loved to read to us from Saint Paul's Letters. She loved the messages all right; but she also stressed the beauty of the language—the King James version. Decades later, when I was working in the South with poor black and white families, I was to hear many of my mother's favorite biblical passages recited again and again—now by men and women considerably harder pressed by fate than she had ever been.

It was somewhat hard for me, as a boy (and maybe it will always be hard for me), to distance myself from what I heard read from the Bible at home, and at church as well. My mother was not one to permit those old philosophical polarities, transcendence as against immanence, to keep their respective territories at a substantial distance from each other. She was always pushing us back and forth, making a connection between the sin of pride, as mentioned in the Bible, and one or another aspect of our daily lives, my brother's and mine. I recall a rather good report card I brought home when in the sixth grade. I gave it to her with a smile, and she noticed the look on my face with more interest, I soon realized, than she gave the string of A's and the favorable comments from Marjorie H. Ellis, the friendly yet demanding teacher I then had. What followed was a brief but pointed sermon on "vanity," as in Ecclesiastes 1:2: "Vanity of vanities, saith the preacher, vanity of vanities, all is vanity."

I hope I don't caricature in retrospect a reasonably happy childhood when I mention that I would know to say those words to myself even at, say, the age of nine or ten. Memory is selective, and writing about one's memories is also selective. There were long stretches of time when the Bible gave way to—yes, Richard Halliburton, a great hero of my childhood. He was the wandering adventurer, always anxious to see something new, then write about what he had experienced. Once, in a fit of analytic assertiveness, I tried to anticipate an observation my mother might make about Halliburton—his pride. She would have no part of the stratagem. *My* pride was really at work. God and God alone was to judge others. I must scrutinize myself. But what about you, Mother? I stood there, wondered that, silently. I rode on my bike later that day and asked myself the question; but of course, when I got home I buried my angry curiosity. To this day, though, the subject returns to mind. No wonder I have found the recent discussions in our cultural life of "narcissism" all too tempting—a familiar way, indeed, of giving vent to the demands of a rather muscled conscience.

In college it was no leap at all, of course, from such a background to work with Perry Miller, who gave so much of his life to literary and historical studies of the Puritan tradition. I loved taking his courses on the social and intellectual history of eighteenth- and nineteenth-century New England. He also gave a course on Christian existentialist writers—especially Kierkegaard, whose cranky, psychologically penetrating writings were just then (1950) appearing in available English. I would go see Miller in his Widener Library office, listen to him expound on John Winthrop's vision, on Jonathan Edwards and the Great Awakening of 1740, on strange, idiosyncratic Sören of mid-nineteenth-century Copenhagen, the last of those an intellectual anti-intellectual, an anti-authoritarian skeptic who wrote glowingly *(Fear and Trembling)* about Abraham's test of faith, a willingness to offer his son Isaac in sacrifice. I also received help from Miller when I wrote my major paper on William Carlos Williams—his doctor stories, his first book of *Paterson.* It was Miller who suggested I send the essay to Rutherford, New Jersey. "I can't do that," I well remember saying. In reply I heard: "You don't have the money for the postage?"

In that exchange much of what we'd been studying—Augustine and Pascal, and here in America, Thomas Hooker and Cotton Mather—came into sharp focus. Now, in a college building, I was hearing the same admonition—true, the suggestion was more slanted—I used to hear in my parents' home: pride and its many lives. Only Miller was less wedded to the Christian orthodoxy of my earlier experience. He was, after all, a *student* of those Puritan divines; he saw their struggles and tried to make tolerant, twentieth-century (but deeply appreciative) sense of them. Moreover, he was especially sensitive to the dilemma of the Puritans, whose "errand in the wilderness," as he put it, had come to naught. John Winthrop and his followers had expected to build their famous "city on a hill" in order to set an example to others, left behind. They came here expecting to report back, so to speak, as those who go on an errand anticipate doing. But the "errand" turned out to be the start of a nation's destiny, and American Puritanism has had to find its own peculiar way ever since, one mere point of view in a world whose proclaimed essence (toleration of all creeds) is in such ironic contrast to the fierce self-righteousness that prompted those early-seventeenth-century Atlantic crossings.

Santayana gave us a "last Puritan," but Miller knew that elements of the Puritan character have persisted—if nowhere else, in the commanding presence of a tradition of scholarship, to which he has contributed a significant part, indeed. And as some of us have read the old Puritan texts, and the new commentaries on them by twentieth-century scholars, we have found ourselves confronted by paradoxical assumptions we'd long (and unsuccessfully) struggled with, well before arriving at Harvard College in the middle of the twentieth century. The Puritans were, of course, radical Christians; but they were also intensely connected to this world's successes—which, in their thinking, were a prophetic sign of what was to come once the biggest valley of all is crossed, and a final reckoning is made. Obsessed with God's judgment, they worked exceedingly hard to please Him. A spiritual faith became, in everyday life, a matter of relentless labor. A dramatic departure from earthly indulgence became an unqualified acceptance of earthly responsibilities.

I go into the above (and was, I fear, educated at home and school to do so endlessly) because, with Perry Miller's help, I tried hard to settle the matter once and for all, and move on, so to speak. Put differently, I kept trying, while at college, to figure out what was proper, what was suitable—given a stern religious and philosophical heritage which demanded the right to scrutinize carefully what we have learned to call a person's "occupational choice" and "life style." In college I was active at tutoring children who came to a building we called then a "settlement house." I went to a prison and taught math to a class of ten men, whose "sinfulness," a word my mother often uses, could only be edifying to a fellow sinner. I headed a successful blood drive. Meanwhile, interestingly, I shunned politics, and political analysis. My father was (is) conservative, and I saw no reason to question that way of seeing things. And if I had, there would no doubt have been this maternal rejoinder, which I'd heard many times at home: "Nothing can be done without God's help." If we are to change the world, we'd better appeal to Him first!

No wonder William Carlos Williams was, for me (in his life and his work), both a refuge and a reprimand. For an activist (of sorts) prig such as myself, here was a man to emulate—a physician, a writer, a social historian; and to fear, if not find alarmingly "evil," because so unashamedly sensual. I can still remember Miller's question: "Are you sure you don't want to write your thesis on T. S. Eliot?" Yes, I wanted to do so; I loved Eliot's *Four Quartets.* But I said no, I was sure I wanted to stick with Williams. I wanted to look at Williams's "doctor stories," published as *Life Along the Passaic River;* and I wanted to look at *Paterson,* the first book of which had been published while I was an undergraduate.

Williams was no hero for a straitlaced, pious youth—"uptight," we'd now say. Or maybe he was just the hero needed. I found his prose and poetry brutally upsetting and confusing. I was scared enough, I now realize, to resort to psychological name-calling, well before I would possess the requisite technical vocabu-

lary. Williams was weird! So are we, Miller reminded me in his
tactful yet blunt manner. Why was Williams weird? I wondered.
Why are we all weird? Miller would ask, genuinely puzzled.

When I met the writing doc I learned that he earned, every
day, his wide-eyed trenchant glimpses at all sorts of people, places,
things. He was brusque, quick-tongued, impatient of cant. I was
full of that: long-winded announcements and pronouncements
called a thesis, and delivered to a very busy man—who, yet, was
patient enough to stop and take a seemingly tolerant (though no
doubt sharp) look at a particular stranger. He was also extremely
hard working, and obviously much beloved by hundreds of men,
women, children: a street-wise city doc who had given his all to
dozens and dozens of ordinary families, and who had managed,
meanwhile, to learn from them so very much. I loved going with
him on his house calls, running up the narrow steps, often broken
down, of tenement houses, and seeing in the cramped apartments,
through his eyes, so much vitality and power and resourcefulness,
and not least, drama.

I suppose it was a flimsy reason to become a doctor—the wish
to emulate a newly obtained hero—but I made it mine with a
certain vengeance: well-developed Puritan instincts put to work
once again, now in the service, however, of an explosive disregard
of my earlier version of the very localism W. C. Williams so strenuously championed. I wanted out of the "New England mind." And
not incidentally, I wanted out of New England. I applied to two
medical schools: Cornell and Columbia, both in Manhattan, across
the river from Paterson and Rutherford. I told Philip Miller, the
biochemist who interviewed me (at Columbia's College of Physi-
cians and Surgeons, known as "P & S"), that I wasn't sure what
kind of doctor I wanted to be, or even if I "really" wanted to be
a doctor. He took me up, immediately and unforgettably, on that
adverb. He said this, tersely: "That's why you came here, to find
out if it's 'real.' " I wondered what "it" was—my professional
desire, my ambition, my entire life?

I had further cause so to wonder when I began studying medi-
cine at P & S. I carried Williams's poems around with me, as I went
from laboratory to laboratory, and increasingly gave more attention to his words than to the dreary dissections I had to perform,
or the microscopic slides I had to learn to comprehend. I was

beginning to have a "problem"; I was having trouble with "motivation." I not only contemplated withdrawal from medical school, I initiated it with the dean.

The interview I had with him was, in the retrospect of today, an anticlimactic farce, though at the time, and for years later, it seemed to be the most significant moment of my life. I had already had second thoughts as I approached his office: what would I do after leaving medical school? Teach W. C. Williams poems to schoolchildren in Paterson! But could I get such a job? How long would I last at it? Not least, what would be the reaction of my parents—whom I'd so gladly left behind in Boston, but who seemed so close to me as I waited for the dean to see me? When he did, I felt as if I were in our old living room back home, a Beethoven record or two out on the table, the Bible not too far away, my father's slide rule in sight. The dean's name was Willard Rappleye, and he stared at me, and I withered away. He boomed out his annoyance: I had been given a much coveted chance, I had obviously been a good college student, yet now I was squandering time, behaving in an eccentric, if not a stupid, way. What was "wrong"? I didn't know. He did. I was trying to romanticize life. I was fighting medical school with poetry, and I would end up, if I didn't watch out, with neither—looking for a job in the telephone company, I was told!

I remember sitting there and thinking of telephones, lots of them. Would I repair them, assign them to customers, send out bills for their use? In New York, or in Boston? All the while I had to keep my ears cocked, because the dean went on and on: the story of his life meant to remind me of what mine should be like. I had heard a version of this speech from my scientist, agnostic father for many years—a secular version, actually, of the religious "tales" I'd heard my mother tell us children. God's Will becomes Responsibility, and, too, Civic Obligation, and, too, a Purpose in Life, something we all need. Such advice used to calm me, reassure me, but at that moment a heavy anxiousness fell upon me. The dean had been at his job for many years, he reminded me, and he'd seen others like me falter. They had all regretted what had happened. They had all become, yes, tragedies. I was on the brink of sacrificing a Calling. I'd best realize that we don't usually get second chances. From his office I could see the dark, muddy waters of the

Hudson—only for me they were the Styx, and a ferryboat was waiting, ready to go.

Some anger of childhood, so constantly renounced, returned in force. But only for a moment. I quickly surrendered to the dean, agreed in my mind to become a compliant, zealous medical student. Soon I was directing a newfound scorn toward "literary types," an expression the dean had used. In that regard W. C. Williams could be of considerable help. He was forever railing against all types of phonies in the academic and artistic worlds. His contempt for aesthetes is an outspoken part of *Paterson,* from its very start:

> To make a start,
> out of particulars
> and make them general, rolling
> up the sum, by defective means—
> Sniffing the trees,
> just another dog
> among a lot of dogs. What
> else is there? And to do?
> The rest have run out—
> after the rabbits.
> Only the lame stands—on
> three legs. Scratch front and back.
> Deceive and eat. Dig
> a musty bone.

The result of that "crisis" of mine was a reasonably successful medical career, culminating in pediatric, then psychiatric training. Later I would combine the two in a third residency: child psychiatry. I was going to be of "service"—to the point that I began, during my postgraduate specialty training, thinking of places to go. India? Africa? Latin America? Wherever there were needy patients and few doctors! On the other hand, I had a military obligation which could not be avoided. In the 1950s there was a so-called doctors' draft. We had to reckon, all of us, with two years for Uncle Sam. I began wondering in 1957, as that two-year span of time approached, how I might end up spending it.

By then I had become involved in a major pediatric and psychiatric project—the last, perhaps, of its kind. We had a severe polio epidemic in Boston during 1955, and with no vaccine then available, there were fearful consequences. At one point, an entire floor of the Massachusetts General Hospital, where I was a resident, was covered with iron lungs. I became intensely involved with those patients, medically and psychologically. I became *too* involved. Their imprisonment struck some chord in my head. I found myself, in off hours, reading Kafka, Dostoevski. Williams seemed almost a pastoral writer when compared with these two. It was a banality when my psychoanalyst brought it up, but so are most of the questions that we ask our psychiatric patients: "Who felt imprisoned more, your polio patients or you?"

I resented such questions for a long while. They were asked in New Orleans, where I began a "training analysis" at the New Orleans Psychoanalytic Institute, having been sent south to do my air force medical work at nearby Keesler Air Force Base, in Biloxi, Mississippi. But no matter my opinion, I kept hearing such questions while lying on my back, making "free associations." Soon enough, I was virtually fighting my way to that doctor's office. The city of New Orleans had become seized by racial violence; mobs roamed the streets; the police seemed paralyzed, if not anxious to let those mobs, segregationist in nature, have all the freedom they wished to have. I found myself, at times, late for my appointed analytic hour—and thereby inclined to discuss what I was seeing in order (of course!) to explain my tardiness.

One day I saw some black children being heckled—even as, a few months earlier, I'd seen some black adults being attacked for trying to swim in the Gulf Coast water of Biloxi's ample beaches. The children were trying to enter a supposedly desegregated school, but were being greeted with such violent street opposition and such police indifference, with respect to protection, that they had to turn back, accompanied by their obviously alarmed parents. I wondered aloud, to my analyst, why it was all happening—a city virtually paralyzed by hysterical fear, because four six-year-old children had been ordered into two elementary schools by a federal judge who was trying to obey a Supreme Court decision. My analyst was himself a Southerner, but impatient with and angered by what he saw happening to a city he dearly loved. When I told him I had thought of stopping my car, and getting into a conversation with some of the white people in the mob I had seen, and then trying to talk with the black children who had to face that mob, I expected to hear my reasons, if not motives, subjected to close scrutiny. Instead (I remember the moment, the words, so very well, even now) I was told this: "Good idea!"

I gulped. A good idea, maybe—but easier mentioned, dreamed of, than done! The next day I was to see the same scene —and drive on. But now I had come to the troubled neighborhood with no analytic hour hovering over me, hence plenty of time. When I was about a mile from the mob scene, I stopped my car and sat and thought. What to do? How to do it? I put on the radio, to a station that offered jazz; I'd been somewhat knowledgeable about it long before I came south, and by then knew some good jazz bars, some good jazz jukeboxes in some neighborhood bars. I didn't like the jazz I heard—*modern* jazz, and no good to my ears! I turned the radio off. I played my own jazz in my head: Louis Armstrong doing "If I Could Be with You." Then I decided to get out of the car, walk to the school, stand there and watch. No harm could come of that. At least I'd be on the street, and I could see and hear what was going on for longer than the minute or two a slow-moving car allowed—or a television news report.

Soon enough I was near the crowd, and they were screaming bloody murder. They were going to avenge the white race. They were going to kill the "little nigger." They were going to go get the federal judge too—and he'd be taught a lesson, all right. There was more, much worse. About two hundred people, feeling betrayed by history, were shouting, pushing, declaring again and again: Never! After a few minutes I decided I'd better leave. This was no place for me to be—ever! I started walking back to my car. I remembered words my mother used to teach us, words that come up, over and over, in the Book of Common Prayer: loving-kindness, charity, the grace of God. I remembered Perry Miller at Harvard, telling us what it was like to be in the American army unit that liberated one of the German concentration camps. I remembered old Doc Williams and his way of sitting with poor people, exchanging a joke or two with them—and later, writing down what he'd heard, the stuff (those remembered phrases) of some of his poetic lines, or of the dialogue in his stories. And I remembered my analyst's observation—that it was a "good idea" for us to learn how others, caught up in the social turmoil of our times, manage to think and do.

It took many days, days of confusion and vacillation and apprehension and agitation, but eventually I managed to make a beginning of sorts—to what would become a certain kind of working life. I got to meet and talk with some of the white people who ranted at Ruby, and I got to speak with her too; and I got to stay in the South for years, rather than escape it quickly and forever upon discharge from the air force. I've often wondered what prompted me to get involved with those small, much harassed black children, and their persistent tormentors—what in my life, my "personality," as we, alas, choose to put it. As I've written this essay, I've tried to touch upon some of those influences—the moral imperatives of a particular family's life, the professorial voices that resonated to that life, the encouragement of a writing doctor, who showed me how he drew strength and knowledge in the course of his home visits, and not least, the encouragement of another doctor, who dared break ranks, at a critical juncture, with what he would smilingly describe later as "the rules of technique." Still, as any novelist knows, and as some in my own profession aren't so happy to know, there are always the mysteries—no matter our determination to banish them with deterministic theory: fate, luck (good and bad), chance, and yes, circumstance. As Ruby got older, I had fairly serious talks with her, and not only about *her* life. Once she asked me: "What would have happened to you if there hadn't been all the trouble back then in our city?" I hesitated long and hard. I told her I honestly didn't know how to answer her question. I told her it's difficult for any of us to know what we'd have been like, where we'd have gone, how we'd have lived this life, *if* a given X or Y or Z event hadn't happened, or *if* a certain person hadn't crossed our path.

Not original, that line of reasoning. Yet for our children, and for us too, a trite reminder may not always be an insulting waste of time. As Ruby once put it: "The Lord grabbed us all, that year, me and you and the people who said they wanted to kill me, and the people who wrote to me and told me they were praying for me. The Lord grabbed us, and that was a big thing to happen." An "influence," one might say—the sight of a vulnerable child assuming an impressive destiny, and the sound of her voice, saying words such as those, words that make one, still, wonder at the mystery of a child's humble intelligence, as I think we were long ago admonished to do by an itinerant Galilean preacher who saw in the innocence of children a hopeful sign of sorts for the rest of us.

The Last Quixote

Marginal Notes on the Gospel According to Samuel Beckett

ROBERT COOVER

Robert Coover grew up in southern Illinois and was educated at the universities of Indiana and Chicago. His early fiction included *The Origin of the Brunists, The Universal Baseball Association: J. Henry Waugh, Prop.*, and *Pricksongs & Descants.* During the 1970s, Coover lived in England, where he completed the massive satire on American politics *The Public Burning,* which was published by Viking Press, after having been under contract to several other publishers. His most recent work of fiction is *Spanking the Maid* (Grove Press).

It is difficult to do this thing, to speak of Beckett. Indeed, he makes it difficult to speak at all. "To name, no, nothing is namable, to speak, nothing is speakable, what then, I don't know, I shouldn't have started." Nothing justifies the betrayal of silence, he tells us, so earnestly in fact we cannot hear the silence for the admonition; yet at the same time there is the compulsion to speak: "strange pain, strange sin . . . , you must go on, I can't go on, I'll go on." "The act," Beckett explains to Georges Duthuit in their "Three Dialogues" on painters (*Transition,* 1949), "is of him who, helpless, unable to act, acts, in the event paints, since he is obliged to paint." Why is he obliged to paint? "I don't know." A senseless endeavor and to no end, yet understandable.

How go on then? Well, it is sanity gives us license, call it sanity, call it a gift. Imagine, in the wise of exemplary microcosms (we are in a time, like Dante's, that tends to think that way again), not a circle, but just a center, without a circumference. Those who strike out for the edge are kept in Magdalen Mental Mercyseats, as are those who stay at home (the center is empty, of course, and they just fall through). The rest of us pass our lives, or something like them, fearfully encircling the voided core, minds averted, complaining of hemorrhoids, corruption, and climatical malice, clawing our eyes out (not in penance or in rage, but as a specific), indulging our appetite for motion, habit, and whoopee, lashing one another with our tethers. And what we trip over we speak of, because why not? The fool and his banana peel—the artist, as they call it in the famous Mr. B and Mr. D routines, and his occasion. The incontinent artist. Any occasion. A corpse, for example, or a concept. A catalogue, a cunt, a Christian. Or some inscrutable ternary, some longed-for memory, some sweet disaster. Or even somebody, e.g., Samuel Beckett. (Between first writing this paragraph and revising it, I came on three different writers who, in speaking of Beckett, had recourse to the same image of parading around a dimensionless core. Beckett, after Pim, would smile at the congruity of course, "scraps of that ancient voice," a myth locked into us by language, "the remnants of a pensum one day got by heart and long forgotten. . . ." Yet maybe more ancient than that even, yes, it may be a myth conferred upon us by our own nucleic acids, we can imagine anything if it comes to it.) Here then this ordeal, grope in a panic in the mud, speak of Beckett. "And me, about me . . ."

It chanced that I entered upon my own novitiate about the same time, in 1957, that *Evergreen Review* entered upon theirs. Such occasions, whether for magazines or for writers, are rife with audacities and manifestos, clumsy and contentious searchings for a new way with the dead words, a sifting through the silly clutter of one's earlier history for something of value and an eclectic embrace of all eccentric visions from abroad—for a while, for me, *Evergreen* was about the only game in town. And in their first issues, they published Beckett's "Dante and the Lobster," "Ten Poems from *Echo's Bones*," and "From an Abandoned Work." This latter fragment, appropriately, was about a setting forth ("I was young then, feeling awful. . . . Feeling really awful, very violent"), a setting forth that was painful and ridiculous, mainly into the head and through words ("words have been my only loves, not many"), rich with pratfalls and paradox, and animated by a new kind of run-on phrasing, self-conscious, self-deprecating, self-contradictory, not unlike that of the stand-up comedian: "I was made of course and still am, but harmless, I passed for harmless, that's a good one."

Others might have discovered Beckett even earlier, yes, of course they did, who am I to speak for others? After all, I bought a lot of dirty green books in Paris in the mid fifties, but I didn't buy *Watt,* and they tell me it was there before I got there. Just as well, for I wouldn't have liked it, as I didn't much like it when, much later and an enthusiast, I read the Grove Press edition. And then, what about *Waiting for Godot,* and *Molloy,* and *Malone Dies,* they'd been out a long time, yes, face it, Beckett was famous, I was late as always, I who was at that same time discovering for the world the likes of Kafka and Henry Miller and Lorca and Sartre and Dylan Thomas. Dostoevski. William Shakespeare. I was very busy.

Such, anyway, was my first encounter with Beckett, and over the decades that have, in the hard world, transpired, I, like Bom (he must have heard something, nearly got my name right, Malone heard it: "And it doesn't matter to my head, in the state it is in, but the man carrying it says, Eh Bob easy!, out of respect perhaps, for he doesn't know me, he didn't know me, or for fear of hurting his fingers"), have crawled back to him from time to time, can opener at the ready . . . and did he know, flat out in the muck there, the poor saintly bastard, that having heard him out, I got up after, took a bath, and went to the movies? If in fact there seems to be more of Beckett here than me, if quoting him seems to be my only way of getting on with it, it's because his epigrams have held up the walls of my studies all this time, one of *my* voices after all, no longer his, I say it as I hear it. . . .

> And I shall resemble the wretches famed in fable, crushed beneath the weight of their wish come true . . .

> But not a word and on with the losing game, it's good for the health . . .

> Yes, it's all easy when you know why, a mere matter of magic.

> A trace, it wants to leave a trace, yes, like air leaves among the leaves, among the grass, among the sand, it's with that it would make a life . . .

That passed the time, I was time, I devoured the world.

that's right, wordshit, bury me

At the end of the fifties, I was a student of sorts at the University of Chicago, and there was a lot of Beckett suddenly around just then, the whole trilogy, plus *Godot* and *Endgame,* reprints of the early novels, and *Evergreen* was publishing something or other every couple of issues. Even our own *Chicago Review,* being torn apart by the inane controversies that eventually set up, in protest, *Big Table,* managed to print a piece of *The Unnamable,* and a troupe of traveling actors brought *Endgame* to Mandel Hall. I remember that after the play, I made some contemptuous remark about Beckett's weakness for hayseed humor ("the old folks at home"), and a really nasty argument ensued; no, I was not the first to discover Beckett. It might even be said he made it in spite of me.

Students are Beckett's natural audience, maybe the only one he's got. His is a secret text for initiates: rebellious, blasphemous, romantic ("let me down, shadow and babble, to an absence less vain than inexistence"), intransigently nihilistic, raucously scatological, a glimpse (from purgatory, where students live) into the living death of the bourgeois dreamworld, including the bourgeois novel, counsel and preparations. Though serious ("I was born grave as others syphilitic"), he turns his "wild beast of earnestness" loose on the grand "Where now? Who now? . . . Questions, hypotheses, call them that" of the student's dark passage, and makes them seem pretty funny, terrible maybe, too terrible for the silly Billy Graham world, but funny. He plays like a juggler with big words like *uniparous* and *mensuration* and *apnoea* and *emunction,* mixing them up joyfully with boghouse barbarisms, often pretending he doesn't know what he's doing. He lets a parrot reduce Locke's "Nothing in knowledge except by discernment" to a mere *"Nihil in intellectu,"* and warns the scholar: "No, don't pretend to seek, don't pretend to think, just be vigilant, the eyes staring behind the lids, the ears straining for a voice not from without, were it only to sound an instant, to tell another lie." He worries over improbable syllogisms, "clarifies" an object or idea right out of existence as a string of clauses undo each other in happy succession, makes the exercise of memory and logic seem like a game for idiots, and insists on more than a mind built like "an indefatigable apparatus

for doing sums with the petty cash of current facts." He turns
Sartre's *Néant* into comedy and, with what one writer calls his
"frantic precision," shoots panic into the dry stuff of the logical
positivists. As for pilgrimages and catechisms, the student's lot,
well, if *How It Is* is too much of a drag, see Moran's brief encounter
with the farmer at the end of *Molloy* ("Such sentiments could not
fail to please a cattle breeder"). And for the dropout: "He began
to talk. He was right. Who is not right? I left him."

Beckett offered us, me, I can only say me, offered me, in those
days, a way of going on, of making art, without affirmation; he
guided me when Christ and Tennessee Williams failed, served me
as exemplar, wise man, and fool, kidded away my self-pity, and did
what little he could to humble my brash posturings. He was wonderful at odd abrupt transitions between different fictional levels,
at ironic echoes and parallels, funny games with numbers, names,
and logogriphs. Of course, he also pandered to my own awkward
fumblings with the inconsonance between words and their refer-
ents, making mere ineptitude seem meaningful (and maybe it was),
pandered as well to my transient love of travels and trials ("in the
toils of that obscure assize where to be is to be guilty"), to my
aggressive inclination for obscurantism and academic gags, ab-
struse puns, rhetorical parody, that look-ma-no-hands virtuosity,
and even, because he sometimes wrote so awfully (*Murphy* especially, and the Belacqua stories—why didn't someone tell him to
quit?), he pandered to my pride. His creatures fleshed out the
newly encountered antinomies for me, and it was through Beckett
that I arrived at Joyce, Dante, Proust, Swift, even Cervantes; a
wanderer discovering Troy by way of Philadelphia, I owed him a
lot. He taught me patience (one needs it to read him, and that's
no disparagement) and obedience, and above all he helped scrub
the canvas clean: "No, no souls, or bodies, or birth, or life, or
death, you've got to go on without any of that junk, that's all dead
with words, with excess of words, they can say nothing else. . . ."

There was a lot of dissatisfaction in the air then with the
traditional novel, I think there was, I felt it anyway, even the best
of them seemed somehow irrelevant, social allegories unadaptable
to the sudden dissolutions upon us, but when self-critical (not
often), I supposed all that to be just part of the old generational
comedy, the adolescent cutting loose from his fathers by chopping

off their balls, and too easily bored by what was intelligent and difficult. But then, at Chicago, the philosopher Richard McKeon turned my restless gaze for a moment on the history of ordered discourse, and I saw, or thought I saw, that the fashion of the world was indeed changing, not only were we about to leave behind the recent age of expression, of analysis, of words and deeds, for another frantic go at the strange instable stuff we stood on, more *Weltanschauung* explorations, but in fact a whole cycle of innocence and experience, begun in the Enlightenment, was drawing to an exhausted—even frightened—close. And sure enough, the cry was abroad, philosophers asking for a New Enlightenment, theologians for a New Age of the Spirit, psychologists throwing out the old distinction of sanity and madness, in the same manner that physicists were having done with matter and energy, historians getting rid of history itself, ecologists metamorphosing all our progressive assumptions into imminent disasters, and as for the young of the sixties, it seemed to be less in their heads than in their blood.

So I was hardly surprised to find, some time later, Beckett telling Duthuit (those three little dialogues and the chapter on Murphy's three zones have become for the intrepid Beckett explorer, I'm afraid, what "The Whiteness of the Whale" chapter has been for the Melville people): "Others have felt that art is not necessarily expression." He wants no more vain efforts to extend art's repertory, this "straining to enlarge the statement of compromise," choosing instead "to submit wholly to" (imitate?) "the incoercible absence of relation . . . between the artist and his occasion." Yet, though "there is nothing to express, nothing with which to express," etc., there is still "the obligation to express": Beckett stands at the end of a collapsing era, telling us how it is ("for he had to") as the old structures sink away in the timeswamp, behaving now like an action painter—all breathless flow, process, inexplicable change ("What was that I said? It does not matter")—now like an abstract expressionist, painting absences, white on white. He undoes all our ancient notions about character, plot (history), setting ("—but to hell with all this fucking scenery," grumps Malone), and his entire opus might be thought of, from one point of view, as the relentless annihilation of "point of view." In *Texts for Nothing IV:*

He has me say things saying it's not me, there's profundity for you, he
has me who say nothing say it's not me. . . . If at least he would dignify
me with the third person, like his other figments, not he, he'll be satisfied
with nothing less than me, for his me. . . . His life, what a mine, what a
life, he can't have that, you can't fool him, ergo it's not his, it's not him,
what a thought, treat him like that, like a vulgar Molloy, a common
Malone, those mere mortals, happy mortals, have a heart, land him in that
shit. . . .

Don Quixote has taken mortally ill. The promise of new adventures does not restore him. "I feel that I am rapidly sinking," he
tells the merciless voices, "let us put aside all jesting." No longer
Quixada, Quesada, Quixana, Quixote, or the shepherd Quixotiz,
but now Quixano, Alonso the formerly Good ("a good man, at
bottom, such a good man, how is it nobody ever noticed it?"), he
calls for a witness and a scribe, and having stated his preambles
and commended his soul to heaven, he stretches his battered body
to full length in the bed and says: "I shall soon be quite dead at
last in spite of all. Perhaps next month. Then it will be the month
of April or of May. For the year is still young, a thousand little signs
tell me so. Perhaps I am wrong, perhaps I shall survive Saint John
the Baptist's Day and even the Fourteenth of July, festival of freedom. Indeed I would not put it past me to pant on to the Transfigu-
ration, not to speak of the Assumption. . . ."

I did not explore Cervantes' books in any thoroughgoing
way until poverty reduced me to teaching them at a small college
some years ago, and I found my passage marked with a thousand
recognitions from my life with Beckett, the impotent old clown
caught up in the mad toils of earnestness sallying forth on his
decrepit vehicle to essay the impossible in the name of vanished
hopes ("The most cunning part in a comedy," says Don Quixote
soberly, "is the clown's"), yes, I knew him, and the wonderful
rhetorical comedy, the clichés and perverted proverbs, puns and
name games, the intransigent adherence to ludicrous strategies,
the hat tricks and whimsical outdated getup, the stories-within-
stories (and where was Cervantes behind all his "I"s?), the pup-
pets and the mock heroics, the slapstick, thumpings, and hollow
victories, even little consonances like Lady Pedal and the Duch-
ess, the stampede of pigs, the penance in the wilderness, the love

letters, yes, Beckett's gentlemen were all Quixotes (or vice versa), Malone especially, aha, there was the pivotal narrative, I decided, Malone was The Last Quixote, what an idea, or what was left of him anyway, now moribund and hopelessly addled, bedridden, "I have lived in a kind of coma," M/Q confesses, nothing new to report yet babbling on, three and a half centuries later. "And what can have changed him so? Life perhaps, the struggle to love, to eat, to escape the redressers of wrong." And if the invention of the Novel ("Wrong, very rightly wrong. You invent nothing . . .") could be witnessed in the vibrant space between *Don Quixote* Part I and Part II, I thought so, an occasion coinciding with the commencement of this our perishing Era of what shall we call it, of Science and History let us say (if we're to believe the latter—traps everywhere!), so now was Beckett finishing the old form off in *Malone Dies,* or thus I told my classes for fear otherwise of falling silent.

More: the whole narrative trilogy, Beckett's, might be read, I went on, as a gloss on Quixote's first sally, the forgotten one, the absurd one, Sancho (from whom the new novel proceeds) not yet in the picture, the old boy (after a bit of foreplay with names and costumes) slipping out heroically under cover of night, clip-clopping down the road, prattling to himself in the high style, dignifying whores and sharpers, misinterpreting all the signs picked up by his stricken senses, so paralyzed by his fantasy that he has to be spoon-fed, getting heads broken and hides whipped in the cause of love and goodness (Cervantes even makes a joke along the way about the sun being hot enough "to dissolve his brains, if he had had any left"—"Perhaps it is liquefied brain," says the narrator of *The Unnamable* of the tears streaming down his cheeks), finally ending up prostrate on an open plain, the ludicrous victim of life and muleteers, rolling about helplessly, singing out gallantries from the *Abencerraje.* In similar fashion, Malone's Macmann, growing restless stretched out in the rain, starts "flinging himself from side to side as though in a fit of the fever, buttoning himself and unbuttoning and finally rolling over and over in the same direction, it little matters which," but instead of recitations from the Age of Romance, Macmann's oratory springs from realism and its Cartesian logic, from the Age of the Novel:

And as he rolled he conceived and polished the plan of continuing to roll on all night if necessary, or at least until his strength should fail him, and thus approach the confines of this plain which to tell the truth he was in no hurry to leave, but nevertheless was leaving, he knew it. And without reducing his speed he began to dream of a flat land where he would never have to rise again and hold himself erect in equilibrium, first on the right foot for example, then on the left, and where he might come and go and so survive after the fashion of a great cylinder endowed with the faculties of cognition and volition. And without exactly building castles in Spain for that

Cervantes, happy with the world's mechanics, cause and effect, history, logic, dutifully returns and polishes off the scene (the battle with the "gallant Biscayan") that he interrupts mid-phrase like that, but Beckett, breaking free, if free is the word, never returns to Macmann in the rain. "In his country the problem —no, I can't do it. The peasants. His visits to. I can't . . . There is a choice of images." We see the new synthesis created by Cervantes disintegrating before our eyes (Quixote's lance reduced to a crutch, a stick—"I thought I was turning my stick to the best possible account, like a monkey scratching its fleas with the key that opens its cage"—and finally a pencil stub; and when even that is momentarily lost, history itself drops out: "I have spent two unforgettable days of which nothing will ever be known . . ."), and this disintegration is partly because Beckett is absorbing his theses and antitheses in negation, not affirmation: "There at least is a first affirmation, I mean negation, on which to build." Malone is reduced to "eat and excrete . . . live and invent." The alliance of vision and scatology (as Molloy says, "dreaming and farting"), common to all revelations since John the Seer's, was for Cervantes merely one of countless consequences of his turning away from the imitation of Beauty to attempt instead the incarnation of ideas in something resembling the world of men, and he gets a lot of liberating fun out of it (though for that matter, Cervantes is still bowdlerized to this very day—the children have to be protected from Sancho filling his pants at the fulling mill in an un-Christian funk), but for Malone it has become a basic principle, and home itself for the narrator of *How It Is. Don Quixote* was a sallying forth from the confining irrelevant wrap of the Platonic spheres of Truth and Beauty into process, discovery, possibility, but in Beckett's books and plays we are caught up again in the vicious circles, digestive cycles, the nothing new ("what vicissitudes within what changelessness") of what Nathan Scott calls this "late, bad time that begins sadly and desperately [Mr. Scott is a theologian] to be spoken of as 'post-modern,' or even 'post-Christian.' " "The Beckett trilogy," Hugh Kenner writes, "takes stock of the Enlightenment, and reduces to essential terms the three centuries during which those ambitious processes of which Descartes is the symbol and progenitor . . . accomplished the dehumanization of man."

For Cervantes, at the outset of the process, the novel was a kind of new resolution, a way to get on with it in a suddenly changing world, a way to escape the darkness of the old literature, the old dead language; for Beckett, at the end, it is, as he says, "mortal tedium," but since all knowledge may be seen as a dialogue between man and his fictions, "all these words, all these strangers, this dust of words" is as good a place as any to make a start. Indeed, it is probably less tedious for him than he claims, for just as much of the energy of *Don Quixote* derives from Cervantes' own nostalgia for the chivalric romances, so do Beckett's books tend to make it from page to page by the strength of his transparent Irish affection for old-fashioned storytelling. . . .

No, grave, I'll be grave, I'll close my ears, close my mouth and be grave. And when they open again it may be to hear a story, tell a story, in the true sense of the words, the word hear, the word tell, the word story. I have high hopes, a little story, with living creatures coming and going on a habitable earth crammed with the dead, a brief story, with night and day coming and going above, if they stretch that far, the words that remain, and I've high hopes, I give you my word.

But the story we get, as we're getting there in *Texts for Nothing*, is the story of the novelist cut off from his form. As Beckett's voices launch narratives, drop them, ruminate on trivia, then suddenly, as though in a twinge of conscience or terror, pick them up again, change persona and place, leap over transitions, suffer contradictions, just as abruptly become disgusted and give it all up, cry out again, hurry on, etc., the reader is dragged through all the fitful emotions (including both boredom and hysteria, or something at the edge of it, maybe the two shared sensations of our times, as we move helplessly and meaninglessly toward annihilation) of the novelist's so-called creative process, only to arrive at the negative denouement that it's all been for nothing:

But my notes have a curious tendency, as I realize at last, to annihilate all they purport to record.

Beckett, writes Scott, "stands against the whole tradition in literature . . . which represents the novel as a type of genuinely empirical examination of human experience." But of course, at the same time, it *is* an empirical examination of human experience for all that, for although he reverses traditional novel habits, begins with death, concludes with prefaces, exposes his inventions, turns love into macrocosmic tyranny, the bizarre multiplier of human misery, dissolves character, thought, and action into the mere flow of language, it is still a faithful report from the voices,

The things one has to listen to, I say it as I hear it,

news from the real world, and if "the voices, wherever they come from, have no life in them," well, that's how it is, and more empirical than most of the wishful thinking that passes elsewhere for history. Moreover, one might well expect to find the seed of the new literature within the destruction of the old—the ingenious hidalgo of La Mancha taught us this after all—and in Beckett's effort to find what he called "a form that accommodates the mess," he has seemed to point us down a few new paths. Unlike the existentialists who preceded him, for example, writers like Kafka and Sartre and Camus, who paint an absurd world in logical language and syntax, Beckett has attempted a more mimetic art, leading us away from expression and back to imitation, creating a fiction that is metaphysical not merely in subject matter but in form as well—in fact, as Beckett reminds us, in art at least they are and must be the same thing. And this applies to the artist as well as to his artifact. Art, he says in his essay on Proust, must avoid the easy delusions of formalism and open a window on the real through self-exploration, through suffering, which he calls "the main condition of the artistic experience," thereby reviving in us all the old romantic dreams of the literary product as a revelation, the literary act as an attempt to reach the absolute:

The only fertile research is excavatory, immersive, a contraction of the spirit, a descent. The artist is active, but negatively, shrinking from the nullity of extracircumferential phenomena, drawn in to the core of the eddy.

Maybe the most impressive thing about Samuel Beckett, in spite of all the self-mockery, is his great sense of vocation, his almost awesome obedience of that ancient instinct to listen and report, in a time when no effort of the rational or imaginative apparatus can provide us one acceptable reason for, well, for going on with life itself, much less doing it the hard way . . .

And indeed the silence at times is such that the earth seems uninhabited . . .

He is like those great sculptors who spend whole lives in the relentless pursuit of some impossible quality, a glance, a gesture, a pygmalion, a leg, and who end up giving us not so much objects, as a process, humbling, archetypal, preceptive—for whatever else Beckett's art is, it is a lifelong parable on what writing itself is all about, not so much a new narrative genre or rhetorical fashion as a kind of eightfold path for the maker—which is all of us, after all, if we're not afraid of madness—on his way to failure, an exemplary settling down into the Self through all its pseudoselves and posturings, disguises, imaginative displacements, with no illusions, doubting even the wherewithal. "What is incomparable in this great solitary oeuvre," he himself wrote about another man, an Irish painter, "is its insistence upon sending us back to the darkest part of the spirit that created it and upon permitting illuminations only through that darkness." The supreme master, he has said, "submits to what cannot be mastered . . . *and trembles.*" Reporter, clown, and seer: he is like Hesiod's paradigmatic poet who celebrates his age, provides relief from sorrow, and serves as a prophet of religious truth. And thus, as we might expect, like our ancient father Don Quixote as well (perhaps, in spite of everything, an immortal after all), who once upon a time—having been flogged unmercifully by a gang of *desalmados Yangueses,* flung over an ass, laid out on a wooden plank, busted in the face till his old jaws were bathed in blood, trampled in the ribs and thrown senseless to the floor, had his beard grabbed by a lawman and his head cracked with blows from the officer's oil lamp, poisoned himself with homemade magic balsam that emptied him out violently from both ends—could still, with all the dignity of a great clown, stagger away toward new adventures, reminding his disciple: "Be quiet and have patience, for a day will come when you will see with your own eyes how fine a thing it is to follow this profession!"

In Praise of What Persists

GEORGE DENNISON

George Dennison's articles, reviews, and fiction have appeared in a wide range of publications. His nonfiction book, *The Lives of Children,* was one of the seminal texts in the alternative education movement and has been widely translated. His one-act plays have been produced in the Off Broadway theater in New York and in repertory theaters in other cities. A collection of short fiction, *Oilers and Sweepers,* was published by Random House in 1979. He was born in 1925, was educated at Columbia University, the New School for Social Research, and New York University. He lives with his wife and three children in central Maine.

I

There was something about our town, and about that time (the years of the Depression), that allowed us young ones incredible freedom. (Others, too, have remarked on this.) We roved in little bands almost at will. For years I was able to come and go at night from my second-story bedroom, and later from the wonderful garret, by climbing over the roof, sliding down the rainspout, and stepping down the ivy trellis, which was as good as a ladder. My last year in high school was a time of happiness: football, track, erotic love, and social life. It ended abruptly at graduation. I was seventeen. I enlisted in the navy, applied for and was assigned to engineering school at Columbia University. World War II was in its third year. After the war I went home again, but my conflicts with my father were severe, and within two months I moved to New York. I had neither family nor friends there. I was lonely and confused, but the city itself was exciting and was far more humane than it is today. I went back to school on the G.I. Bill, made a few friends, discovered politics, art, etc., and repudiated much too much of my past, as converts do. I earned a living, in the meantime (and did for years), at blue-collar jobs. I liked the people I encountered in that work, but in fact I had no choice: the decorum and subservience of white-collar jobs were intolerable to me. And I kept going to school.

I remember the elderly, short, broad, impassive Italian who, with the gestures of a mime (he didn't speak English), showed me how to use a pick and shovel and wheelbarrow. And I remember powerful Joe Moody, the black laborer who lived in Harlem, and who on another job took me aside and said, "They goin' fire you 'less you shape up. Now you look here . . ." and showed me how to use the jackhammer, the star drill and sledgehammer, how to mix cement, how to carry a hundred and twenty-eight pounds of bricks with two tongs, how to walk so that shoulder loads and dangling loads wouldn't lame my back.

After a term at Columbia, I transferred to the New School for Social Research, then a tiny, quite remarkable place, with many refugee faculty and veteran students, and there I encountered two unforgettable teachers, William Troy and Meyer Schapiro.

The New Criticism, in these years, had passed its zenith, but its attitudes were everywhere, as were the attitudes of Eliot. *Partisan Review* was in its ascendancy.

Troy was not a New Critic. He was too modest to compete with his authors, too respectful of the spirit of form, too discursive and aware of history. Without being in the least hieratical, he was impressed by the recurrence of archetypal myth in works of art; and he was skeptical of the utility of psychoanalysis as a tool of criticism.

The meagerness of Troy's output was as well known to other critics as its excellence. After his death, when his collected essays were at last published, I learned from Allen Tate's introduction that rivals who were not his intellectual peers would raid Troy's classes for ideas, and hurry into print with little fractions of the thought that poured out of him when he talked. During those same years there was another lecturer in literature at the New School, whose capacities were by no means contemptible, yet who typified the spiritless careerism one found in such plenty in the little magazines. Neither his published work nor his lectures lacked insight, yet he lapsed continually into mere pietisms, and into critical formulations that took many things for granted and that in that sense were glib. He would pause in his lecture, as if words could not do justice to a matter of deep feeling. His face would take on a look of sincerity and suffering, almost of victimization, and he would hesitate and stammer in such a way as to imply that some deep mystique of the life of the mind lay just beyond his capacity for expression. That this sort of thing was the mere pseudoself of career no one doubted. What mattered was that he used it as the shrine or setting of the works under discussion. One wished he wouldn't do that. It was diminishing . . . and it made us squirm.

Troy was different. His mind, his character, his spirit (so one was convinced), deeply needed the impress of those other spirits that lived in works of literature and thought. His great intelligence had not made him immodest. Nor did he confront us as the custodian and explicator of culture, but as a man among men, some of whom were students, and some geniuses, long dead. Hearing Troy was always good, always meaningful. We were grateful to him. He was a remote, often overwrought man, yet he was much and affectionately admired by his students.

One incident stands out in my memory, it was so moving.

Troy lectured in the big hall, and the hall was invariably crowded. Among the students was one who was spastic. We were aware of him, but usually he was silent. Once or twice he ventured the briefest of comments. And then one night he plunged into speech.

Some complicated exchange was under way. Troy had just answered a student, and now turned to this one.

I was able to follow only a few of the spastic student's words. The point he was making was complex, and was filled with the qualifications and exceptions that we students seemed unable to speak without. Moreover, he was knowledgeable and intelligent and wanted urgently to be heard. The silence while he spoke became painful. Troy looked at him intently and began to sweat. The writhing and churning of throat, tongue, and jaw were extreme. I could not understand the words at all. The terrible effort went on and on. One began to fear for both of them. I became aware that my inability to distinguish syllables was due in good part to egotism; that is, I was impatient, I disliked the fellow, I was embarrassed. All I could hear was a tortured moaning, a lurching and crooning that registered muscular convulsions accurately enough but had nothing to do with thought or speech . . . except that strange, disembodied tones of asseveration and questioning rose out of it and hovered there briefly.

Troy had come around the lectern to the edge of the platform and was leaning forward. His eyes were wide and his face was flushed and moist. At last the voice fell silent. We many students, scarcely breathing, could not take our eyes from Troy, though we wanted to spare him the slightest additional pressure.

Troy nodded to the student. "Let me see if I've understood you," he said—and he recapitulated everything, ending, "Do I have it right?"

The student bobbed his head and said, "Yes . . . yes . . ."

Troy proceeded to answer the argument, and a large, very quiet breath found its way through the hall. I know that many others were as moved as I, and as proud as I of our teacher.

Twice Troy showed me kindnesses that meant much to me. Both were letters praising papers I had written for him. The second was in response to a paper on Dylan Thomas, who as yet had not been dealt with at any length (scarcely at all) in American publications. I handed in the paper so late that Troy was obliged to take it with him on vacation. There came a letter that not only forbore to reprove me as I deserved, but included the names of editors for me to contact, and his own note of recommendation. I was working by then with a gang of masons and steamfitters in the basement of a huge apartment building in Brooklyn. It was a sweltering day. I was mixing cement in the courtyard, and to my astonishment was summoned to the nearby candy store by one of the neighborhood kids who had learned my first name. My wife (long since divorced) had somehow located that number. She was elated, and in a moment so was I, since what she read to me on the phone was the generous and wholly unexpected letter from William Troy.

We exchanged two postcards and two brief letters over the next few years. When Paul Goodman's *Empire City* was published, I sent a copy to Troy, who in one of his lectures had mentioned very favorably an early story of Paul's. I had hoped that he would like the book and perhaps review it, and we corresponded again on this occasion. Not long afterward I received a letter from the New School. They were contacting former students of Troy's. He had undergone surgery for cancer. Blood donors were needed. I went with several others to replace blood that he had used . . . and was appalled to learn that the operation had been a laryngectomy and that Troy was mute. A year or so later we learned that he had died.

In 1948 I attended Meyer Schapiro's evening lectures in the history of modern art. This was the year of de Kooning's first one-man show, and of Arshile Gorky's tragic suicide.

It would be presumptuous of me to attempt to praise learning and genius of the order of Schapiro's. But I can indicate, at least sketchily, the kind of excitement he stirred in us during those lectures. He was not like a man who has amassed knowledge and opinion and then imparts them, but like a great traveler who has seen wonders and tells of them with an utterly winning animation. I learned in time that every artist of consequence in the city had sought him out; and I believe that it was this quality of delight, of delighted engagement, that drew them to him.

The lights would go down; a bolt of color would flash through the darkness; we would recognize one or another painting on the projection screen . . . and Schapiro's extraordinary voice would begin its high-speed arias of scholarship and creative discernment, in which one heard continually (and miraculously) the happy babbling of a child.

It was this last that set him apart in his genius, and that allowed him (so I believe) to escape the abstract formulations that are the usual penalties of the analytical process; allowed him, I should say, to handle analysis with the descriptive élan of a poet-naturalist.

The delight one heard in Schapiro's voice had the qualities and the status of moral virtue, like the patience of Freud, or the modesty of Proust. It seemed unaware of itself. It seemed to be commanded by the phenomena, and in that respect seemed quite egoless. In all these ways it was harmonious with fundamental qualities of the masterworks hovering up there in the darkness.

The egotism of painters is notorious. The means by which the phenomena of self are subdued and universalized are perhaps not

so well known. The brush stroke of a minor painter may be filled
with personality, with "flair" (the later Vlaminck), but the brush
stroke of Cézanne, though it cannot be imitated, has been generalized, and can be taken as a characteristic of the human mind under
certain conditions of demand. The brush stroke of Van Gogh,
similarly, though it is thoroughly his own, has been moved from
selfhood toward archetypal things, and actually acquires almost
the status of a symbol. Scarcely any aspect of great technique
displays ego; and if one could put words to the deep-lying fascina-
tions that sustain whole lifetimes of grand invention, what a simple
minded (or simple-beyond-the-mind), strange, and entirely universal conversation it would be, as if in every painter there were
a fascinated cat peering by the hour at running water. "Don't you
love red?" "I do. I love it in all its shades and hues, and always
have. I love yellow too." "Yes, yellow is glorious. And blue . . ."
"Blue is a fascinating color. I love blue." "I am thinking of lemon
yellow." "I too. I never cease thinking of lemon yellow. I have
always thought of lemon yellow and always will, especially when I
am thinking of blue, and of the possibilities of certain pinks."
"Pinks are wonderful. There are *saturated* pinks . . ." "Pinks are
glorious. . . ."

What one finds in every masterwork is a vertical range (to put
it this way) that begins in the fascination of the fascinated cat and
rises without hiatus (like the Great Chain of Being) to a kind of
godhead of intellect and spirit. This was what we sensed to be the
nature of the paintings Schapiro showed us and talked about. And
soon enough we saw (rarity of rarities!) that it was the nature of
his lectures as well.

Everyone who speaks or writes of Schapiro praises his erudi-
tion. We students, too, in the degree that we could, expressed our
great bedazzlement. But one heard in our voices, as we emerged
from those lectures, a kind of élan, a momentarily liberated and
clarified spirit, touched lightly by gaiety, that one does not ordinarily hear at the doors of colleges, but that is indeed the aftereffect
of masterworks of public art: drama, dance, opera, concert. It
dawned on us finally that this evanescent spoken form—The
Schapiro Lecture—was an artifact of high art. I do not mean that
because of excellence, superior organization, etc., these lectures
resembled art. I mean that they possessed the attributes, the kinds

and quantities and proportions, the subordinations and eminences, that one finds in works of art, and only in works of art. And they were masterpieces.

The New York painters in those days were still venturing toward unprecedented things. Schapiro only rarely lent his authority to any contemporary work, yet his presence in the city, the irradiation of the city by his own dazzling art, seemed to be endlessly encouraging to artists. There were always painters at his lectures. Many followed him for years.

A mere handful of galleries then were exhibiting the new art. Betty Parsons' was one. By chance I came to know some of the artists there. Charles Egan's gallery was another. In the spring of '48, Egan mounted the first one-man show of the work of Willem de Kooning. . . .

II

The immediate postwar years were a time of grim discoveries. The true extent of the Holocaust was becoming known. (We began to see it as a wound to mankind as a whole.) New revelations of Nazism, Fascism, and Stalinism deepened our sense of human monstrousness. So, too, did our perception (it was gradual) of the atomic bombing of Hiroshima and Nagasaki . . . and the firebombing of Dresden . . . and the destructive hypocrisy of the Nuremberg Trials. . . . The list might go on and on. Anxiety and doubt were not unreasonable states.

At the same time, energy (and pent-up energy) had been released. One felt it especially in the arts. A complex revolution had been under way for years, and now entered a period of great success.

It was in this year, at the show of de Kooning at the Egan gallery, that the abiding great pleasure of painting came into my own life; more than a pleasure—an affinity and a second language, a tonic and support.

These were the black-and-white paintings that since then, of course, have become well known. I sat in front of them all day long, absolutely amazed. Amazed, moved, spellbound, mystified, exhilarated. They did truly speak *to* me and speak *for* me in ways that I sensed and trusted, but that were inexplicable, and that I never had encountered before. Some need, some intellectual/spiritual hunger or incompletion, was being met and answered for the first time. This is the kind of thing that happens probably only in one's early maturity, and that only the art of one's own time can bring about. From the emotions I felt, I derived a certain aesthetic. The paintings did provoke that effort (in many people). They were mysterious. They had been stripped utterly of recognizable forms, yet did not seem arbitrary, or merely decorative, or "poetic." On the contrary, they were powerfully objective, immediate, and, as it were, *factual*.

There were no illusions of objects, but there were forms of a sort, and pseudoforms, shapes that did not quite establish planes or continuous surfaces, and that seemed to flicker in complex relationships with one another. In a radical departure from representation (in which figures and backgrounds are fixed once and for all), these shapes and brush strokes were capable of being both figures and grounds. They were in contrapuntal, or dialectical, relations with one another, and they kept pushing and attracting one's gaze this way and that over the plane of the painting, as if by bursts of energy. That this movement should be unarrestable, and that one should nevertheless feel quite secure in a sense of the whole, seemed to imply that the artist had taken some ongoing process, or illusion of process, or metaphor of process, some doing or searching as his subject and overall form. It was as if each painting were a grand metaphor for the powers that ordinarily create our certainties of recognition—powers of mind, tradition, sight, ego, animal faith. But these forces were seen here only as a vitalism; that is, were seen in a state preceding the life of forms, drawn back, as it were, from proprioception, as if to say that history had rendered the old forms false.

I asked permission to write my term paper on this show at the Egan, though it lay outside the purview of Schapiro's course. A mutual acquaintance spoke to de Kooning (who didn't have a phone), and relayed back to me a direct quotation: "Sure. Tell him to come on over." Things were that simple then.

His studio was a small loft in an old building on Fourth Avenue, in Booksellers Row, one flight up, with grimy large windows overlooking the street. I remember the large kerosene heater in the back.

It was the simplest sort of workshop, cared for but decrepit, with no amenities of any kind beyond a hot plate for coffee, chipped cups, and sugar in a blue Maxwell House can. On the other hand, by the windows up front (and in strong colors now) there was the great luxury-of-the-eye/luxury-of-the-spirit that seems attainable only to plastic artists. I mean the work itself, the work in progress, with all its attendant studies on paper, taking up both space and consciousness.

De Kooning's paintings had not yet become beautiful; they were still taming untamed things, and were at their maximum activity in relation to the observer. A decade later, having established themselves not as events in our psyches but as psyche itself, the same works would begin to appear beautiful. What one felt in 1948 was power . . . that is, immediacy, demand, great impress of mind. It was dazzling to me to sit there and listen to de Kooning, in his wonderfully outgoing, forthright, *goodly* way, say things about Cézanne and Picasso that (it seemed to me) only a fellow artist could see and say; and it was wonderful to glance aside continually at the large painting on the work wall—that unfinished living thing that seemed to be making its way in time as authentically as we ourselves.

Something in my response to his work pleased him, as I suppose it must be pleasing to an artist when the intuitive aspects of his own work prove themselves in the responses of another person, especially when that person comes from a milieu outside the artist's own, and is of a different generation. For the next two or three years I visited de Kooning occasionally in his studio and saw the development of paintings that since then have become famous. Whatever understanding I have of art and artists began in those years. And that I should have commenced my own experience of these things as a beneficiary of Meyer Schapiro and Willem de Kooning I count among the lucky chances of my life.

III

If I had been able to solve the formal problems of this piece, and to write it as I had conceived it, that is, disjointedly and entirely episodically, I would have begun and ended with memories of love. Or so I believe. That first conception may have been illusory. What

I envisioned was a kind of mosaic, cut loose from time but not from the affections of memory.

We had eaten, had had dessert, and were sitting with second cups of coffee at the small round table near the windows of my loft overlooking the Hudson. I began the quiet, urgent, resentful, angry, utopian, generalized harangue that was familiar to many desirous men and hesitant women of that time, arguing against the mores that, I thought, were holding her back.

She listened with a bowed head. Finally she raised her eyes and looked at me.

"If you want to go to bed with me," she said, smiling shyly, actually wondering about it, "why don't you say nice things to me?"

We had been separated. We made love at great length, hungry for each other. She collapsed in the large easy chair by the bed and I on the bed, and we fell asleep instantly.

But I didn't want to close my eyes. She lay curled and turned in the chair, her legs drawn up, her hip resting on one side, and her torso facing me. There was no desire left in me, yet I wanted to look and look, she was so beautiful and so beautifully asleep, her head drooping as easily as a child's on one shoulder and all those shapely limbs relaxed and glowing with good health. But my eyes closed with a heaviness I couldn't withstand.

The struggle went on in my sleep. I remembered something that had made me happy and that I wanted to wake up for . . . and my eyelids would struggle open, and there she lay, and I would look at her again without wanting to cease, but my eyes would close. . . .

I wrote a number of pages in this style, describing certain long-enduring memories and putting them in sequences more faithful (I thought) to the action of memory in the present than to their place in time. But this conception of form was a consequence of intending chiefly praise; and the real action of memory very soon destroyed it. I mean that the memories that rushed forward out of the past—of love, and scenes of family life—aroused emotions that, even at this remove, were deeper than praise could reach, and that demanded a form far beyond the scope of what I had conceived. This became clear to me after I had finished the sequence below, which was the last that I attempted in this spirit.

In the morning, at the hotel (I am going back now to the idea of the mosaic), Becky commented on the elegant people she had seen the night before when she had walked past the Opéra with Mabel. She said something that made us smile, though it was exactly what a five-year-old would notice and an adult would not: "Their hands and faces were so clean!" At Chartres cathedral that afternoon a funeral party entered at the front portals. The casket was placed on sawhorses near the entrance and its velvet covering was removed. Several men carried baskets and large wreaths of flowers to the altar, and then bearers lifted the casket and led the procession. We could hear the prayer and song.

Michael, who was a year and a half old, shrieked with excitement. I quieted him, but in fact the sound seemed not to have been disturbing, the place itself is so powerful and continually absorbs so many things.

Becky said to me, "Is there a person in the box?"

"Yes, a dead person."

She was quiet for a while, then whispered, "Do people have clothes on when they're dead?"

I explained to her that someone dressed the dead person for burial. She asked if it was a man or a lady in the box. We listened to the prayers. I said to her, "When they leave the cathedral they'll go to a cemetery and dig a hole and put the box in and fill up the hole with dirt." She wanted to go and watch.

At supper Michael burst into song as soon as he began eating. He does it often.

At the hotel that evening, Susan, who was nine, fell asleep in the large chair and began to snore. Looking down at her, I could see my mother's features in her profile. For three days my mother had breathed like that, unconscious, and then had died. From time to time I still saw her dead face vividly. I had knelt by the bed with a mirror, to see if any vapor of breathing might mark it, then had taken her head in my arms. The memory of her parting from me, her last expression of love, seemed to be with me continually.

The night before her last day of consciousness, the cancer reached her brain. My brother and sister had both gone back to their families. Mabel and the children, too, had gone home. My mother was too weak to stand or feed herself. I stayed with my father and together we cared for her. It was during this time that I gave up, for real, the anger with him that had put a five-year gap in our relations. A nurse came to the house briefly every day, an intelligent, vigorous, gentle, compassionate Southern woman in her early middle age, and she and my mother, who was also Southern, grew fond of each other. On this last day of consciousness my mother awakened to find that she could not make her tongue form words. The nurse bathed her lightly in the hospital bed we had rented, and changed the sheets. I brought in the mail. My mother tried to speak to the nurse, but a slurred, guttural sound came out, and she stopped trying. She reached up and stroked the back of the woman's head, trying to make the expression in her eyes take the place of speech. The woman touched my mother's cheek with the palm of her hand, bent closer, and kissed her forehead. She was crying soundlessly as she left, holding her head so that my mother couldn't see.

I sat by the bed and read to her, as I had done every day, glancing at her often to notice if she was dozing. She had been in pain for weeks and had borne it without complaint. Morphine was available now, but we hadn't used it. She lay there with her eyes open and a reflective look on her face.

I became aware that she was looking at me. Very slowly, since all movement was painful to her, she extended her hand toward mine. I put my hand in hers and she drew it to her face laboriously and pressed it against her lips, kissing it. She held it there a long while, looking at me steadily with intent, earnest eyes. That night her coma began, and for three days she breathed noisily and unconsciously.

We drove south from Chartres. The immensities of the cathedral had produced in me a weighted silence that would need time and many returns to find its way into feelings and words. In any event, I hadn't thought of my mother's death at Chartres. But in Matisse's chapel in Vence, to which I went alone, and which I took immediately to be in some way his self-designed tomb—so elegiac and calm it was in its unperturbed awareness of death—I was shaken, all the cloudy sorrows rose, and I wept in a way that surprised me, then was calm, breathing easily in the spirit of the place.

Writers on Matisse have called him hedonistic, as if the sensual and pleasurable impulses in his work were unaccompanied by mind, or had no need of mind. But just the opposite is true. The sensuality he shows us is approved by mind, is suffused with it, as by a light. One feels this in the chapel at Vence. The stained-glass windows are staggeringly beautiful, but one comes upon them in a setting of great simplicity, of whiteness and light, and their own colors and patterns are such that they do not seem at all to be in rivalry with the natural beauty of the world, but are the mind's images and memories of it. They are elegiac. (The great windows at Chartres are as if hurled into being out of darkness. Stories can be gleaned from their images, but in the same way that weather can be read in the sky. The windows were not meant to be *grasped* by the mind. Nor does one feel, at Chartres, the departure and leave-taking of individual death, but recurrence, eternity, and mystery.)

Matisse was not a practicing Catholic. If he was religious, it was not in any churchly way. The black stick figures of the *Stations of the Cross* on the wall of white tiles are nothing but notations or diagrams of a great myth. But he can be serious about that diagram. The diagram is what remains to those of us who don't believe in miracles. Some Italian women among the tourists were disappointed. They wanted the full-blown Passion they were used to. But what floods of fabrics, metals, woods, gestures, textures, the artist would have found himself confronting in order to accommodate that wish!

Death ceases to be a fate, a distant ending, and becomes a presence. Room has been made for it. I don't mean that one *accepts* death here (who can refuse it?), but that death *is* here, and is one of the great conditions of consciousness. Matisse's triumph is that all this that is so calm and beautiful is not merely lyrical, but profoundly objective.

The small little flame flickering silently in the hanging lamp seemed incredibly alive, so vulnerable, vulnerable to a mere breath, yet intense and insistent, not at all overwhelmed by these beauties of art, but actually, very quietly, more powerful.

What a marvelous conception to place it at this height, and to isolate it to this degree! A flame *is* one of the great single objects of human experience.

And this, too, is Matisse's triumph: to have acted upon us in such a way that this little flame becomes seeable. It is like Proust's triumph (that one among thousands) in *Remembrance* to have made the word *farewell* actually hearable in the person of an admirable and loving woman.

IV

It was while writing of my mother's death that I began to see how many things I should have to omit were I to confine myself to praise, and how many others (she herself) I could not even approach. Cursing might do more justice to the awfulness and real power of the world.

I thought of the protracted times of loneliness and severe disappointment, bleak years that certainly left their mark, if one could see.

But I can scarcely hold my thoughts on those times. I think instead of the things I did that brought about change, always engagement in the lives of others. The first such engagement (after a considerable apprenticeship) was as a lay psychotherapist with severely disturbed children, so-called juvenile schizophrenics. The second was a more general engagement years later, which included social-political activism.

In the fall of '67 I wrote of the Pentagon demonstration shortly after getting back from it. Rereading that piece today, I see that certain things were invisible to me then, and that others have changed in value.

I still remember what a beautiful Indian summer day it was, and how elated we were, marching in our dense, long column. Our numbers emboldened us and cheered us enormously. When the march ended in the lower parking lots, scarcely anyone stayed to hear the speakers, but moved on to the Pentagon, some strolling and others running. We passed a grassy little park cordoned off by MP's in neat uniforms, wearing white helmets and carrying clubs. A long-legged youth, of the kind that one sees in Harvard Square, dashed out into the green. Several of the MP's chased him. His light fall coat was flapping out behind him and he grinned and zigzagged this way and that. Many hundreds of us, perhaps several thousands, came to the edge of the field and stood among the small trees and ornamental shrubs, watching. There was some laughter and some youthful cheering. The runner was fast. What he seemed to want to do (there was nothing else that *could* be done) was to elude the MP's, rejoin his friends, and go on to the Pentagon. But he was thrown to the ground, face down. Two MP's knelt on each of his arms, two on each of his legs, another on the small of his back. He must have believed at that moment, as we did, that he would be lifted bodily and thrown from the park, or perhaps would be arrested. But an MP with a club came running toward him. We began screaming, "No! No!" and then a gasp rose from our throats. The MP swung the weighted club fiercely across the youth's skull. The youth's body arced upward violently, and lay there shaking unconsciously in dreadful spasms. He was carried away on a stretcher, both arms trailing limply from the sides. Later, when the demonstrators reached the steps and ramps of the Pentagon, they were stopped by armed troops with outthrust bayonets. One heard frantic shouts of "Don't push!" Tear gas drifted here and there. Two groups, neither very large, overturned light barricades and pressed into the VIP parking lot before the walls of the building itself. These groups were immediately sealed off by many hundreds of troops who rushed out of hiding. We sat down, moved close to one another, and faced the troops. Three youths dashed for the main doors. They were knocked to the ground and encircled by a group of soldiers, who leaned over them, pounding downward with the butts of their rifles. Late that night, small groups of us still remained in the positions we had taken before the walls of the Pentagon. There were more beatings. But *beating* is not the right word for these blows of rifle butts. Bones were broken, gristle smashed, organs injured. During one of these assaults (there were two, each involving several soldiers and several seated demonstrators) a U.S. marshal pushed through the soldiers and struck ragingly with his club at the already prostrate bodies. It was the same man who that afternoon had pulled a youth from a flatbed truck and assaulted him. The youth, we had learned, was still unconscious at the hospital. Most of the arrests, which began shortly after midnight, were accompanied by blows of the marshals' clubs, especially to the heads and shoulders of the young women. My friends and I agreed to wait until the last moment, that is, until it seemed that we ourselves were about to be clubbed and arrested. An ambulance and a paddy wagon moved slowly up our ramp. We thought that the time had come. We got up and walked away. It was around one o'clock in the morning.

A small press conference was arranged early the next day, and I went with some friends in a taxi to meet a reporter from the *Washington Post.* A couple of strangers rode with us, who also had stories to tell. I was describing to them, in an overwrought and still astonished voice, the viciousness of the unprovoked assaults I had seen, when I became aware that our driver was listening to me. He was a large, grave black man, and was looking at me in the rearview mirror. I turned to him, that is, to his image, and amplified what I had been saying, ending with some such statement as, "They were just sitting there. They were beaten for nothing, nothing."

His eyes looked steadily and noncommittally into mine, and he said in a neutral voice, "Is that so?"

The import of that odd tone silenced me immediately. I realized that what I had just described to him so emotionally—"beaten for nothing, nothing"—had been for centuries a commonplace in the community of blacks.

For me it was a moment of revelation. I had thought that I understood the situation of the blacks, at least in part, but I saw that I was grossly ignorant. And I saw that the things I did not know were of a kind that I could not ever know; and that whatever the psychic stresses of my character and way of life, the mere facts of race and of class privilege spared me dangers that many blacks had no choice but to fear.

The Pentagon demonstration has been powerful in my life. The moral and physical bravery and the goodwill of the dissenting young people moved me deeply. I passionately wanted to believe in the possibility of a better world . . . and to see so much generosity of spirit, so much helpfulness and youthful optimism, moved me continually to admiration and hope. I know now that I overestimated many things as wildly as the greenest youth, and that I underestimated badly the berserk momentum of the forces we refer to so clumsily as *the government,* and *the economy.* Nevertheless, the exaltation of seeing so many individual and concerted actions in which morality, reason, and courage were joined—in which, that is to say, the ulterior hopes of social life were actually visible—hasn't faded from my memory, and won't. I still feel proud of those young people. I still feel grateful that I was there and was able to see and feel the spirit they brought to life.

Certain aspects of those events have changed for me. In a rather abstract way, I might have said at the time: Yes, the soldiers and marshals come from working-class communities; there's class hatred here. What I couldn't have known then was that those obviously true words were in fact an almost empty formula, certainly in my own mouth, but also in the literate arguments I was acquainted with at the time. For years I had made my living at blue-collar jobs. Few (none, actually) of the artists, intellectuals, bohemians, and wastrels I knew had a similarly sustained experience. But my knowledge of working-class life was dreadfully incomplete. For almost a decade and a half now, I have been living among members of the rural working class, and though I have shared only a few of their interests and not any of their tribulations, I have made some friends and have come to know more than I did of working lives, though I still have much to learn. I realize now, for one thing, that the demonstrators at the Pentagon, myself included, were fatally unaware of the people in the uniforms. We were deliberately and acutely aware that there *were* people in the uniforms. We didn't blame them for the war, or even for following the orders that obligéd them to stand in front of us with bayonets thrust in our faces. There were many touching instances of awareness, compassion, and reaching out across the barriers. But these very moments betrayed the inability of the privileged young even to imagine the experiences of lives so different from their own. The expressions of compassion were authentic, and at the same time were innocent projections and idealizations, creating fictive persons who possessed freedom of choice and a wide range of possibilities. In this fellow feeling there was no awareness (and there could not be any) of the background of penury, enforced ignorance, and boredom shared by many of those in uniform; or of the absolute need for employment; or of the inexorable coercion in essential matters; or of the bitterness of having been always the losers in the worker-producing mills of the public schools. There were no working-class people among the demonstrators. Merely to be there was a sign of privilege. At one point there was a chant of "Join us! Join us!" It was deeply felt, was heart-wrenching in its yearning for a just and loving society—yet those were probably the bitterest of all words to the soldiers, who might have replied, "What are you asking? Do you realize the punishment?

Can you help us at all? Will your parents guarantee us a living, as they do you, until we can make our own? Will they pay our rent, buy our food, pay our doctor and dentist bills, send us to expensive schools, introduce us to their friends and their friends' friends so that superior employment and social power will always be ours? Is this what you mean by 'Join us!'?"

Hidden among the impressive moral convictions of the young demonstrators there really was an ulterior conviction that their way of doing things *in its entirety* was correct and unarguably superior to the (largely unknown) ways of the lower classes. I doubt that many were aware that their own quite leisurely habits of critical response, which seemed so natural, so clearly the very pattern of human spontaneity, were actually artifacts of privilege and education; and that the same habits of mind would be perceived by many members of the working class as hazardous luxuries, or mere sources of pain. The middle-class psychological fashions of the time extolled "sensitivity," "openness," expression of (as opposed to inhibition of) feeling and emotion. Working men and women, during those same years, as now, knew that their material survival and all possible advancement rested on one primary virtue: the ability to endure stoically discomfort, boredom, and, often, pain. Many methods of desensitization were familiar to them.

The Pentagon demonstration has meant many things to me.

I would say the same of the earlier civil rights march of 1963. I had been leading an exceedingly private life, isolated and lonely, and found myself abruptly in a vast throng, largely black, that was animated by the most extraordinary public spirit. It was militant, yet it was a spirit of reason. And in fact, the event itself was a monument of social peace, absolutely staggering in its effect on everyone I knew.

This began a period in my life (it was the second) in which I did join forces with other people and work toward a common good.

And when I think of it, I believe that it was actually on the momentum of the civil rights march that I went to work a bit later at a small school in a poverty neighborhood in New York, from which there came a book, and a family of my own, and a hugely altered way of life.

V

Thinking and writing of the past has made the idea of *self* more and more elusive. Perhaps it is only in action that self becomes real to us . . . except that the more vital the action, the more *self* recedes from consciousness. As an object of our own awareness it seems to consist almost entirely of otherness.

Dilemmas of self—self as object, self as terrain, self as stylistic deliberation—all these permeate the art of our century. The master poet of these stresses (and certainly they are stresses) is probably Jean Genet. His novels, especially the first and the last, were important to me at one time. What effect they had I don't know. I do know that my unhappiness made me an acute reader of them. I had experienced a revival of love with a woman I had already suffered for, and whose childishness was disastrously like my own. Our relationship failed again, this time definitively. But much else in my life had failed. I was looking at the world from a great distance, and with painful yearning.

Genet's grown-up homosexual loves are like figures in a childish landscape after some horrible disaster has occurred. They are heroes of rejection, they are *modes* of rejection; and having dismissed the world, care about nothing but love, or rather the affects of love, and in fact only certain of those. Some of his dazzling scenes are given settings that are incomprehensible except as states of mind. It is as if infantile fantasies of rage have been converted into architecture, or rather landscape, just at the moment the rage is beginning to subside. The mother has been consumed, the father annihilated. Some such disasters seem to be preconditions for Genet's starry nights of heart's ease.

Genet's inventions would be staggeringly vindictive were it not for the fact that he consciously affirms the underlying unconscious violence which in certain kinds of homosexuals creates obsessions and fetishistic objects of love. He affirms it precisely because it dissolves the ties of community, and therefore can be used as one of several levers to pry the world away from himself, the world having already cast him out and imprisoned him for life in a cell.

What an amazing invention this criminal pursuit of sainthood is that he announces in *Our Lady of the Flowers!* And what an extraordinary ancillary subject he discovers in his solitude: the phenomenology of the creative imagination; that is, the imagination under the stress of need and desire, and in the act of making art!

As did many of the artists I admired, Genet worked in such a way as to utilize the very dilemmas of self-consciousness that had paralyzed so many others, and in which I was suffering terribly at the time. His aesthetics, moreover, were harmonious with, were actually *functions* of, the primary action (the *plot!*) of assaulting selfhood, that is, assaulting his own past, eradicating it. The dynamics of the assault actually became the basis of his legend. Whatever its perversity, it was a triumph of will and pride, and I knew, or believed, that if I could carry out a similar assault, I would be free. Of course I could not. And more time had to pass before I learned my error. What I had wanted was not to be free of the past (a wish that actually seemed blasphemous to me), but to be free of the suffering of having lived it. I did not understand that freedom of this kind demands a spiritual labor, and not a labor merely of the mind.

The emotions of reading Genet were unique. I admired him and envied him the energy and eloquence of intellectual violence, but I never felt the love for him that I have felt for Proust and Tolstoy; and never felt a moment of the liberation I have experienced so often with Proust, laughing aloud in the sheer elation of unencumbered spirit. On the contrary, I distrusted Genet, and took very seriously the criminal aspect of his work as well as its peculiar honor and courtliness. Too, the polemical, natureless, encapsulated aspects of that consciousness were evident to me, and these set real limits to his powers. Nevertheless, no author at that time could have gripped me more.

Once one begins to praise the works that have mattered, that have made a shock in the soul (a sonic boom: the projectile has traveled far quite silently, and suddenly the pressure wave occurs), there is probably no end to it, since they keep happening, and are numerous anyway. But I see that four great artists who have been presences in my life—Proust, Cézanne, Van Gogh, Genet—have been heroes of solitude, and models of solitude.

Solitude, moreover, has been a theme in their work.

Van Gogh paints the portraits of real things (sunflowers, for example) in such a way as to produce symbols—which can't be done except in solitude and alienation. At the same time, because it is a religious enterprise and makes a spiritual use of everyday things, it is broadly accessible to other people. The harshness and anger, the headlong acting out of eccentric passions, the earnestness and lucidity and decency of speech of the letters, the opacity of action, the strange, childlike modesty toward experience, the terrible grief of his collapses into madness (as he called it) and the helplessness immediately afterward, his self-conscious yearning for communion with other artists, which he was in no way fitted to achieve—all these that ordinarily would be the man himself, and that are surely an achingly human presence, are somehow not attached to the underlying essential spirit one wants to call "Van Gogh," and that achieved only a wraithlike passage through the world.

VI

Perhaps one would not write at all if it were not such an excellent means of escaping the self, writing being the conduit, simultaneously, of unconscious life, human speech, and traditional forms.

I have had the experience several times of transposing dreams to paper, in stories and poems. And when I worked with the severely disturbed children, I found that dreaming was both an accompaniment and an aid.

I was deeply engaged in that work, and am still very proud of what I accomplished. Often, in order to go out in the evening (this was the period of my second marriage) I had to sleep in the late afternoon to recover from the six hours of intensive engagement with just two children. Frequently I dreamed of them, all sorts of things, including strategies, "cures," and changed behaviors. In one dream a brain-damaged boy who was unable to organize the neural and muscular activity needed for speaking but achieved only an explosive, chaotic jabbering spoke to me quietly in a rapt voice, a breathless, whispering voice marked by a strange gasping that seemed deliberate and actually efficient. In my dream I saw that he had gained control of his breathing by complex muscular strategies of his chest and abdomen. Some such strategies, organized into a physical program and extended over a period of months, did actually prove helpful to him, though not, of course, to the wonderful degree that the dream had projected.

In another dream, a twelve-year-old boy named Christopher, who never spoke to anyone, but who did speak aloud occasionally when he thought he was alone—brief phrases in a gruff, abrupt voice that sounded like the voice of his father—spoke to me in a joyous sweet voice that combined the happiness of infancy with the vocabulary and intelligence of the age of twelve. He explained to me why he behaved as he did—why he secluded himself from the others, why he wouldn't look at anyone, why he draped one arm up and across his head so that the palm dangled down and covered his ear; why he leaned his head continually to one side. The dream was long and complex, with many other figures in it, and a scene of birth, or in any event the arrival of a baby. I woke up more bedazzled by the dream than instructed by it. Nothing in it seemed usable. The wonderful explanations evaporated. And so I stopped thinking about it. But after work the next day, driving Christopher home (his mother was ill), I began playing a number game, a counting game on a very primitive level, and I played it in such a way as to give his usual silences the status of responses, just as one does with an infant. We came to a complex intersection. I missed the tail end of a three-way light and we had to wait. Suddenly I heard beside me the voice I had heard in my dream. The voice counted quite swiftly and easily up to fifty, and then—apparently because Christopher had become aware that he was speaking—gasped and fell silent.

During this period I worked as a lay therapist also with adults in group therapy. When the period as a whole came to an end, the end was presaged by a dream of the children. The dream saddened me and disturbed me. It was touched faintly by horror—but it made my feelings inescapably clear to me.

I dreamed that it was napping time at the little school. I had used to rest when the children rested, sitting by this one or that one, and perhaps briefly stroking or patting them. In my dream it was as if the children had been transformed into glassified dolls, as inert as bowling pins. I laid each one down. The feel and look of those hard, glossy, highly colored surfaces was both fascinating and appalling, but the momentum of the dream didn't falter, and when I awakened, though I was disturbed (I felt both guilt and fear), I knew that I was going to stop all these activities of psychotherapy, and try once again to find my way as a writer.

Years later, I dreamed the two following dreams during the same night, and wrote them down in the morning, not to analyze them (I detest that relationship, that proportion, or disproportion, between self-interested ratiocination and the achieved poetry of the unconscious), but to make them at home, to finish delivering the letter that had been sent to me.

I dreamed that I was walking down the main street of my hometown. (I hadn't been there for decades.) I was nearing the intersection at the center of town, walking downhill on the sidewalk. There weren't any cars in the street. Merce Cunningham, whom I had never met but whose work I had followed from the beginning, suddenly appeared in the street, wearing the white overalls and tennis shoes of one of his dances. He called to me, "Here's that dance you like . . ." and executed about twenty seconds' worth of his one-minute soft-shoe dance. I was delighted, and responded in kind, that is, with a mini-ovation. The dream was delightful and buoyant. Thinking of it later, I was encouraged by its linking of this boyhood place with a figure from my adult life of alienation.

That same night I dreamed that I was running down long, grassy terraces, and leaping down broad flights of garden stairs that appeared in the terraces. It was a deep rich summer night of grass and trees, a dark sky, large houses with lighted windows, which resembled the houses of my hometown. My sense of my age —as in the other dream—was not a sense of period, or time, but simply a sense of my body, which was buoyant and strong, as in adolescence. The mood of the dream was somber, actually sad, yet everything was luminous, as if some glowing, pulsing energy, without producing light, had created a brightness in the air. Some tragedy had occurred in one of the houses, and my awareness of myself had a great deal to do with this tragedy. As I came to each flight of stairs in the grassy terraces, I leaped from the topmost steps, and assuming an ardent posture, like a dancer, glided through the air in long, soaring leaps. I held my arms forward, with clenched fists, arms not quite parallel but opened toward the sides and slightly elevated. I executed this same leap at each flight of stairs, but some leaps were called Winged Victories and others Winged Griefs.

El Salvador:
An Aide-Mémoire

CAROLYN FORCHÉ

Carolyn Forché's first book of poems, *Gathering the Tribes*, won the Yale
Series of Younger Poets Award in 1976. Subsequently she received fellow-
ships from the Guggenheim Foundation and the National Endowment for
the Arts. Between 1978 and 1980 she made numerous trips to El Salvador,
where she worked as a journalist and human rights advocate. In 1981 her
second book of poems, *The Country Between Us*, received the di Castagnola
Award and was chosen as the Lamont Selection of the Academy of American Poets. It was published in 1982 by Harper & Row.

I

The year Franco died, I spent several months on Mallorca translating the poetry of Claribel Alegría, a Salvadoran in voluntary exile.
During those months the almond trees bloomed and lost flower,
the olives and lemons ripened, and we hauled baskets of apricots
from Claribel's small *finca*. There was bathing in the *cala*, fresh
squid under the palm thatch, drunk Australian sailors to dance
with at night. It was my first time in Europe and there was no better
place at that time than Spain. I was there when Franco's anniversary passed for the first time in forty years without notice—and the
lack of public celebration was a collective hush of relief. I traveled
with Claribel's daughter, Maya Flakoll, for ten days through An-
dalusia by train, visiting poetry shrines. The *gitanos* had finally
pounded a cross into the earth to mark the grave of Federico
Garcia Lorca, not where it had been presumed to be all this time,
not beneath an olive tree, but in a bowl of land rimmed by pines.
We hiked the eleven kilometers through the Sierra Nevada foot-

hills to La Fuente Grande and held a book of poems open over the silenced poet.

On Mallorca I lost interest in the *cala* sunbathing, the parties that carried into the morning, the staggering home wine-drunk up the goat paths. I did not hike to the peak of the Teix with baskets of *entremesas* nor, despite well-intentioned urgings, could I surrender myself to the island's diversionary summer mystique.

I was busy with Claribel's poems, and with the horrific accounts of the survivors of repressive Latin American regimes. Claribel's home was frequented by these wounded: writers who had been tortured and imprisoned, who had lost husbands, wives, and closest friends. In the afternoon, more than once I joined Claribel in her silent vigil near the window until the mail came, her "difficult time of day," alone in a chair in the perfect light of thick-walled Mallorquín windows. These were her afternoons of despair, and they haunted me. In those hours I first learned of El Salvador, not from the springs of her nostalgia for "the fraternity of dipping a tortilla into a common pot of beans and meat," but from the source of its pervasive brutality. My understanding of Latin American realities was confined then to the romantic devotion to Vietnam-era revolutionary pieties, the sainthood of Ernesto Che rather than the debilitating effects of the cult of personality that arose in the collective memory of Guevara. I worked into the late hours on my poems and on translations, drinking "101" brandy and chain-smoking Un-X-Dos. When Cuban writer Mario Benedetti visited, I questioned him about what "an American" could do in the struggle against repression.

"As a *North*american, you might try working to influence a profound change in your country's foreign policy."

Over coffee in the mornings I studied reports from Amnesty International–London and learned of a plague on Latin exiles who had sought refuge in Spain following Franco's death: a right-wing death squad known as the "AAA"—Anti-Communista Apostólica, founded in Argentina and exported to assassinate influential exiles from the southern cone.

I returned to the United States and in the autumn of 1977 was invited to El Salvador by persons who knew Claribel. "How much do you know about Latin America?" I was asked. Then: "Good. At least you know that you know nothing." A young writer, politically unaffiliated, ideologically vague, I was to be blessed with the rarity of a moral and political education—what at times would seem an unbearable immersion, what eventually would become a focused obsession. It would change my life and work, propel me toward engagement, test my endurance and find it wanting, and prevent me from ever viewing myself or my country again through precisely the same fog of unwitting connivance.

I was sent for a briefing to Dr. Thomas P. Anderson, author of *Matanza,* the definitive scholarly history of Salvador's revolution of 1932, and to Ignacio Lozano, a California newspaper editor and former ambassador (under Gerald Ford) to El Salvador. It was suggested that I visit Salvador as a journalist, a role that would of necessity become real. In January 1978 I landed at Ilopango, the dingy center-city airport which is now Salvador's largest military base. Arriving before me were the members of a human rights investigation team headed by then Congressman John Drinan, S.J. (Democrat of Massachusetts). I had been told that a black Northamerican, Ronald James Richardson, had been killed while in the custody of the Salvadoran government and that a Northamerican organization known as the American Institute for Free Labor Development (AIFLD, an organ of the AFL-CIO and an intelligence front) was manipulating the Salvadoran agricultural workers. Investigation of the "Richardson Case" exposed me to the sub-rosa activities of the Salvadoran military, whose highest-ranking officers and goverment officials were engaged in cocaine smuggling, kidnapping, extortion, and terrorism; through studying AIFLD's work, I would learn of the spurious intentions of an organization destined to become the architect of the present agrarian reform. I was delivered the promised exposure to the stratified life of Salvador, and was welcomed to "Vietnam, circa 1959." The "Golden Triangle" had moved to the isthmus of the Americas, "rural pacification" was in embryo, the seeds of rebellion had taken root in destitution and hunger.

Later my companion and guide, "Ricardo," changed his description from "Vietnam" to "a Nazi forced labor camp." "It is not hyperbole," he said quietly. "You will come to see that." In those first twenty days I was taken to clinics and hospitals, to villages, farms, prisons, coffee mansions and processing plants, to cane mills and the elegant homes of American foreign service bureaucrats, nudged into the hillsides overlooking the capital, where I was offered cocktails and platters of ocean shrimp; it was not yet known what I would write of my impressions or where I would print them. Fortuitously, I had published nationally in my own country, and in Salvador "only poetry" did not carry the pejorative connotation I might have ascribed to it then. I knew nothing of political journalism but was willing to learn—it seemed, at the time, an acceptable way for a poet to make a living.

I lay on my belly in the *campo* and was handed a pair of field glasses. The lenses sharpened on a plastic tarp tacked to four maize stalks several hundred yards away, beneath which a woman sat on the ground. She was gazing through the plastic roof of her "house" and hugging three naked, emaciated children. There was an aqua plastic dog-food bowl at her feet.

"She's watching for the plane," my friend said. "We have to get out of here now or we're going to get it too." I trained the lenses on the woman's eye, gelled with disease and open to a swarm of gnats. We climbed back in the truck and rolled the windows up just as the duster plane swept back across the field, dumping a yellow cloud of pesticide over the woman and her children to protect the cotton crop around them.

At the time I was unaware of the pedagogical theories of Paulo Freire *(Pedagogy of the Oppressed),* but found myself learning in situ the politics of cultural immersion. It was by Ricardo's later admission "risky business," but it was thought important that a few Northamericans, particularly writers, be sensitized to Salvador prior to any military conflict. The lessons were simple and critical, the methods somewhat more difficult to detect. I was given a white lab jacket and, posing as a Northamerican physician, was asked to work in a rural hospital at the side of a Salvadoran doctor who was paid two hundred dollars a month by her government to care for one hundred thousand *campesinos.* She had no lab, no X ray, no whole blood, plasma, or antibiotics, no anesthetics or medicines, no autoclave for sterilizing surgical equipment. Her forceps were rusted, the walls of her operating room were studded with flies; beside her hospital, a coffee-processing plant's refuse heaps incubated the maggots, and she paid a *campesina* to swish the flies away with a newspaper while she delivered the newborn. She was forced to do caesarean sections at times without enough local anesthetic. Without supplies, she worked with only her hands and a cheap ophthalmoscope. In her clinic I held children in my arms who died hours later for want of a manual suction device to remove the fluid from their lungs. Their peculiar skin rashes spread to my hands, arms, and belly. I dug maggots from a child's open wound with a teaspoon. I contracted four strains of dysentery and was treated by stomach antiseptics, effective yet damaging enough to be banned by our own FDA. This doctor had worked in the *campo* for years, a lifetime of delivering the offspring of thirteen-year-old mothers who thought the navel marked the birth canal opening. She had worked long enough to feel that it was acceptable to ignore her own cervical cancer, and hard enough in Salvador to view her inevitable death as the least of her concerns.

I was taken to the homes of landowners, with their pools set like aquamarines in the clipped grass, to the afternoon games of canasta over quaint local *pupusas* and tea, where parrots hung by their feet among the bougainvillea and nearly everything was imported, if only from Miami or New Orleans. One evening I dined with a military officer who toasted America, private enterprise, Las Vegas, and the "fatherland," until his wife excused herself and in a drape of cigar smoke the events of "The Colonel" were told, almost a *poème trouvé*. I had only to pare down the memory and render it whole, unlined, and as precise as recollection would have it. I did not wish to endanger myself by the act of poeticizing such a necessary reportage. It became, when I wrote it, the second insistence of El Salvador to infiltrate what I so ridiculously preserved as my work's allegiance to Art. No more than in any earlier poems did I choose my subject.

The following day I was let into Ahuachapán prison (now an army *cuartel*). We had been driving back from a meeting with Salvadoran feminists when Ricardo swung the truck into a climb through a tube of dust toward the run-down fortification. I was thirsty, infested with intestinal parasites, fatigued from twenty days of ricocheting between extremes of poverty and wealth. I was horrified, impatient, suspicious of almost everyone, paralyzed by sympathy and revulsion. I kept thinking of the kindly, silver-haired American political officer who informed me that in Salvador, "there were always five versions of the truth." From this I was presumably to conclude that the truth could not therefore be known. Ricardo seemed by turns the Braggioni of Porter's "Flowering Judas" and a pedagogical genius of considerable vision and patience. As we walked toward the gate, he palmed the air to slow our pace.

"This is a criminal penitentiary. You will have thirty minutes inside. Realize, please, at all times where you are, and whatever you see here, understand that for political prisoners it is always much worse. O.K."

We shook hands with the chief guard and a few subordinates, clean-shaven youths armed with G-3s. There was first the stench: rotting blood, excrement, buckets of urine, and corn slop. A man in his thirties came toward us, dragging a swollen green leg, his pants ripped to the thigh to accommodate the swelling. He was introduced as "Miguel" and I as a "friend." The two men shook hands a long time, standing together in the filth, a firm knot of warmth between them. Miguel was asked to give me a "tour," and he agreed, first taking a coin from his pocket and slipping it into the guard station soda machine. He handed me an orange Nehi, urging me somewhat insistently to take it, and we began a slow walk into the first hall. The prison was a four-square with an open court in the center. There were bunk rooms where the cots were stacked three deep and some were hung with newsprint "for privacy." The men squatted on the ground or along the walls, some stirring small coal fires, others ducking under urine-soaked tents of newspaper. It was suppertime, and they were cooking their dry tortillas. I used the soda as a relief from the stench, like a hose of oxygen. There were maybe four hundred men packed into Ahuachapán, and it was an odd sight, an American woman, but there was no heckling.

"Did you hear the shots when we first pulled up?" Ricardo asked. "Those were warnings. A visitor—behave."

Miguel showed me through the workrooms and latrines, finishing his sentences with his eyes: a necessary skill under repressive regimes, highly developed in Salvador. With the guards' attention diverted, he gestured toward a black open doorway and suggested that I might wander through it, stay a few moments, and come back out "as if I had seen nothing."

I did as he asked, my eyes adjusting to the darkness of that shit-smeared room with its single chink of light in the concrete.

There were wooden boxes stacked against one wall, each a meter by a meter, with barred openings the size of a book, and within them there was breathing, raspy and half conscious. It was a few moments before I realized that men were kept in those cages, their movement so cramped that they could neither sit, stand, nor lie down. I recall only magnified fragments of my few minutes in that room. I was rooted to the clay floor, unable to move either toward or away from the cages. I turned from the room toward Miguel, who pivoted on his crutch and with his eyes on the ground said in a low voice, *"La oscura,"* the dark place. "Sometimes a man is kept in there a year, and cannot move when he comes out."

We caught up with Ricardo, who leaned toward me and whispered, "Tie your sweater sleeves around your neck. You are covered with hives."

In the cab of the truck I braced my feet against the dashboard and through the half-cracked window shook hands with the young soldiers, smiling and nodding. A hundred meters from the prison I lifted Ricardo's spare shirt in my hands and vomited. We were late for yet another meeting, the sun had dropped behind the volcanoes, my eyes ached. When I was empty the dry heaves began, and after the sobbing a convulsive shudder. Miguel was serving his third consecutive sentence, this time for organizing a hunger strike against prison conditions. In that moment I saw him turn back to his supper, his crutch stamping circles of piss and mud beside him as he walked. I heard the screams of a woman giving birth by caesarean without anesthetic in Ana's hospital. I saw the flies fastened to the walls in the operating room, the gnats on the eyes of the starving woman, the reflection of flies on Ana's eyes in the hospital kitchen window. The shit, I imagined, was inside my nostrils and I would smell it the rest of my life, as it is for a man who in battle tastes a piece of flesh or gets the blood under his fingernails. The smell never comes out; it was something Ricardo explained once as he was falling asleep.

"Feel this," he said, maneuvering the truck down the hill road. "This is what oppression feels like. Now you have begun to learn something. When you get back to the States, what you do with this is up to you."

Between 1978 and 1981 I traveled between the United States and Salvador, writing reports on the war waiting to happen, draw-

ing blueprints of prisons from memory, naming the dead. I filled
soup bowls with cigarette butts, grocery boxes with files on American involvement in the rural labor movement, and each week I took
a stool sample to the parasite clinic. A priest I knew was gang-
raped by soldiers; another was hauled off and beaten nearly to
death. On one trip a woman friend and I were chased by the death
squad for five minutes on the narrow back roads that circle the city;
her evasive driving and considerable luck saved us. One night a
year ago I was interviewing a defecting member of the Christian
Democratic Party. As we started out of the drive to go back to my
hotel, we encountered three plainclothesmen hunched over the
roof of a taxicab, their machine guns pointed at our windshield.
We escaped through a grove of avocado trees. The bodies of
friends have turned up disemboweled and decapitated, their teeth
punched into broken points, their faces sliced off with machetes.
On the final trip to the airport we swerved to avoid a corpse, a man
spread-eagled, his stomach hacked open, his entrails stretched
from one side of the road to the other. We drove over them like
a garden hose. My friend looked at me. *Just another dead man,* he
said. And by then it had become true for me as well: the unthinkable, the sense of death within life before death.

II

"I see an injustice," wrote Czeslaw Milosz in *Native Realm;* "a
Parisian does not have to bring his city out of nothingness every
time he wants to describe it." So it was with Wilno, that Li-
thuanian/Polish/Byelorussian city of the poet's childhood, and so
it has been with the task of writing about Salvador in the United
States. The country called by Gabriela Mistral "the Tom Thumb
of the Americas" would necessarily be described to Northamericans as "about the size of Massachusetts." As writers we could
begin with its location on the Pacific south of Guatemala and west
of Honduras and with Ariadne's thread of statistics: 4.5 million
people, 400 per square kilometer (a country without silence or
privacy), a population growth rate of 3.5 percent (such a population would double in two decades). But what does "90 percent
malnutrition" mean? Or that "80 percent of the population has no
running water, electricity, or sanitary services"? I watched women

push feces aside with a stick, lower their pails to the water, and
carry it home to wash their clothes, their spoons and plates, themselves, their infant children. The chief cause of death has been
amoebic dysentery. One out of four children dies before the age
of five; the average human life span is forty-six years. What does
it mean when a man says, "It is better to die quickly fighting than
slowly of starvation"? And that such a man suffers toward that
decision in what is now being called "Northamerica's backyard"?
How is the language used to draw battle lines, to identify the
enemy? What are the current euphemisms for empire, public defense of private wealth, extermination of human beings? If the
lethal weapon is the soldier, what is meant by "nonlethal military
aid"? And what determined the shift to helicopter gunships,
M-16s, M-79 grenade launchers? The State Department's white
paper entitled "Communist Interference in El Salvador" argues
that it is a "case of indirect armed aggression against a small Third
World country by Communist powers acting through Cuba."
James Petras in *The Nation* (March 28, 1981) has argued that the
report's "evidence is flimsy, circumstantial or nonexistent; the reasoning and logic is slipshod and internally inconsistent; it assumes
what needs to be proven; and finally, what facts are presented
refute the very case the State Department is attempting to demonstrate." On the basis of this report, the popular press sounded an
alarm over the "flow of arms." But from where have arms
"flowed," and to whom and for what? In terms of language, we
could begin by asking why Northamerican arms are weighed in
dollar value and those reaching the opposition measured in ton-
nage. Or we could point out the nature of the international arms
market, a complex global network in which it is possible to buy
almost anything for the right price, no matter the country of origin
or destination. The State Department conveniently ignores its own
intelligence on arms flow to the civilian right, its own escalation of
military assistance to the right-wing military, and even the discrep-
ancies in its final analysis. But what does all this tell us about who
is fighting whom for what? Americans have been told that there is
a "fundamental difference" between "advisers" and military
"trainers." Could it simply be that the euphemism for American
military personnel must be changed so as not to serve as a mne-
monic device for the longest war in our failing public memory? A

year ago I asked the American military attaché in Salvador what would happen if one of these already proposed advisers returned to the U.S. in a flag-draped coffin. He did not argue semantics.

"That," he said, smiling, "would be up to the American press, wouldn't it?"

Most of that press had held with striking fidelity to the State Department text: a vulnerable and worthy "centrist" government besieged by left- and right-wing extremists, the former characterized by their unacceptable political ideology, the latter rendered nonideologically unacceptable, that is, only in their extremity. The familiar ring of this portrayal has not escaped U.S. apologists, who must explain why El Salvador is not "another Vietnam." Their argument hinges, it seems, on the rapidity with which the U.S. could assist the Salvadoran military in the task of "defeating the enemy." Tactically, this means sealing the country off, warning all other nations to "cease and desist" supplying arms, using violations of that warning as a pretext for blockades and interventions, but excepting ourselves in our continual armament of what we are calling the "government" of El Salvador. Ignoring the institutional self-interest of the Salvadoran army, we blame the presumably "civilian" right for the murder of thousands of *campesinos*, students, doctors, teachers, journalists, nuns, priests, and children. This requires that we ignore the deposed and retired military men who command the activities of the death squads with impunity, and that the security forces responsible for the killings are under the command of the army, which is under the command of the so-called centrist government and is in fact the government itself.

There are other differences between the conflicts of El Salvador and Vietnam. There is no People's Republic of China to the north to arm and ally itself with a people engaged in a protracted war. The guerrillas are not second-generation Vietminh, but young people who armed themselves after exhaustive and failed attempts at nonviolent resistance and peaceful change. The popular organizations they defend were formed in the early seventies by *campesinos* who became socially conscious through the efforts of grass-roots clergymen teaching the Medellín doctrines of social justice; the precursors of these organizations were prayer and Bible study groups, rural labor organizations and urban trade unions. As the military government grew increasingly repressive, the opposition widened to include all other political parties, the Catholic majority, the university and professional communities, and the small-business sector.

Critics of U.S. policy accurately recognize parallels between the two conflicts in terms of involvement, escalation, and justification. The latter demands a vigilant "euphemology" undertaken to protect language from distortions of military expedience and political convenience. Noam Chomsky has argued that "among the many symbols used to frighten and manipulate the populace of the democratic states, few have been more important than terror and terrorism. These terms have generally been confined to the use of violence by individual and marginal groups. Official violence, which is far more extensive in both scale and destructiveness, is placed in a different category altogether. This usage has nothing to do with justice, causal sequence, or numbers abused." He goes on to say that "the question of proper usage is settled not merely by the official or unofficial status of the perpetrators of violence but also by their political affiliations." State violence is excused as "reactive," and the "turmoil" or "conflict" is viewed ahistorically.

It is true that there have been voices of peaceful change and social reform in El Salvador—the so-called centrists—but the U.S. has never supported them. We backed one fraudulently elected military regime after another, giving them what they wanted and still want: a steady infusion of massive economic aid with which high-ranking officers can ensure their personal futures and the loyalty of their subordinates. In return we expect them to guarantee stability, which means holding power by whatever means necessary for the promotion of a favorable investment climate, even if it requires us to exterminate the population, as it has come to mean in Salvador. The military, who always admired "Generalissimo Franco," and are encouraged in their anti-Communist crusade, grow paranoid and genocidal. Soldiers tossed babies into the air near the Sumpul River last summer for target practice during the cattle-prod roundup and massacre of six hundred peasants. Whole families have been gunned down or hacked to pieces with machetes, including the elderly and the newborn. Now that the massacre and the struggle against it have become the occasion to "test American resolve," the Salvadoran military is all too aware of the security of its position and the impunity with which it may

operate. Why would a peasant, aware of the odds, of the significance of American backing, continue to take up arms on the side
of the opposition? How is it that such opposition endures, when
daily men and women are doused with gasoline and burned alive
in the streets as a lesson to others; when even death is not enough,
and the corpses are mutilated beyond recognition? The answer to
that question in El Salvador answers the same for Vietnam.

III

We were waved past the military guard station and started
down the highway, swinging into the oncoming lane to pass slow
sugar cane trucks and army transports. Every few kilometers, pa-
trols trekked the gravel roadside. It was a warm night, dry but close
to the rainy season. Juan palmed the column shift, chain-smoked,
and motioned with his hot-boxed cigarette in the direction of San
Marcos. Bonfires lit by the opposition were chewing away at the
dark hillside. As we neared San Salvador, passing through the
slums of Candelaria, I saw that the roads were barricaded. More
than once Juan attempted a shortcut, but upon spotting military
checkpoints, changed his mind. To relieve the tension, he dug a
handful of change from his pocket and showed me his collection
of deutsche marks, Belgian francs, Swedish öre and kronor, holding each to the dashboard light and naming the journalist who had
given it to him, the country, the paper. His prize was a coin from
the Danish reporter whose cameras had been shot away as he
crouched on a rooftop to photograph an army attack on protest
marchers. That was a month before, on January 22, 1980, when
some hundred lost their lives; it was the beginning of a savage year
of extermination. Juan rose from his seat and slipped the worthless
coins back into his pocket.

Later that spring, Rene Tamsen of WHUR radio, Washington,
D.C., would be forced by a death squad into an unmarked car in
downtown San Salvador. A Salvadoran photographer, Cesar
Najarro, and his *Crónica del Pueblo* editor would be seized during
a coffee break. When their mutilated bodies were discovered, it
would be evident that they had been disemboweled before death.
A Mexican photojournalist, Ignacio Rodriguez, would fall in August to a military bullet. After Christmas an American free-lancer,

John Sullivan, would vanish from his downtown hotel room. Censorship of the press. In January 1981, Ian Mates would hit a land mine and that South African TV cameraman would bleed to death. In a year, no one would want the Salvador assignment. In a year, journalists would appear before cameras trembling and incredulous, unable to reconcile their perceptions with those of Washington, and even established media would begin to reflect this dichotomy. Carter policy had been to downplay El Salvador in the press while providing "quiet" aid to the repressive forces. Between 1978 and 1980, investigative articles sent to national magazines mysteriously disappeared from publication mailrooms, were oddly delayed in reaching editors, or were rejected after lengthy deliberations, most often because of El Salvador's "low news value." The American interreligious network and human rights community began to receive evidence of a conscious and concerted censorship effort in the United States. During interviews in 1978 with members of the Salvadoran right-wing business community, I was twice offered large sums of money to portray their government favorably in the American press. By early 1981, desk editors knew where El Salvador was and the playdown policy had been replaced by the Reagan administration's propaganda effort. The right-wing military cooperated in El Salvador by serving death threats on prominent journalists, while torturing and murdering others. American writers critical of U.S. policy were described by the Department of State as "the witting and unwitting dupes" of Communist propagandists. Those who have continued coverage of Salvador have found that the military monitors the wire services and all telecommunications, that pseudonyms often provide no security, that no one active in the documentation of the war of extermination can afford to be traceable in the country; effectiveness becomes self-limiting. It became apparent that my education in El Salvador had prepared me to work only until March 16, 1980, when after several close calls I was urged to leave the country. Monsignor Romero met with me, asking that I return to the U.S. and "tell the American people what is happening."

"Do you have any messages for [certain exiled friends]?"

"Yes. Tell them to come back."

"But wouldn't they be killed?"

"We are all going to be killed—you and me, all of us," he said quietly. A week later he was shot while saying mass in the chapel of a hospital for the incurable.

In those days I kept my work as a poet and journalist separate, of two distinct *mentalidades,* but I could not keep El Salvador from my poems because it had become so much a part of my life. I was cautioned to avoid mixing art and politics, that one damages the other, and it was some time before I realized that "political poetry" often means the poetry of protest, accused of polemical didacticism, and not the poetry which implicitly celebrates politically acceptable values. I suspect that underlying this discomfort is a naive assumption: that to locate a poem in an area associated with political trouble automatically renders it political.

All poetry is both pure and engaged, in the sense that it is made of language but it is also art. Any theory that takes one half of the social-aesthetic dynamic and accentuates it too much results in a breakdown. Stress of purity generates a feeble aestheticism which fails, in its beauty, to communicate. On the other hand, propagandistic hack work has no independent life as poetry. What matters is not whether a poem is political, but the quality of its engagement.

In *The Consciousness Industry,* Hans Magnus Enzensberger has argued the futility of locating the political aspect of poetry outside poetry itself, and that:

Such obtuseness plays into the hands of the bourgeois esthetic which would like to deny poetry any social aspect. Too often the champions of inwardness and sensibility are reactionaries. They consider politics a special subject best left to professionals, and wish to detach it completely from all other human activity. They advise poetry to stick to such models as they have devised for it, in other words, to high aspirations and eternal values. The promised reward for this continence is timeless validity. Behind these high-sounding proclamations lurks a contempt for poetry no less profound than that of vulgar Marxism. For a political quarantine placed on poetry in the name of eternal values itself serves political ends.

All language, then, is political; vision is always ideologically charged; perceptions are shaped a priori by our assumptions and sensibility is formed by a consciousness at once social, historical, and aesthetic. There is no such thing as nonpolitical poetry. The time, however, to determine what those politics will be is not the moment of taking pen to paper, but during the whole of one's life. We are responsible for the quality of our vision, we have a say in the shaping of our sensibility. In the many thousand daily choices we make, we create ourselves and the voice with which we speak and work.

From our tradition we inherit a poetic, a sense of appropriate subjects, styles, forms, and levels of diction; that poetic might insist that we be attuned to the individual in isolation, to particular sensitivity in the face of "nature," to special ingenuity in inventing metaphor. It might encourage a self-regarding, inward-looking poetry. Since Romanticism, didactic poetry has been presumed dead and narrative poetry has had at best a half life. Demonstration is inimical to a poetry of lyric confession and self-examination, therefore didactic poetry is seen as crude and unpoetic. To suggest a return to the formal didactic mode of Virgil's *Georgics* or Lucretius's *De Rerum Natura* would be to deny history, but what has survived of that poetic is the belief that a poet's voice must be inwardly authentic and compelling of our attention; the poet's voice must have authority.

I have been told that a poet should be of his or her time. It is my feeling that the twentieth-century human condition demands a poetry of witness. This is not accomplished without certain difficulties; the inherited poetic limits the range of our work and determines the boundaries of what might be said. There is the problem of metaphor, which moved Neruda to write: "the blood of the children/flowed out onto the streets/like . . . like the blood of the children." There is the problem of poeticizing horror, which resembles the problem of the photographic image that might render starvation visually appealing. There are problems of reduction and oversimplification; of our need to see the world as complex beyond our comprehension, difficult beyond our capacities for solution. If I did not wish to make poetry of what I had seen, what is it I thought poetry was?

At some point the two *mentalidades* converged, and the impulse to witness confronted the prevailing poetic; at the same time it seemed clear that eulogy and censure were no longer possible and that Enzensberger is correct in stating: "The poem expresses in exemplary fashion that it is not at the disposal of politics. That is its political content." I decided to follow my impulse to write narratives of witness and confrontation, to disallow obscurity and conventions, which might prettify that which I wished to document. As for that wish, the poems will speak for themselves, obstinate as always. I wish also to thank my friends and *compañeros* in El Salvador for persuading me during a period of doubt that poetry could be enough.

My Father's Love Letters

TESS GALLAGHER

Tess Gallagher is the author of two books of poetry, *Instructions to the Double* and *Under Stars,* both from Graywolf Press. She has recently completed a book of short stories, some of which will appear in *The New Yorker, Antaeus,* and *North American Review.* Her essays have appeared in the *Atlantic Monthly, Parnassus,* and *Ironwood.* She teaches undergraduate poetry writing and literature courses at Syracuse University.

It's two days before Christmas and I have checked myself into the Dewitt Ranch Motel. "We don't ask questions here," says the manager, handing me the key to number 66. I let him think what he thinks.

The room is what I need, what I've been imagining for the past two days—a place with much passing and no record. I feel guilty about spending the money, but I've trusted my instincts about what it will take to get this writing done. For the past week I've been absorbed with student manuscripts and term papers. At the finish, I discover I have all but vanished. Coming to the motel is a way to trick myself out of anonymity, to urge my identity to rise like cream to the top again.

I had known from the first moments of being asked to write about my influences as a writer that I would want to get back to the child in me. For to talk of influences for a writer is essentially to trace the development of a psychic and spiritual history, to go back to where it keeps starting as you think about it, as an invention of who you are becoming. The history which has left its deepest imprint on me has been an oral and actual history and so involves my willingness at a very personal level. It involves people no one

will ever know again. People like the motel room I write this in, full
of passing and no record. The "no record" part is where I come
in. I must try to interrupt their silence. Articulate it and so resur-
rect them so that homage can be paid.

To speak of influences, then, is not to say "Here, try this,"
only "This happened and this is what I think of it at this moment
of writing."

I want to begin with rain. A closeness, a need for rain. It is the
climate of my psyche and I would not fully have known this if I had
not spent a year in Arizona, where it rained only three glorious
times during my entire stay there. I begin with rain also because
it is a way of introducing my birthplace on the Olympic peninsula
in Washington State, the town of Port Angeles. The rain forest is
a few miles west. The rain is more violent and insistent there. Port
Angeles lies along the strait of Juan de Fuca and behind the town
are the Olympic Mountains. The Japanese current brings in warm
air, striking the mountains, which are snow-covered into June.

It is a faithful rain. You feel it has some allegiance to the trees
and the people, to the little harbor with its long arm of land which
makes a band of calm for the fishing boats and for the rafts of logs
soon to be herded to the mills. Inside or outside the wood-frame
houses, the rain pervades the temperament of the people. It brings
an ongoing thoughtfulness to their faces, a meditativeness that
causes them to fall silent for long periods, to stand at their windows looking out at nothing in particular. The people don't mind
getting wet. Galoshes, umbrellas—there isn't a market for them
here. The people walk in the rain as within some spirit they wish
not to offend with resistance. Most of them have not been to
Arizona. They know the rain is a reason for not living where they
live, but they live there anyway. They work hard in the logging
camps, in the pulp mills and lumberyards. Everything has a wet-
ness over it, glistening quietly as though it were still in the womb,
waiting to be born.

Growing up there, I thought the moss-light that lived with us
lived everywhere. It was a sleepy predawn light that muted the
landscape and made the trees come close. I always went outside
with my eyes wide, no need to shield them from sun bursts or the
steady assault of skies I was to know later in El Paso or Tucson.

The colors of green and gray are what bind me to the will to write poems.

Along with rain and a subdued quality of light, I have needed the nearness of water. I said once in an interview that if Napoleon had stolen his battle plans from the dreams of his sleeping men, then maybe I had stolen my poems from the gray presence of water.

The house I grew up in overlooks the eighteen-mile stretch of water between Canada and America at its far northwest reach. The freighters, tankers, tugs, and small fishing boats pass daily; and even at night a water star, the light on a mast, might mark a vessel's passage through the strait. My father was a longshoreman for many of these years and he knew the names of the ships and what they were carrying and where they came from: the *Kenyo Maru* (Japanese), the *Eastern Grace* (Liberian), the *Bright Hope* (Taiwan), the *Brilliant Star* (Panamanian), the *Shoshei Maru* (Japanese)—pulp for paper, logs for plywood, lumber for California. He explained that *Maru* was a word that meant that the ship would make its return home. I have been like these ships, always pointed on a course of return to this town and its waters.

On Saturdays my father would drive my mother and my three brothers and me into town to shop and then to wait for him while he drank in what we called the "beer joints." We would sit for hours in the car, watching the townspeople pass. I noticed what they carried, how they walked, their gestures as they looked into the store windows. In other cars were women and families waiting as we were, for men in taverns. In the life of a child, these periods of stillness in parked cars were small eternities. The only release or amusement was to see things, and to wonder about them. Since the making of images is for me perhaps ninety percent seeing and ten percent word power, this car seeing and the stillness it enforced contributed to a patience and a curiosity that heightened my ability to see. The things to be seen from a parked car were not spectacular, but they were what we had—and they promoted a fascination with the ordinary. My mother was an expert at this: "See that little girl with the pigtails. I bet she's never had her hair cut. Look there, her father's taking her in there where the men get their hair cut." And sure enough, the little girl would emerge twenty minutes later, eyes red from crying, one hand in her father's and the other clutching a small paper sack. "The pigtails are in there."

Every hour or so my mother would send me on a round of the taverns to try for a sighting of my father. I would peck on the windows and the barmaid would shake her head *no* or motion down the dim aisle of faces to where my father would be sitting on his stool, forgetting, forgetting us all for a while.

My father's drinking, and the quarrels he had with my mother because of it, terrorized my childhood. There is no other way to put it. And if coping with terror and anxiety are necessary to the psychic stamina of a poet, I had them in steady doses—just as inevitably as I had the rain. I learned that the world was not just, that any balance was temporary, that unreasonableness could descend at any minute, thrashing aside everything and everyone in its path.

Emotional and physical vulnerability was a constant. Yet the heart began to take shelter, to build understandings out of words. It seems that a poet is one who must be strong enough to live in the unprotected openness, yet not so strong that the heart enters what the Russian poet Akhmatova calls "the icy calm of unloving." Passion and forgiveness, emotional fortitude—these were the lessons of the heart I had no choice but to learn in my childhood. I wonder now what kept me from the calm of not loving. Perhaps it was the unspoken knowledge that love, my parents' love, through all was constant, though its blows could rake the quick of my being.

I was sixteen when I had my last lesson from the belt and my father's arm. I stood still in the yard, in full view of the neighbors. I looked steadily ahead, without tears or cries, as a tree must look while the saw bites in, then deepens to the core. I felt my spirit reach its full defiance. I stood somehow in the power of my womanhood that day and knew I had passed beyond humiliation. I felt my father's arm begin to know I had outleaped the pain. It came down harder. If pain could not find me, what then would enforce control and fear?

I say I entered my womanhood because I connect womanhood with a strong, enduring aspect of my being. I am aware, looking back, that women even more than children often serve a long apprenticeship to physically inflicted threat and pain. Perhaps because of this they learn more readily what the slave, the hostage, the prisoner, also know—the ultimate freedom of the spirit. They learn how unreasonable treatment and physical pain may be turned aside by an act of the will. This freedom of spirit is what has enabled poets down through the ages to record the courage and hopes of entire peoples even in times of oppression. That women have not had a larger share in the history of such poetry has always seemed a mystery to me, considering the wealth of spiritual power that suffering often brings when it does not kill or maim the spirit. I can only assume that words have been slow in coming to women because their days have, until recently, been given over so wholly to acts, to doing and caring for.

I did not feel sorry for myself during these periods of abuse and I did not stop loving. It was our hurt not to have another way to settle these things. For my father and I had no language between us in those numb years of my changing. All through my attempts in the poems, I have needed to forge a language that would give these dead and living lives a way to speak. There was often the feeling that the language might come too late, might even do damage, might not be equal to the love. All these fears. Finally no choice.

The images of these two primal figures, mother and father, condense now into a vision of my father's work-thickened hands, and my mother's back, turned in hopeless anger at the stove where she fixed eggs for my father in silence. My father gets up from the table, shows me the open palms of his hands. "Threasie," he says, "get an education. Don't get hands like these."

Out of this moment and others like it I think I began to make a formula which translates roughly: words = more than physical power = freedom from enslavement to job-life = power to direct and make meaning in your own life.

There were few examples of my parents' having used words to transcend the daily. The only example was perhaps my father's love letters. They were kept in a cedar chest at the foot of my bed. One day I came across them, under a heap of hand-embroidered pillowcases. There were other treasures there, like the deer horn used to call the hounds when my father had hunted as a young man. The letters were written on lined tablet paper with a yellow cast to it. Written with a pencil in a consistently erratic hand, signed "Les" for Leslie and punctuated with a brigade of *XXX XX*'s. I would stare at these *X*'s, as though they contained some impenetrable clue as to why this man and woman had come together. The letters were mainly informational—he had worked here, was going there, had seen so-and-so, would be coming back to Missouri at such and such a time. But also there was humor, harmless jokes some workman had told him, and little teasings that only my mother could have interpreted.

My mother's side of the correspondence was missing, probably because my father had thrown her letters away or lost them during the Depression years when he crossed the country, riding the rails, working in the cotton fields, the oil fields, and the coal mines. My mother's lost letters are as important to remember as those I found from my father. They were the now invisible lifeline that answered and provoked my father's heart-scrawl across the miles and days of their long courtship. I might easily have called this essay "My Mother's Love Letters," for they would have represented the most articulate half of the correspondence, had they been saved. That they are now irrevocably lost, except to the imagination, moves them into the realm of speculation. The very fact that my mother had saved my father's love letters became a sign to me as a child that love·*had* existed between my parents, no matter what acts and denials might come after.

As with my parents, invisible love has been an undercurrent in my poems, in the tone of them, perhaps. They have, when I can manage it, what Marianne Moore called iodine and what I call turpentine. A rawness of impulse, a sharpness, a tension, that complicates the emotion, that withholds even as it gives. This is a proclivity of being, the signature of a nature that had learned perhaps wrongheadedly that love too openly seen becomes somehow inauthentic, unrealized.

My father's love letters were then the only surviving record of my parents' courtship and, indeed, the only record that they ever loved each other, for they never showed affection for one another in front of us. On a fishing trip years after I'd left home, my father was to remark that they had written to each other for over ten years before they married in 1941.

My father's sleep was like the rain. It permeated the household. When he was home he seemed always to be sleeping. We saw him come home and we saw him leave. We saw him during the evening meal. The talk then was of the ILWU longshoremen's union and of the men he worked with. He worked hard. It could be said that he never missed a day's work. It was a fact I used in his defense when I thought my mother was too hard on him after a drinking bout.

Stanley Kunitz has seen the archetypal search for the father as a frequent driving force for some poets, his own father having committed suicide before his birth. It occurs to me that in my own case, the father was among the living dead, and this made my situation all the more urgent. It was as if I had set myself the task of waking him before it was too late. I seemed to need to tell him who he was and that what was happening to him mattered and was witnessed by at least one other. This is why he has been so much at the center of my best efforts in the poems.

The first poem I wrote that reached him was called "Black Money," this image taken from the way shoveling sulfur at the pulp mills had turned his money black. He had come to visit me in the Seattle apartment where I lived as a student and I remember telling him I'd written this poem for his birthday. I had typed it and sealed it into an envelope like a secret message. He seemed embarrassed, as if about to be left out of something. Then he tore the envelope open and unfolded the poem. He handed it back to me. "You read it to me," he said. I read the poem to him and as I read I could feel the need in his listening. I had finally reached him. "Now that's something," he said when I'd finished. "I'm going to show that to the boys down on the dock."

As the oldest child, I seemed to serve my parents' lives in an ambassadorial capacity. But I was an ambassador without a country, for the household was perpetually on the verge of dissolving. I cannot say how many times I watched my father go down the walk to the picket fence, leaving us forever, pausing long enough at the gate to look back at us huddled on the porch. "Who's coming with me?" he would ask. No one moved. Again and again we abandoned each other.

Maybe this was the making of my refugee mentality. And perhaps when you are an emotional refugee you learn to be industrious toward the prospect of love and shelter. You know both are fragile and that stability must lie with you or it is nowhere. You make a home of yourself. Words for me and later poems were the tools of that home-making.

Even when you think you are only a child and have nothing, there are things you have, and as Sartre has already told us, one of these things is words. When I saw I had words and that these could affect what happened to me and those I loved, I felt less powerless, as though these might win through, might at least mediate in a life ruled as much by chance as by intention.

These ambassadorial skills I was learning as a child were an odd kind of training for the writing of poems, perhaps, but they were just that. For in the writing of the poem you must represent both sides of the question. If not in fact, then in understanding. You must bring them into dialogue with one another fairly, without the bias of causes or indignation or needing too much to be right. It requires a widening of perspective, away from oversimplification—the strict good or bad, wrong or rightness of a situation. The sensibility I've been attempting to write out of wants to represent the spectrum of awareness. In this way the life is accounted for in its fullness, when I am able.

I have spoken of words as a stay against unreasonableness, and they are often this—though more to one's solitude than to the actual life. My father came to his own words late, but in time. I was to discover that at seventy he could entertain my poet friends and would be spoken of afterward as someone exceptional in their experience. He told stories, was witty, liked to laugh. But in those early days, my father was not a man you could talk with. He would drive me to my piano lessons, the family's one luxury, without speaking. He smoked cigarettes, one after the other. He was thinking and driving. If he had had anything to drink during these times it was best to give him a wide berth. I was often afraid of him, of the violence in him, though like the rain, tenderness was there, unspoken and with a fiber that strangely informed even the unreasonable. If to be a poet is to balance contraries, to see how seemingly opposite qualities partake of, in fact penetrate, each other, I learned this from my combative parents.

This long childhood period of living without surety contributed in another way to my urge to write poetry. If I had to give one word which serves my poetry more than any other, it might be

"uncertainty." Uncertainty which leads to exploration, to the artic-
ulation of fears, to the loss of the kind of confidence that provides
answers too quickly, too superficially. It is the poet's uncertainty
which leaves her continually in an openness to the possibilities of
being and saying. The true materials of poetry are essentially invisible—a capacity for the constant emptying of the house of the
word, turning it out homeless and humbled to search its way toward meaning again. Maybe "poem" for me is the act of a prolonged beginning, one without resolution except perhaps musically, rhythmically—the word "again" engraved on the fiery
hammer.

After my youngest brother's death when I was twenty, I began
to recognize the ability of poetry to extend the lives of those not
present except as memory. My brother's death was the official
beginning of my mortality. It filled my life, all our lives, with the
sense of an unspoken bond, a pain which traveled with us in memory. It was as though memory were a kind of flickering shadow left
behind by those who died. This caused me to connect memory
firmly to the life of the spirit and finally to write poems which
formalized the sharing of that memory.

I have been writing about my progress toward a life in words
and poems, but my first love was actually paint. As a child I took
great pleasure in the smell of linseed, the oil of it on my fingers,
the tubes of oil paint with their bands of approximate color near
the caps, the long-handled brushes. I had heard somewhere that
artists taught themselves by copying other painters. But the only
paintings we had in the house were those in some Bible books a
salesman had sold my mother. I began to copy these with oil colors
onto some rough paper I'd found in a boxcar near the paper mill
below our house. I remember especially my painting of Jacob
sleeping at the foot of a heavenly stairway, with several angels
descending. They each had a pair of huge wings and I wondered
at the time why they didn't just fly down, instead of using the stairs.
The faces of these angels occupied a great deal of my efforts. And
I think it is some help to being a poet to paint the faces of angels
when you are ten.

I finished the Jacob painting and sent it to my grandfather in
Missouri. He was a farmer and owned a thousand-acre farm of
scrub oak, farmland, and riverbed in the Ozarks. My mother had

been raised there. Often when she had a faraway look about her, I imagined she was visiting there in her thoughts.

Children sometimes adopt a second father or mother when they are cut off from the natural parent. Porter Morris, my uncle, was the father I could speak with. He lived with my grandparents on the farm in Windyville, Missouri, where I spent many of my childhood summers. He never married, but stayed with the farm even after my grandparents had died. He'd been a mule trainer during the Second World War, the only time he had ever left home. He loved horses and raised and gentled one for me, which he named Angel Foot because she was black except for one white foot.

I continued to visit my grandfather and my uncle during the five years of my first marriage. My husband was a jet pilot in the Marine Corps. We were stationed in the South, so I would go to cook for my uncle during the haying and I would also help stack the hay in the barn. My uncle and I took salt to the cattle. We sowed a field with barley and went to market in Springfield with a truck-load of pigs. There were visits with neighbors, Cleydeth and Joe Stefter or Jule Elliot, when we sat for hours telling stories and gossiping. Many images from my uncle's stories and from these visits to the farm got into the long poem "Songs of the Runaway Bride" in my first book.

My uncle lived alone at the farm after my grandfather's death, but soon he met a woman who lived with her elderly parents. He began to remodel an old house on the farm. There was talk of marriage. One day my mother called to say there had been a fire at the farm. The house had burned to the ground and my uncle could not be found. She flew to the farm, what remained of her childhood home. After the ashes had cooled, she searched with the sheriff and found my uncle's skeleton where it had burned into the mattress springs of the bed.

My mother would not accept the coroner's verdict that the fire had been caused by an electrical short-circuit, or a fire in the chimney. It was summer and no fire would have been laid. She combed the ashes looking for the shotgun my uncle always kept near his bed and the other gun, a rifle, he hunted with. They were not to be found. My mother believed her brother had been mur-dered and she set about proving it. She offered a reward and soon after, a young boy walking along the roadside picked my uncle's billfold out of the ditch, his name stamped in gold on the flap.

Three men were eventually brought to trial. I journeyed to Bolivar, Missouri, to meet my parents for the trial. We watched as the accused killer was released and the other two men, who had confessed to being his accomplices, were sentenced to five years in the penitentiary for manslaughter. Parole would be possible for them in two to three years. The motive had been money, although one of the men had held a grudge against my uncle for having been ordered to move out of a house he'd been renting from my uncle some three years before. They had taken forty dollars from my uncle, then shot him when he could not give them more. My parents and I came away from the trial stunned with disbelief and anger.

I tried to write it out, to investigate the nature of vengeance, to disarm myself of the anger I carried. I wrote two poems about this event: "Two Stories" and "The Absence." Images from my uncle's death also appeared in "Stepping Outside," the title poem of my first, limited-edition collection. I began to see poems as a way of settling scores with the self. I felt I had reached the only possible justice in the writing out of my anger and the honoring of the life that had been taken so brutally. The *In Cold Blood* aspect of my uncle's murder has caused violence to haunt my vision of what it is to live in America. Sometimes, with my eyes wide open, I still see the wall behind my grandfather's empty bed, and on it, the fiery angels and Jacob burning.

I felt if my uncle, the proverbial honest man, could be murdered in the middle of the night, then anything was possible. The intermittent hardships of my childhood were nothing compared to this. I saw how easily I could go into a state of fear and anger which would mar the energy of my life and consequently my poems for good. I think I began, in a steady way, to move toward accepting my own death, so that whenever it would come before me as a thought, I would release myself toward it. In the poems I've written that please me most, I seem able to see the experience with dead-living eyes, with a dead-living heart.

Fasting is another activity of the past four years that may have strengthened this out-of-body consciousness in me and ultimately in my poems. At least once a year and sometimes more often, I have done extensive fasting, sometimes on water alone (fifteen days) and sometimes on juices (eight to ten days). During these periods I don't do much. I don't write. It is as important sometimes *not* to write as it is to write. I try to stay alone during the fasting. An island of calm forms around me and many things in my life and in the lives closest to me become clear. It is a time to adjust my vision about what matters, what I should give my energy to.

Time during fasting takes on a slower dimension, in which the events seem more in agreement with their space, and the mind need not feel like a room full of accordions, as it often does in so-called normal times. My own sense of time in poems approximates what I experience in my life—that important time junctures of past and present events via memory and actual presences are always inviting new meanings, revisions of old meanings, and speculation about things still in the future. These time shifts are a special province of poems because they can happen there more quickly, economically, and convincingly than in any other art form, including film. Film is still struggling to develop a language of interiority using the corporeal image, while even words like *drum* or *grief* in poems can borrow inflection from the overlap of words in context, can form whole new entities, as in a line from Louise Bogan's poem "Summer Wish": "the drum pitched deep as grief."

Since my intention here has been to emphasize experiential influences rather than literary ones, I must speak of the Vietnam War, for it was the war that finally caused me to take up my life as a poet. For the first time since I had left home for college, I was thrown back on my own resources. My husband and I had met when I was eighteen and married when I was twenty-one. I was twenty-six when he left to fly missions in Vietnam. I'd had very little life on my own. It became a time to test my strengths. I began working as a ward clerk in a hospital, on the medical floor. I did this for about five months, while the news of the war arrived daily in my mailbox. I was approaching what a friend of that time called an "eclipse." He urged me to leave the country. It was the best decision I could have made, as I look back now.

My time in Ireland and Europe during the Vietnam War put me firmly in possession of my own life. But in doing this, it made my life in that former time seem fraudulent. The returning veterans, my husband among them, had the hardship of realizing that many Americans felt the war to be wrong. This pervasive judgment was burden to us both and one that eventually contributed to the dissolution of our marriage.

I began to experience a kind of psychic suffocation which expressed itself in poems that I copied fully composed from my dreams. For a while, this disassociation of dream material from my life caused the messages to go unheeded. But gradually my movement out of the marriage began to enact the images of dissolution in the poems. It was a parting that gave me unresolvable grief, yet at the same time allowed my life its first true joys as I began a full commitment to my writing. I think partings have often informed my poems with a backward longing, and it was especially so with this one.

I returned to Seattle in 1969 and began to study poetry with David Wagoner at the University of Washington. My family did not understand what I was doing. Why should I divorce and then go back to college to learn to write poetry? It was beyond them. What was going to become of me now? Who would take care of me?

Trees have always been an important support to the solitude I connect with the writing of poetry. I suspect my affection and need of them began in those days in my childhood when I was logging with my parents. There was a coolness in the forest, a feeling of light filtering down from the arrow-shaped tops of the evergreens. The smell of pitch comes back. The chain-saw snarl and a spray of wood chips. Sawdust in the cuffs of my jeans. My brothers and I are again the woodcutter's children. We play under the trees, but even our play is a likeness to work. We construct shelters of rotten logs, thatch them with fireweed, and then invite our parents into the shelters to eat their lunches. We eat Spam sandwiches and smoked fish, with a Mountain Bar for dessert. After a time, my parents give me a little hatchet and a marking stick so I can work with them, notching the logs to be cut up into pulpwood to be made into paper. My brothers and I strip cones from the fallen trees, milking the hard pellets with our bare hands into gunnysacks, which are sold to the Forestry Department for ten dollars a bag. There is a living to be made and all of us are expected to do our share.

This word *share* has become a sadly lost word in American life.

Children seem not to be taught sharing as we were. It seems a part of my attitude toward being a poet—that my writing serve not only my own life but the lives of others, the community at large.

When I think of it now, it is not far from the building of those makeshift shelters to the making of poems. You take what you find, what comes naturally to the hand and mind. There was the sense with these shelters that they wouldn't last, but that they were exactly what could be done at the time. There were great gaps between the logs because we couldn't notch them into each other, but this allowed us to see the greater forest between them. It was a house that remembered its forest. And for me, the best poems, no matter how much order they make, have an undercurrent of forest, of the larger unknown.

To spend one's earliest days in a forest with a minimum of supervision gave a lot of time for exploring. I also had some practice in being lost. Both exploring and being lost are, it seems now, the best kind of training for a poet. When I think of those times I was lost, it comes back with a strange exhilaration, as though I had died, yet had the possibility of coming back to life. The act of writing a poem is like that. It is that sense of aloneness which is trying to locate the world again, but not too soon, not until the voice has made its cry, "Here, here, over here," and the answering voices have called back, "Where are you?"

My mother and father started logging together in 1941, the year my mother traveled from Missouri by bus to marry my father. As far as she knows, she was the only woman who worked in the woods, doing the same work the men did. She was mainly the choker-setter and haul-back. She hauled the heavy steel cable, used to yard the logs into the landing, out over the underbrush to be hooked around the fallen trees. My mother's job was a dangerous one because the trees, like any dying thing, would often thrash up unexpectedly or release underbrush which could take out an eye or lodge in one's side. She also lifted and stacked the pulpwood onto the truck and helped in the trimming of the branches. She did this work for seven years.

There is a photograph of my mother sitting atop two gigantic logs in her puffed-sleeved blouse and black work pants. It has always inspired me with a pride in my sex. I think I grew up with the idea that whatever the rest of the world said about women, the woman my mother was stood equal to any man and maybe one better. Her labor was not an effort to prove anything to anyone. It was what had to be done for the living. I did not think of her as unusual until I was about fourteen. I realized then that she was a wonderful mechanic. She could fix machines, could take them apart and reassemble them. None of the mothers of my friends had such faith in their own abilities. She was curious and she taught herself. She liked to tinker, to shift a situation or an object around. She had an eye for possibilities and a faculty for intuitive decision-making that afterward looked like knowledge. I feel I've transferred to the writing of poems many of my mother's explorative methods, even a similar audacity toward my materials.

"What happened to those letters?" I ask my mother over the telephone. I don't tell her I'm at the Dewitt Ranch Motel writing this essay. I don't tell her I'm trying to understand why I keep remembering my father's love letters as having an importance to my own writing.

"Well, a lot of them were sent to the draft board," she says. "Your dad and I were married November of forty-one. Pearl Harbor hit December seventh, so they were going to draft your father. A lot of men was just jumping up to get married to avoid the draft. We had to prove we'd been courting. The only way was to send the letters, so they could see for themselves."

"But what happened to the letters?"

"There was only about three of them left. You kids got into them, so I burnt them."

"You burnt them? Why? Why'd you do that?"

"They wasn't nothing in them."

"But you kept them," I say. "You saved them."

"I don't know why I did," she says. "They didn't amount to anything."

I hang up. I sit on one of the two beds and stare out at an identical arm of the motel which parallels the unit I'm in. I think of my father's love letters being perused by the members of the draft board. They become convinced that the courtship is authentic. They decide not to draft him into the war. As a result of his having written love letters, he does not go to his death, and my birth takes place. It is an intricate chain of events, about which I had no idea at the start of this essay.

I think of my father's love letters burning, of how they might never have come into their true importance had I not returned to them here in my own writing. I sit in the motel room, a place of much passage and no record, and feel I have made an important assault on the Great Nothing, though the letters are gone, though they did not truly exist until this writing, even for my parents, who wrote and received them.

My father's love letters are the sign of a long courtship and I pay homage to that, the idea of writing as proof of the courtship —the same blind, persistent hopefulness that carries me again and again into poems.

Cartoons

JOHN GARDNER

John Gardner was the author of novels, stories, children's books, scholarly books, opera libretti, and scripts for radio, TV, and film. He taught literature and creative writing at the State University of New York, Binghamton. He was killed in a motorcycle accident in September 1982. He was forty-nine.

Trying to figure out the chief influences on my work as a writer turns out to be mainly a problem of deciding what not to include. I grew up in a family where literary influence was everywhere, including under the bridge on our dirt road, where I kept my comic books. My father was (is) a memorizer of poetry and scripture, a magnificent performer in the old reciter tradition. (I once did a reading in Rochester, New York, near Batavia, where I grew up. After I'd finished, several people remarked that I was a wonderful reader—"though not quite up to your father, of course.") He did readings of everything from Eddie Guest to Shakespeare and the Book of Job at the monthly Grange meetings, in schools, churches, hospitals. While he milked the cows, my mother (who'd once been his high school English teacher) would read Shakespeare plays aloud to him from her three-legged stool behind the gutter, and he would take, yelling from the cow's flank, whatever part he'd decided on that night—Macbeth, King Lear, Hamlet, and so on. My mother was a well-known performer too, except she mainly sang. She had one of those honey-sweet Welsh soprano voices and sang everything from anthems to the spirituals she'd learned from an old black woman who took care of her during her childhood in Missouri. Often my mother performed in blackface, with a red bandanna, a practice that may sound distasteful unless you understand she wasn't kidding, she was authentic, flatting, quarter-toning, belting it out; she was amazing. They frequently worked together, my mother and father, and were known all over western New York. Sometimes they were in plays—my mother often directed—and wherever they went, riding around in the beat-up farm truck or just sitting in the kitchen, they sang, always in harmony, like crazy people.

The house was full of books, very few of them books that would now be thought respectable, aside from the Shakespeare and Dickens. My parents read aloud a lot—the narrative poems of Scott, miles of Longfellow, spooky stories by Edgar Allan Poe, the poems of Tennyson and Browning, also rather goofy religious writers (I loved them; what did I know?) like Lloyd C. Douglas and some woman whose name escapes me now, who wrote Jesus-filled love stories with titles like *A Patch of Blue*. My grandmother, who was bedridden through much of my childhood, was especially fond of this religious lady, and one of my more pleasant chores was to read her these tender little novels. The climax was always the moment the boy shyly touched the girl's hand. I've never found anything more sexually arousing than that Jesus-filled, long-delayed touch. I mean it was smut, it nearly made me a pervert, and not a court in the land that could nail her.

My favorite authors, at least when I was eight to eighteen, were in what might be described as the nonrealistic tradition: God, Dickens, and Disney. One of my less pleasant chores when I was young was to read the Bible from one end to the other. Reading the Bible straight through is at least seventy percent discipline, like learning Latin. But the good parts are, of course, simply amazing. God is an extremely uneven writer, but when he's good, nobody can touch him. I learned to find the good parts easily (some very sexy stuff here too), and both the poetry and the storytelling had a powerful effect on what I think good fiction ought to be. Dickens I ran into when I was in my early teens, when I began to find the Hardy boys tiresome and unconvincing. I never liked realism much, but the irrealism of two boys having long conversations while riding on motorcycles (I was big on motorcycles myself) was more than I could put up with. Running across Dickens was like finding a secret door. I read book after book, and when I'd finished the last one I remember feeling a kind of horror, as if suddenly the color had gone out of the world; then luckily I discovered that when you went back to one of the ones you had read first, you couldn't remember half of it, you could read it again and find it even better, so life wasn't quite as disappointing as I'd thought. For me at that time, Disney and Dickens were practically indistinguishable. Both created wonderful cartoon images, told stories as direct as fairy tales, knew the value of broad comedy spiced up with a little weeping. I have since learned that Dickens is occasionally profound, as Disney never deigns to be; but that was not why I valued Dickens or have, now, a bust of him in my study to keep me honest. Unconsciously—without ever hearing the term, in fact—I learned about symbolism from Dickens and Disney, with the result that I would never learn to appreciate, as I suppose one should, those realistic writers who give you life data without resonance, things merely as they are. Dickens's symbolism may never be very deep—the disguised witches and fairy princesses, Uriah Heep and his mother flapping around like buzzards, or all the self-conscious folderol of *A Tale of Two Cities*—but in my experience, anyway, it spoils you forever for books that never go *oo-boom*.

There were other important influences during this period of my life, probably the most important of which was opera. The Eastman School of Music presented operas fairly often (and of course played host to traveling opera companies, including the Met). From Dickens and Disney (not to mention God), it took no adjustment to become opera-addicted. The plots of most operas (not all, heaven knows) are gloriously simpleminded, or to put it more favorably, elemental; the stage is nothing if not a grand cartoon (Wagner's mountainscapes and Norns, Mozart's crazies, Humperdinck's angels, the weirdness and clowning that show up everywhere from *La Bohème* to *The Tales of Hoffman*). I was by this time playing French horn, and of course I'd always been around singing. So I got hooked at once—hence my special fondness now for writing libretti.

By the time I reached college, my taste was, I'm afraid, hopelessly set. Predictably I was ravished by Melville—all those splendid cartoon images, for instance Ahab and the Chinese coolies he's kept hidden until the first time he needs to lower away after whale

—and of course by Milton, who must be considered one of the all-time great cartoonists, as when Satan

> Puts on swift wings, and toward the Gates of Hell
> Explores his solitary flight; sometimes
> He scours the right hand coast, sometimes the left,
> Now shaves with level wing the Deep, then soares
> Up to the fiery concave touring high. . . .

(It's true, Milton's a little boring now and then, and Milton teachers often don't properly value the cartoonist in him, and want to know things about *Paradise Lost* that only some kind of crazy could get seriously interested in; but never mind.) I'm afraid the embarrassing truth is that the whole literary tradition opened out, for me, from Disney and his kind. I got caught up in the mighty cartoons of Homer and Dante (much later Virgil and Apollonius), the less realistic eighteenth- and nineteenth-century novelists (Fielding, Smollett, Collins, and the rest), the glorious mad Russians (Tolstoy, Dostoevski, Bely), and those kinds of poets who fill one's head with strange, intense visions, like Blake, Coleridge, and Keats.

For me, the whole world of literature was at this time one of grand cartoons. I thought of myself mainly as a chemistry major and took courses in English just for fun. I guess I thought literature was unserious, like going to the movies or playing in a dance band, even an orchestra. It did not seem to me that one ought to spend one's life on mere pleasure, like a butterfly or cricket. Beethoven, Shakespeare, Richard Strauss, Conan Doyle, might be a delight, but to fritter away one's life in the arts seemed, well, not quite honest. Then I came across the New Criticism.

At the first college I went to (for two years) I'd read nearly all of the Modern Library, partly for fun, partly because I felt ignorant around my fellow students, people who could talk with seeming wisdom about Camus and Proust, Nietzsche and Plato. I soon discovered they hadn't really read what they claimed to have read —they'd just come from the right part of town. But I'd never in any serious sense "studied" literature. (I took a couple of courses where one was examined on what Carlyle and Newman said, without much emphasis on why or to whom.) When I moved to Washington University in Saint Louis I got a whole new vision of what literature was for—that is, the vision of the New Criticism. Like the fanatic I've always been, I fell to analyzing fiction, digging out symbols and structural subtleties, learning about "levels" and so on. I don't say this was a foolish activity—in fact, I think the New Critics were basically right: it's much more interesting and reward- ing to talk about how literature "works" than to read biographies of the writer, which is mainly what the New Criticism replaced. Working with the famous Brooks and Warren books, I began to love things in fiction and poetry that I'd never before noticed, things like meaning and design, and like all my generation, I made the great discovery that literature is worthwhile, not a thing to be scorned by serious puritans but a thing to be embraced and turned cunningly to advantage. I learned that literature is good for you, that writers who are not deeply philosophical should be scorned, and that *phanopoeia* is for the small-minded. I began to read realists —two of whom I actually liked, Jane Austen and James Joyce—and I began to write "serious" fiction; that is, instead of writing pleas- ant jingles or stories I desperately hoped would be published in the *Saturday Evening Post* or maybe *Manhunt,* I began shyly eyeing the *Kenyon Review.* With a sigh of relief (though I'd enjoyed them, in a way), I quit math and science and signed up, instead, for courses in philosophy and sociology and psychology, which I knew would make me a better person and perhaps a famous writer, so brilliant and difficult that to get through my books you would need a teacher.

This period lasted longer than I care to admit. On the basis of my earnestness and a more or less astonishing misreading of Nietzsche (I was convinced that he was saying that only fiction can be truly philosophical), I won a Woodrow Wilson Fellowship to Iowa, where I meant to study in the famous Writers' Workshop but soon ended up taking medieval languages and literature, the litera- ture God had been nudging me toward all along: *Beowulf, The Divine Comedy,* the *Gawain* poet, Chaucer. The scales fell from my eyes. My New Critical compulsion to figure out exactly how every- thing works, how every nuance plays against every other, had sud- denly an immense field to plow. I continued to read and think about other literature—I went through a Mann phase, a James phase, and so on—but I found myself spending more and more time trying to figure out medieval works.

It seems to me that when I began working on medieval literature, in the late fifties and early sixties, scholars knew very little about even the greatest works in that literature. No one had really figured out the structure of the works of the *Gawain* poet, not to mention *Beowulf* or the poetry of Chaucer. People were still arguing about whether or not *Beowulf* is a Christian poem; people were still trying to shuffle around *The Canterbury Tales*. The usual New Critical method, which is to stare and stare at the work until it comes clear, was useless on this material, because again and again you found yourself staring at something that felt like a symbol or an allusion, or felt like maybe it ought to be some kind of joke but you couldn't see the humor. To figure out the poem you had to figure out the world it came from—read the books the poets knew, try to understand aesthetic principles abandoned and forgotten centuries ago. One had no choice but to become a sort of scholar.

Literary detective work is always fun, for a certain kind of mind at least, but the work I did on medieval literature, then later classical literature, was for me the most exciting detective work I've ever done or heard of. The thing was, not only did you solve interesting puzzles, but when you got them solved you found you'd restored something magnificent, a work of art—in the case of *Beowulf* or *The Canterbury Tales*—supremely beautiful and noble. One unearthed tricks of the craft that nobody'd known or used for a long, long time—tricks one could turn on one's own work, making it different from anybody else's and yet not crazy, not merely novel. I think every writer wants to sound like him- or herself; that's the main reason one sees so many experimental novels. And of course the risk in the pursuit of newness is that in refusing to do what the so-called tradition does, one ends up doing exactly the same thing everybody else trying to get outside the tradition does. For better or worse (I'm no longer much concerned about whether it's better or worse), I joined up with an alternative tradition, one with which I felt almost eerily comfortable. My church-filled childhood delighted in discovering a Christianity distant enough—in fact, for all practical purposes *dead* enough—to satisfy nostalgia without stirring embarrassment and annoyance, as modern Christianity does. For instance, when one reads about "ensoulment" in a medieval book—that is, when one reads arguments on precisely when the soul enters the fetus, and the argument comes from someone of the thirteenth century—one can read with interest; but when one hears a living Christian hotly debating ensoulment, hoping to be able to support abortion without feelings of guilt, one shrinks away, tries to get lost in the crowd. I found in medieval culture and art, in other words, exactly what I needed as an instrument for looking at my own time and place. I of course never became for a moment a medieval Christian believer, but medieval ideas and attitudes gave me a means of triangulating, a place to stand. And needless to say, medieval literature had built into it everything I'd liked best from the beginning, back in the days of God, Dickens, and Disney: grotesques (cartoon people and places), noble feeling, humor (God was perhaps a little short on humor), and real story-telling.

I said earlier that I'm no longer much concerned about whether the work I have done and am doing is for better or worse. That is not quite as true as I might wish. Egoistic ambition is the kind of weed that grows out of dragon's blood: the more you chop it away, the more it flourishes. But it's true that at a certain point in one's career one begins to face up to one's limitations, and the way to stay sane at such a moment is to soften one's standards a little—find good reasons for approving lumpy but well-intentioned work, one's own and everybody else's. To put all this another way, when I think back now over the influences that have helped to shape the way I write, I notice with a touch of dismay that they were as much bad influences as good ones. I won't criticize God (anyway, he's almost certainly been misquoted), but clearly the influence of Dickens and Disney was not all to the good. Both of them incline one toward stylized gestures. Instead of looking very closely at the world and writing it down, the way James Joyce does, brilliantly getting down, say, the way an old man moves his tongue over his gums, or the way a beautiful woman idly plays with her bracelets, a writer like me, seduced by cartoon vision, tends to go again and again for the same gestural gimmicks, a consistent pattern of caricature (compare the way doors in Dostoevski are forever flying open or slamming). I look over my fiction of twenty years and see it as one long frenzy of tics—endlessly repeated words like *merely* and *grotesque,* a disproportionate number of people with wooden fingers and a dreary penchant for frowning thoughtfully or darting their eyes around like maniacs. I seem incapable of writing a story in which people do not babble philosophically, not really because they're saying things I want to get said but because earnest babbling is one of the ways I habitually give vitality to my short-legged, overweight, twitching cartoon creations. And needless to say, from artists like Dickens and Disney I get my morbid habit of trying to make the reader fall into tender weeping.

The whole New Critical period I went through, and the scholarly period that followed it, betrayed me, I think, into an excessive concern with significance. It's probably the case that novels and stories are more interesting if, in some sense or another, they mean something. But it has begun to dawn on me that—in fiction as in all the arts—a little meaning goes a long way. I think what chiefly made me notice this is the work of my creative writing students. Until about five years ago, I never taught creative writing, only medieval literature and now and then a little Greek. When I began to look hard and often at student writing, I soon discovered that one of the main mistakes in their writing is that students think (probably because they've taken too many English literature courses) that fiction is supposed to tell us things—instruct us, improve us, show us. In a sense, of course, they're right, but only in a subtle and mysterious sense. When one has analyzed every symbolically neat detail in a story like "Death in Venice" or "Disorder and Early Sorrow"—when one has accounted for every verbal repetition, every pattern and relationship, and set down in alphabetical order every thought to be lifted or wrenched from the story—one discovers that when you come right down to it, Mann has told us nothing we didn't know already. More by my writing students' early bad examples (they later get better) than by all the good literary examples I ever read, I've come to see that fiction simply dramatizes. It gives importance to ideas, it seems to me, pretty much in the way the string on which a handful of pearls have been strung gives a kind of importance to the pearls. When I read my earliest, most ingeniously constructed fictions (*The Resurrection* and *Grendel*), I find I can no longer figure the damn things out—would that I'd kept all my charts! Insofar as such books are interesting, for me at least, they're interesting because I like the characters and hope as I reread that life (the rest of the book) won't treat them too badly.

I don't mean, of course, that I intend never again to use symbols or to design my stories so that the reader has the kind of experience William James described with such delight: "There goes the same thing I saw before again." What I do mean is that when I was three or four, or twelve or thirteen, I understood fiction more profoundly than I understood it through most of my writing years. I understood that a story, like a painting, or like a symphony, is one of the most wonderful, one of the most useless things in the world. The magnificence of a work of art lies precisely in the fact that nobody made the artist make it, he just did, and—except when one's in school—nobody makes the receiver read it, or look at it, or listen to it, he just does. The influence of my writing students has been to lead me to understand (or imagine I understand) that art's value is not that it expresses life's meaning (though presumably it does, as do butterflies and crickets), but that it is, simply, splendidly, *there.*

I think of the performances my mother and father would sometimes do at, for instance, the monthly meetings of the Grange. The way the night would go is this: First everybody would crowd into one immense room with trestle tables and white paper tablecloths, the tables all loaded down with food, all the red-faced farmers and their plump wives and children finding folding chairs near friends, and somebody would tap a water glass with the side of his spoon and would say a quick, self-conscious prayer, and then everybody would eat. It was a wonderfully pleasant, social time, lots of jokes and stories and abundant country food; but it wasn't a time they chose solely for its pleasantness: if you wanted to get farmers to come from all over the county late at night, after chores, you had to feed them. Then they'd all go into another room and have their business meeting—how much or how little they should organize, how to keep the feed mills, the truckers, and the United States Congress in line. Nobody much cared for the business meeting, though sometimes somebody would "get off a good one," as they used to say. Then, when the work was done, my mother and father would stand there in the middle of the big, bright room and say poems or sing. How strange it seemed to me that all these serious, hard-working people should sit there grinning for an hour or more, listening, for instance, to my father telling them an endless, pointless story of a ghost in armor, or a ship rescued by pigeons, or somebody called Dangerous Dan McGrew. It was absurd. I wasn't just imagining it. The whole thing was deeply, weirdly absurd. Clearly, if one is to devote a lifetime to doing something as crazy as that, one had better do it well—not necessarily because there is any great virtue in doing it well, but only because, if one does it badly, people may wake up and notice that what one's doing is crazy.

Dark Landscapes

JOHN HAWKES

John Hawkes is the author of a volume of short plays and ten works of fiction, including *The Cannibal, The Lime Twig, Second Skin, The Passion Artist,* and his latest novel, *Virginie: Her Two Lives* (Harper & Row, 1982). He teaches at Brown University and is a member of the American Academy and Institute of Arts and Letters.

My novel *Second Skin* was written in eight swift magnificent months in 1962–63, when my wife and children and I were living in the natural lushness and clarity of an island in the Caribbean. But this novel had its genesis in the distant past of my childhood, was related to other fiction I'd written by that time, appeared to depend on a few strange moments when literal event and imagined event coincided, and underwent an extensive metamorphosis several years before we lived on our tropical island. It was the first novel I knew I wanted to write entirely in the first person; it was a novel I managed to write with ease and pleasure; it was the first novel in which I was explicitly attempting to write comic fiction. So *Second Skin* particularly lends itself to a discussion of landscape and the fictive process.

In brief, this novel is about the futile efforts of its narrator (a fifty-nine-year-old ex-navy lieutenant, junior grade, who is an artificial inseminator of cows on a tropical island) to prevent the suicide of his only daughter, Cassandra. Skipper tells his "naked history," as he calls it, while living in idyllic timelessness on a floating island with his Second World War mess boy, Sonny. As he waits for the birth of Catalina Kate's child, who has been impossibly fathered by both Sonny and Skipper, and as he artificially impregnates great Brahman cows or swims in the clear limpid midnight sea, Skipper recalls how he attempted but failed to save the life of Cassandra, who, on a small cold island off the New England coast, finally jumps to her death from an abandoned lighthouse. The juxtaposition of the two islands, the juxtaposition of Cassandra's death and the eventual birth of Catalina Kate's black child—these are the essential opposites of *Second Skin.* The true sources of interesting fiction no doubt lie buried in inaccessible depths of the psyche. Yet the two islands in *Second Skin* share obvious similarities with two real islands, while many images and the deepest thematic preoccupations of this novel have their shadowy counterparts in memory.

This personal chronology lies behind *Second Skin:* When I was a thin, horseback-riding, asthmatic child of about eight years old, we were living in a small old-fashioned Connecticut village on the edge of Long Island Sound. And one of my earliest and strongest recollections is of a girl, a cousin, who now for me is only myth but whom I loved as a child.

When I was about seventeen, I entered a room in which my father was threatening to commit suicide.

When I was twenty-two, Sophie and I were married at the end of one summer which was all the more beautiful because we lived it in the brilliant barrenness of Montana. It was there in Montana, while waiting for the moment of marriage, that I first turned to fiction and wrote my first short novel, *Charivari,* a highly surrealistic vision of a middle-aged couple, Henry and Emily Van, who are embarking on marriage with all the fear and innocence of youth.

When I was twenty-four and finishing my first novel, *The Cannibal,* and also finishing my last two years at Harvard (I had lost time thanks to the war), Sophie and I became friends with an enormous life-filled humorous artistic man whom we loved until his appalling death.

When I was thirty, I began to teach at Harvard, where Sophie and I became friends with Edwin Honig, who talked even then of an island off the New England coast where he had spent one perfect isolated year writing poetry.

The next year Honig came to Brown. The year after, I too came to Brown. The following spring Sophie and I read Honig's poem "Island Storm." And that was the summer we managed to spend on the island of the poem, and where I began to write a novel which—abortive, unfinished—became the written genesis of *Second Skin.*

Two years later, in the spring, our life-filled friend from Harvard committed suicide. That fall Sophie and our by now four young children and I went to our coral-ringed island in the Caribbean. There at last I had *Second Skin* firmly in mind and wrote it.

Events of the imagination precede and sometimes outdo the events of life. I say this because in the case of the New England island, at least, I had experienced some version of it as a child, imagined a truer version of it as a young man writing *Charivari,* glimpsed in the real island the one I had already written about, found this same island in Honig's poem, then tried to create it one last time from the vantage point of its opposite—which was the serene and spice-scented island in the tropics.

I'm obsessed with the sea and islands, and whereas Donne says that "no man is an island," I believe that we're all islands—inaccessible, drifting apart, thirsting to be explored, magical.

I remember very little about my cousin and me—the slender invisible girl and the skinny child—except that we walked. Again and again I see the two of us walking, merely walking, and always down the same empty lane in the twilight toward the water and, most important, into a great abandoned half-built house on the very edge of that gray darkening ocean. I remember longing in some vague way for the love of my cousin, and it seems to me now that she must have spent all her adolescence taking me on exactly the same thrilling but dreadful walk at the end of each of the days of my childhood.

The monstrous castle-like house that we visited was built so close to the sea and so incompletely that the ocean would suddenly roar up inside the unfinished room where we stood holding hands, great waves smashing onto the black rocks actually visible below us at the edge of the unfinished floor, and then receding and leaving spumes of foam lying around our wet shoes. The wind and the sea used to roar through that hopeless house, and I would be terrified and more in love with my cousin than ever.

I don't know what kind of person she was. She was probably

only an ordinary young girl helping her aunt by occasionally taking her aunt's little boy on a walk. But that same girl led me happily into the terrors of a microcosmic New England, into the world of dead houses with beams like great bones, and toward the ocean that lies vast and ominous at the end of a country road. She embodied what I've feared and yearned for ever since, and the abandoned house she used to take me to is clearly the source of three related visions or images that have obsessed me as long as I can recall: the abandoned lighthouse, the abandoned ocean liner leaning on its side in low tide far from shore, and the New England fishing village on an island.

The island fishing village is something I've long pursued in the imagination, in fiction, in actuality. And in various forms it appears in *Charivari*, "The Nearest Cemetery" (the fragment preliminary to *Second Skin* and written on the island where Edwin Honig had lived), and lastly in *Second Skin*. But I haven't written about the ocean liner and it still remains what it's always been: a personal waking dream in which I stand alone at the edge of a straight empty beach at low tide and gaze with fear and longing at an enormous black ship that looms in awful silence in knee-deep water far from shore. A few lifeboats hang halfway down the side of the ship from their davits; on the ship there is no movement, only the black immensity and the smokeless funnels and the occasional small flash of some piece of metal on the deck or in the rigging. I know that I shall have to walk the entire distance from shore to the listing ship. I know that I shall climb somehow to the tilted deck of the abandoned ship. I know that I must discover its vast world, must pry open some metal door rusted half ajar and enter the ship until I discover what it contains—its treasure, if childhood hopes prevail, or its emptiness, its floating corpses.

The vision, no matter how personal, is one of potential and desolation. It suggests the undiminishing power of childhood experience, defines what I'm most interested in writing about, becomes literal in *Second Skin* when Skipper happens to see a long dark ship drifting past on the horizon and finds himself filled with both joy and dread.

Charivari—the word is the source of our word *shivaree* (the comic and vulgar rites for harassing newlyweds)—is about marriage. In this youthful short novel (whimsical, surrealistic, often poetic in the wrong way), Henry and Emily Van are a strange and lonely pair of middle-aged people newly married. At the hands of each other, and especially at the hands of their aged parents, they undergo a kind of double suffering—of the indignities of middle age and of the vulnerabilities of youth. Whether *Charivari* was at the time an accurate self-portrait thinly veiled in wild distortion and surging prose (since at the time of our marriage I thought of myself as dourly old), or whether it was instead a kind of terrifying glimpse into the future (for some of us innocence persists into middle age), nonetheless *Charivari* evokes universal burdens of desire and anxiety framed in the rituals and conditions of married life.

One of Henry Van's worst fears is the possible loss of Emily, and one section of *Charivari* is devoted to the moment when Henry's fears come true and Emily disappears. In a violent storm and in a small archaic fishing village, Henry catches a sudden dreamlike glimpse of the missing Emily, only to lose her.

The wind shot down the main street, oscillating, shimmering from side to side, pulling with its giant tail armfuls of driving rain from the doldrums; it broke off in tangents to be drawn into a chimney flue, to swirl madly, trapped in a dead end, or to fly swiftly and vertically up the crevice between two houses, to be spent in the still aimless air high above. The main blow beat its way down the narrow street, tearing leaves from trees and rattling windows, smashed between two warehouses and jumped out to sea, tearing frantically at the waves. The rain was almost impenetrable; it beat like nail heads on the rotting wood, and covered cobblestones with a running slime.

Henry lost his nerve. Pummeled he stood heaving to and fro, floundering, flapping wildly, in the middle of the street before her house. His hands shifted and beat the air, thrusting outward to clutch at lost supports, to maintain a precarious balance; he hung by the good graces of the wind. He laughed and felt himself shoving off at last, but he simply couldn't go to the house.

The door opened and she came out and walked easily into the storm. For a moment she was but thirty feet from him. Miraculously the black hat stayed in place. He could almost see the features of the face, oh, Emily, yes, yes, the howling wind, the shadowed mouth open to gasp for air behind that wind, the eyes covered by a constant veil, the hair beating upon the open throat. Fish were being hammered against the logs, clouds collided with mountains of water, the fishing nets tore loose, and wandering, flying, flung themselves on teakwood ribs, sky, and rocks.

For one brief moment his hope and desire came together, to walk up to her, hold her, speak to her, hold the blowing hair. The taste of salt was on his lips. Then he turned and was carried off down the street. Once he turned back and saw that she was following.

This was his gigantic hold, the town of water. He noticed each blurred metallic color or lack of color, each gray and black, each wet shadow, salt and iron of the sea and blood. Drawn to her, he fled from her, happier in each dolphin-winged spasm, careening along with pillaging, battling black birds. To catch fish. To catch grain. To shed the strengthening water. He bent his body and ran disjointedly for cover. The inn door. Pieces of driftwood were pounding on the shore; a deep loud voice from the doldrums. Sailors from Madagascar, ships from the Caribbean, the Puritan, iron hulks from Liverpool, plunging their crimson sails and tarred lines through the surf, they hovered in the harbor. No sun, no moon, only hurling starfish and fine foam, water hauling in the wizened lives.

Leather rots; rubber comes alive; the beach erodes; the fungus grows; the sound of the wailing bell. And always that barely remembered woman behind him, the faint flush of youth and scrubbed cheeks.

This is the first time that my imaginary island fishing village became fictional. Despite embarrassing adverbs, colloquialisms, sentence fragments, still Henry's "town of water" is my own seaside Connecticut village and the empty half-built house echoing with the sound of waves at the water's edge—though while writing *Charivari* I was not thinking about childhood. This passage also reveals the beginnings of my own fictional insistencies (the wind and rain become animated, the writer dwells on images and details of decay and corruption) and reveals the beginnings of my own writing voice (heard in such phrasing as "beat like nail heads on the rotting wood"). But the association of the "barely remembered woman," who is idealized for her "faint flush of youth," with a vast violent world of death, sexlessness, and misogyny is the thematic center of much that I've written. I realized some time ago that the language of *Charivari* had served as an unconscious source for the language of *Second Skin*.

When I first read aloud to Sophie Honig's poem "Island Storm," the island (or lost New England world) of my own preoccupations leapt from the page: I felt that I was a version of the poem's narrator, that I too was surviving the rain and storm in a place I recognized and wanted to be in—despite its cataclysmic chaos, its unavoidable terror. Even then I thought that the poem had already made inevitable our actual journey to the "cold, Atlantic island," as Skipper calls it in *Second Skin.*

Here, then, is "Island Storm":

All morning in the woods I heard the bushes choke
    Among dead boughs that creaked and groaned,
And no other murmur than the flurry of live prey
    Grappling in the wind's slow teeth.
A starling toppled near the river-run, black
    As stone. A garter snake shivered
Up a root and instantly turned brown. It began
    On such a day prophets used
To rave about—"Stiff-necked mankind, remember
    Sodom and God's frown!" Through miles

Of tensing acreage only two eyes peeped when it
    Came down. The road became a falls
Where hubbubs fell to foam across a glazed surrendering
    Of channelled stone. In the hollow beat
Of some annihilating warmth, tumorous old stumps
    Were ground to muck. "Will it be day
Again?" I heard the brittle window ask the lightning
    Flash, and tremble three full hours
As it spoke. Often, while the sea coughed distantly,
    Infamous last words of misanthropes
Ransacked my brain for counter-prayers. Below the eaves,
    Crackling like a greasy frying
Pan, only a floral lampshade quavered hope.

When at last the silence trickled in, I found
    The fungi like great plastered wounds,
The stupefying sweetness everywhere. And when
    The weather turned gigantically
And padded off, I found the world it left nearby:
    On the bloated attic floor
Two drowned mice; through the skylight, one fir
    Permanently bowed; above the flooded
Garden, the first fierce dart of an exploratory crow.

I like the moments of awesome sound in this poem. I like the way the world of nature is first mythologized, or personified, and then "collapsed" to a few palpable details of concrete reality. But I quicken most to the "tumorous old stumps" and to the fungi "like great plastered wounds," since these images make me think of *Charivari* ("Leather rots; rubber comes alive; the beach erodes; the fungus grows; the sound of the wailing bell"), and since this special sympathy for decay, deterioration, destruction (and for the maimed, the victimized), is one of the essential qualities of the imagination, evident as it is in "The Ancient Mariner," say, or in the mammoth bruised and battered and aged tortoises of Melville's *Encantadas*.

On a cold, bright, early summer morning we sailed with our then three young children on an old white fishing boat to the world of "Island Storm." The boat smelled of dead fish and engine fumes; our five-year-old daughter was seasick down below in her mother's arms in the dark and foul-smelling cabin. But still we sailed across eleven miles of brilliant sea and rounded a promontory and for the first time I saw my imaginary fishing village clustered around its shimmering boat-filled harbor (as I had known it would be). This was what the imagination had suddenly and at last produced: the sun, the black shining sea, the cluster of bleached houses, the bright boats, an enormous abandoned white house on another promontory, and overhead the scavenging gulls. Only a few miles from the village, we saw for ourselves the row of "permanently bowed" fir trees from "Island Storm."

That summer we lived on the island, eating blueberry pancakes on a veranda overlooking the sea and a few smaller islands, sleeping in bedclothes that smelled of mothballs in a small clapboard house with wrinkled linoleum on the kitchen floor and a playable wooden pump-organ in one of the small rooms. The privy was like an upended coffin, there were stunted apple trees on the slope between the porch and the sea, we lived in the rhythms of bright sun and heavy fog. We walked, we explored the island, the children painted designs on rocks and pieces of driftwood, and up under the eaves of one of the narrow bedrooms (that smelled of camphor and dead insects) I wrote about fifty pages of a fragment called "The Nearest Cemetery," which immediately preceded *Second Skin*.

The landscape, charged as it was with personal meaning, the landscape at once familiar and unfamiliar, the constant dreamlike appearance of symbols in nature (gigantic rocks like human skulls, foreboding trees), and that strange psychological pull exerted by the unexpected confluence of sloping farmland and open sea—in the context of all this I was, for the first time, prompted to write fiction out of the very world I was living in.

An anecdote, a real woman, and a few rumors cohered to give rise to the story of "The Nearest Cemetery." We hadn't been on the island a week when I heard an anecdote about a local barber who had been accused of molesting a child and had managed to jump overboard and drown himself when he was being taken from the island back to the mainland for arraignment and trial. Then there was a woman, the wife of a summering New Yorker, who daily passed our cottage wearing a pale blue kerchief and waving and calling out in a lovely voice to the children. The rumors were that her sexual trysts occurred everywhere on the island—in culverts, in fields, in dank places among the trees, in abandoned farmhouses filled with rotting mattresses and broken bottles. She was everywhere, we heard, this defenseless and unhappy and smiling woman, and I thought of her as everywhere and pure. I called her the Princess. I used to sit in the privy and think of the Princess or hear her voice, as she called out to our children from the country road, and imagine her blue kerchief which she always wore, when the wind was blowing and when it was calm. The fiction that came to mind was about a woman called the Princess who had a townful of lovers and was murdered by the local barber. My notion was that three men—Captain Red, Blud, Jomo—had all committed crimes for the sake of the Princess, with whom they had experienced extravagant sexuality, and so at the time of the barber's narration were to be imprisoned; and also that the barber, whose love for the Princess was purely imaginary, had finally murdered her in order to preserve his ideal love. The barber was to be imprisoned with the other three, was to spend his days cutting their hair, and his nights talking to himself in his prison cell, obsessed with the dead Princess and with his own wife (Mildred, the New England Puritan) and aware of his own approaching murder by the men who had had a crude capacity to love.

So the mind lies between the echoing coffins of the ears—a barber's ears
—and you try to calm it in the midst of all that roar and whisper while
a shadow falls through the bars and sweeps your chest. But then I raise
my hands; I hold one ear; I hold both of them; I press with my palms.
Because then it is not Mildred's voice I hear—not the voice, though I hear
it often enough—but rather Mildred playing steadily on the church
organ, Mildred pumping her feet, Mildred pushing the keys and Mildred
making the reeds and seagulls shriek. And in each of Mildred's chords is
the heavy harmony of the Lord and bass voice of Mildred's other brother
who died from drink. And I cannot bear to listen. The barber cannot bear
to listen to Mildred pumping and marching with the Lord at the town's
church organ. The Lord and Mildred deafen me. They make me think of
lying dead and naked beside the body of the shipwrecked woman on
Crooked Finger Rock at the height of the gale.

 Short as the watch that ends the night is what I hear, and *Time like an
ever-rolling stream Bears all its sons away* is what I hear, the phrases filling the
mind with their monotony and fear, and *They fly, forgotten, as a dream Dies
at the opening of day*—all of it this booming, this beating of hymn on slick
shingles and empty beach, and the Lord and Mildred are bearing me away
to the Rock. Singing. Bearing off the naked barber to the heart of the
hymn that is the gate, carrying me away at the center, easily, while the
plankton spurts aloft into the dark of the storm, and I fly, while Vinny
cranks his truck in the wind and Mildred sings with the lost brother.

 The barber. But even the barber has his tongue and toes and fingers,
his hidden hair. The barber too has his lungs of twisted and dampened
paper, his ears in which the islands float, his eyes that gleam, his sensitivity to skin, his touch. And sometimes I think I am all water. Hair and
water. What the crack leaps upon, leaping to deform the image further,
is nothing and my shop is on Bloody Clam Shell Island—closed, safely
boarded up—while I am here.

 This is the rhetoric of tormented sexlessness and a punitive
religious preoccupation with death. These are the guilt-ridden
cadences of someone beguiled by but also hating New England
Puritanism, the hymnbook prose (derived from *Charivari*) that
served as the immediate source of the language in *Second Skin.* But
by the summer's end I gave up on the barber, partly because I
couldn't sustain his relentless interior monologue, partly because
I had already heard another anecdote, of a man who was futilely
attempting to thwart his daughter's emotional illness. The selfless
father (who couldn't be entirely blameless for the emotional state

of his daughter) and the deteriorating girl, who was to become the object of her father's steadfast care and unwitting love, obliterated the barber but not his world. For the next two years I thought about this story of an older man's unsuccessful efforts to preserve his daughter's sanity on a New England island.

In the spring of 1962 I came down with pneumonia (when Providence was a place of iron and ice and fever and dead morality rattling in the bitter wind). In that same terrible and often delirious season we heard that our humorous, artistic, life-filled friend from Harvard had committed suicide. Weeks later I knew that I wanted to write a novel about an older man attempting to preserve his daughter not from insanity but from suicide, that the real center of the novel had to be sexuality and suicide, that the novel would be comic, and that I wanted to write it, not in infectious Providence, but on a tropical island.

We fled Providence for the West Indies—where all of our children became violently sick when we drove from the airport over the mountains and through the rain forests to our crescent of perfect beach, and where we flourished (on the beach, in the clear sea, surrounded by wildflowers and hummingbirds and the underwater coral beds of the earth's navel), and where I spent my timeless mornings sitting on a veranda in the trade winds and writing *Second Skin.*

In those eight months of warmth and clarity I felt suspended, free, detached, confident (as if life itself had become a fiction), and it gave me a secret and even crafty pleasure to invoke the cold dark Atlantic island while sitting amidst the light and spices of a tropical world, or to fictionalize Skipper's tropical landscape while having freshly in mind some recently written scene of New England coldness and brutality. Skipper was now a heavy benevolent middle-aged disreputable Prospero creating both his present and his past life on a wandering island of Brahman cows, towering sugar cane, sea fans waving in the depths of the clear water, candles burning at night in a sunken cemetery. The Princess became Skipper's daughter, Cassandra; the barber's wife, Mildred, became the heavy-set seductive landlady who fails to win Skipper and so plots to involve Cassandra with Captain Red and Jomo, knowing that these sexual liaisons will lead inevitably to Cassandra's suicide;

while Captain Red remained the same, as did Jomo—except that I had the pleasure of deciding that Jomo would be one-handed, so that the steel hook that served as his missing hand would also exemplify the ruthlessness of his sexual greed. On the tropical island I believed more strongly than ever that the Atlantic island was filled with men like Jomo and Captain Red. They carried knives, they had long black sideburns, they lolled on the wharves and back roads leading to abandoned trysting places, their skin was made of fish scales—and they were poor, violent, isolated, admirable. In the sun of the tropical island the dangerous death-ridden landscape of the Atlantic island loomed with a beauty quite the equivalent of the Caribbean island paradise.

In *Second Skin* an abandoned lighthouse organizes the fears and longings of childhood. But I still see that lighthouse everywhere in New England—in the form of old houses, fallen tombstones, half-sunken boats, and most of all in the endless long-empty factories, still somehow suggesting the piety and callousness and energy that no longer exist.

Skipper climbs up the inside of the abandoned lighthouse in his futile effort to prevent the last sexual encounter between Jomo and Cassandra. But Jomo and Cassandra have already had their love at the top of the empty lighthouse. Jomo has already fled the scene. Cassandra has already leapt naked from the top of the lighthouse to her death on the rocks below—a fact which Skipper knows but can't admit.

The iron gut of the tower remained intact, and I crawled to the top and crawled back down again without mishap, without a fall. But the damage was done. I knew it was done before I reached the top, and I began to hurry and began to whisper: "Cassandra? He's gone now, Cassandra, it's all right now . . . you'll see. . . ." I heard nothing but the echoing black sky and tiny skin-crawling sounds above me and the small splash, the eternal picking fingers of wave on rock below. "Cassandra?" I whispered, and tried to pull myself up the last few shaky steps, tried to fight down dizziness, tried to see, "you're not crying, are you, Cassandra? Please don't. . . ."

But the damage was done and I was only an old bird in an empty nest. I rolled up onto the iron floor in the smashed head of the lighthouse and crawled into the lee of the low wall and pulled myself into a half-sitting position and waited for the moment when Dog's Head light must tremble and topple forward into the black scum of the rising tide far below.

"Gone, Cassandra? Gone so soon?" I whispered. "Gone with Gertrude, Cassandra? Gone to Papa? But you shouldn't have, Cassandra. You should have thought of me. . . ."

The neat pile of clothing was fluttering a little in the moonlight and it was damp to the touch. . . .

I clutched a couple of the thin rusted stanchions and in the gray moonlight stared out to sea. The shoals were miles long and black and sharp, long serrated tentacles that began at the base of the promontory and radiated out to sea, mile after square mile of intricate useless channels and breaking waves and sharp-backed lacerating shoals and spiny reefs. Mile after square mile of ocean cemetery that wasn't even true to its dead but kept flushing itself out on the flood tide. No wonder the poor devils wanted a lighthouse here. No wonder.

My dark landscapes have included the ruined terrain of a mythical postwar Germany, the vulgar physicalities of an imaginary London, the nightmare fields and villages of a violently invented France, a dead world of central Europe. But the landscape of the imagination is darkest of all.

On Becoming a Writer

EDWARD HOAGLAND

"I've published four collections thus far: *The Courage of Turtles, Walking the Dead Diamond River, Red Wolves and Black Bears,* and *The Tugman's Passage.*" And ten years after the travel book about British Columbia referred to here, I wrote another one—this time of interviews, impressions, and adventures in Africa, called *African Calliope: A Journey to the Sudan.* I've also published three novels, and hope to write a couple more."

I wrote my first poem when I was nine, visiting my grandparents in a rented beach house in La Jolla, California. It was Christmas 1941, and we regularly woke up to the sight of a thousand marines with black grease slicked on their faces storming ashore alongside tanks and jeeps and howitzers from landing barges in front of the house. My mother, the maid, and I would carry out a pitcher of coffee and a plate of doughnuts, and about a dozen of the marines nearest us, after a glance at their sergeant, would politely swallow what they could, before heading into the sandy hills—then, within weeks, no doubt, overseas to the horrific casualties of the amphibious campaign. But my poem was about a frog that lived in the brook behind the house, whose man shape and thin skin in a dangerous, adventurous world had touched my heart in ways a nine-year-old could deal with.

John Steinbeck and Saul Bellow became my special heroes a little later, as I decided I wanted to be a writer; and each, I notice now, chose to write a slapstick tour de force about a slaughter of the innocents in which the innocents were frogs. I shared Steinbeck's affection for dogs as well, and Bellow's for lions and bears (brown Smolak, with teeth like date pits, riding the terrifying roller coaster, clasping the teenaged Henderson). Like Henderson the Rain King, I worked in a circus early on, and at times laid my life between the paws of lions in order to learn from them whatever I could.

Bears now leave their sign within a hundred feet of my house in Vermont, and when I've written about them I've first gone to one of my hunter friends for a chunk of bear meat from his freezer (though I never hunt and am pained by hunting), which I put in a stew pot over a wood fire until the house is full of bear smell, and live on that for the first draft. Though this might not be Bellow's method, a bear that set off on a comparable effort of transubstantiation would probably begin like me.

I believe, incidentally, that those of us who care about bears and frogs haven't much time left to write about them, not just because—among the world's other emergencies—a twilight is settling upon them, but because people are losing their capacity to fathom any form of nature except, in a more immediate sense, their own. We ski or pilot boats and planes, and to reach "deeper" rhythms and ramifications in ourselves seem to prefer sidetracks such as drugs. Even when we speak of a literature that plumbs deep, we tend to mean that it examines narcissism, inertia, reasonless murder, and other modern deadness or griefs which are as recent as they are "deep."

However, very soon I found the world scarier than I am pleased to admit. Visiting my old prep school in Massachusetts on the thirtieth anniversary of my graduation, I didn't tour the wooden dormitories with nostalgia, as I'd expected to, but tiptoed through like Ulysses revisiting Cyclops' cave. Though I'd spoken condescendingly of the school as a place where attendance was taken seventeen times a day and where for my bookishness I'd been assigned to a corridor called The Zoo, I'd always claimed to have been happy there.

In those years, Steinbeck had been my favorite living writer. At his best he wrote with likable clarity, picturing in shorter works like *The Red Pony* and *Cannery Row* boys and men such as I wanted to be. His friendship with the biologist Ed Ricketts, which lay behind the appeal of *Cannery Row* and is described directly in *The Log from the Sea of Cortez*, corresponded to some dream of mine of what friendship between men could be. I hoped for a writer-zoologist's career, so Ricketts—living with a series of girl friends in a laboratory on the oceanfront in Monterey, across the street from a whorehouse, whose inhabitants dropped in on him for advice, and half a dozen chummy bums who slept in a row of rusty steam pipes—seemed enviable. A natural man, he sniffed the food on his fork before he ate and yet worked hard, wading in the great tidal pools to collect specimens with a feeling of citizenship in a vaster, time-stunned concord of sea and sky which most writers have never attempted to convey.

Steinbeck was the first writer I met. It came about because my "Zoo" roommate had an uncle who was designing the Broadway sets for Steinbeck's ill-fated play *Burning Bright* and kindly took the two of us to lunch with him at Sardi's. (My friend would have preferred to talk to Thomas Wolfe, but Wolfe was dead.) Steinbeck turned out to be a thick-shouldered man with a becoming ease and modesty. Neither a bully nor a toady to the headwaiter, he was staying at the Biltmore, and although edgy about his play's title, the late rewrite job he was attempting, and what the critics might say, he had remained enough of a man who cultivated cronies that the night before, he and his secretary had been interrupted by the hotel detective, who'd been tipped off by a prankster to the possibility that he was entertaining a prostitute.

He spoke with choosy fondness of New York City and his miserable first visit, when, fresh from several years of roaming the curriculum at Stanford, he'd worked as a hod carrier on the construction of Madison Square Garden. His upbringing had been middle class—his father the treasurer of Monterey County—so, as he glanced at the two of us in our white shirts and our ties and sport jackets, such as would pass muster at the door of the dining hall at Deerfield Academy, but obviously wanting the wider experiences he and Wolfe had sought, he may have seen himself thirty years earlier.

Thirty years after that lunch, I find my closer friends tend to be women rather than men and that the whores who haunt the waterfront in New York, where I winter, are mostly transvestites, not ladies of the night. I know Steinbeck sentimentalized his perceptions and couldn't account for the fact that the bouncer in Ed Ricketts's whorehouse killed himself with an ice pick, for instance. By long acquaintance with animal-lovers and champions of human underdogs, I know, too, that these enthusiasms which Steinbeck and I shared may hide substantial kinks of character (if never so many as those of people who harbor no sympathy at all for animals and underdogs). But Steinbeck's liberal spirit had its roots in a feeling that everybody should have a fair start—a revolutionary, most American perception which has kept his liberalism fresh.

There is a peculiarly American tradition that families swing "from shirtsleeves to shirtsleeves in three generations." Radicals make conservatives make radicals again. Probably the American dream is so riven with paradoxes (free speech versus "free enterprise," and so on) that its incongruities can be accommodated in no other way. "I must study politics and war so that my sons may . . . study mathematics . . . in order to give their children a right to study painting, poetry, music, architecture," John Adams wrote to his wife, Abigail. The entrepreneur's children—hedged in by the special privileges he won for them—want, instead, "a better world." Or, moving in the opposite direction, the cry has been, "The working class can kiss my arse, I've got the boss's job at last," as generations of new or neo-conservatives have said.

Saul Bellow captured my attention in college. It was not that I pored over his novels with an intensity Cervantes and Tolstoy deserved—not that I learned as much of writing about nature from Steinbeck as from Turgenev, or about solitude from Bellow as from Chekhov. But Bellow, who was warier than Steinbeck, yet readier to blurt out every intimacy, who was unable to write well at length about women but appeared to like women better than men, reached me in a way that mattered. It's important to have living models. That Faulkner, an adornment to world literature, was walking about at the same time we were made an enormous difference to writers who started out in the 1950s. People met him on the stairs at Random House and never afterward could take writing for the movies any more seriously than he did, for example. Though a young American can gawk at Günter Grass, V. S. Naipaul, and Gabriel García Márquez and be astonished at their talent, even in the event that one of them eventually develops into a fiery, tenacious genius on the scale of Faulkner, they are not his countrymen.

If Bellow was no Faulkner, he excelled at making the most of what he had. Nothing went to waste; and being a teacher by profession, he was more at ease with cub writers, less intimidating, though less superbly self-possessed, than Faulkner. I never quite considered that he had the intellectual hardware sometimes ascribed to him, but he caught the temper of his time with marvelous particularity. Also, I felt like him when I read him, and, in person, more akin. Twenty years ago he had not flowered into fashionability. One took a little ribbing on the Upper West Side, in Greenwich Village, and from the East Side *Paris Review* crowd if one did not prefer Mailer to Bellow then. *Time* magazine regarded him as "a smart Jew," he said, and he sounded as though *The New Yorker* could have been Heartbreak House for him, as for so many lesser writers, if he had let it be. Though he hadn't cut himself loose from his roots, as Steinbeck did in moving east, Bellow from his citadel in Chicago in 1964 smelled the poisons of New York's literary scene and, more than Californians like Steinbeck and Saroyan, was pained. ("We made you and we can break you," a New York critic was to tell him during a political disagreement at a White House reception several years later.)

Like Steinbeck in 1950, Bellow was ambitious to branch out to the theater, and he had written a similarly static play, *The Last Analysis,* starring Sam Levene—not, as he had hoped, Zero Mostel, who had had the bad taste to strut the boards in a new presentation called *Fiddler on the Roof* instead. An air of despair pervaded the rehearsals. On the spiderwebby stage set, the desperate actors launched their lines as if still trying to understand them. Bellow's Reynard face had lost its shape and grown irregular in coloring. In his posture he resembled a man awaiting an announced punishment. Indeed, on the night after opening night, the Belasco Theater was already one-fourth empty, though some USO soldiers and sailors had gotten free tickets and stood about during intermission looking bewildered. But Bellow had just had a splendid pair of front-page reviews for *Herzog* in the *New York Times* and the *New York Herald Tribune* book sections to comfort him; and when, cub-like, I asked which spread he liked best, he shrugged, like the writer I wanted him to be. He inveighed against the "professionalism" of American writing, by which he meant drawing from literary, not street-smart, sources, and he said there was "a line of succession," already fearing that he might become an institution and lose his anonymity, as his friend Arthur Miller had for different reasons after marrying Marilyn Monroe. Gingerly, elusive, with his sharp, shy smile, he said that writers were by nature eccentrics, and to accept that, to be honest with oneself, and then not to worry about one's personal reputation.

Cublike, I followed him another time across Central Park from a meeting we had had at the Metropolitan Museum, stutteringly telling him he reminded me of Nathanael West, a flattering comparison he said he hadn't heard before. But at the far edge of the park he stopped and said goodbye so that I wouldn't see where he was going—again, just as, in my secretive way, I imagined I would have done.

Like Bellow, I lived as though life were precarious, as if the roof might fall in. I lived as though I didn't entirely know where next week's meals were coming from, and this not only because I admired Joyce Cary's caricature of the artist's life in *The Horse's Mouth*. My childhood had been teetery, and generally I'd kept a cache of cash around in case I felt a need to hit the road—as would have happened if the threat had been fulfilled that I might be required to put in an extra, postgraduate year at that prep school. With the bad stutter I suffered from, I suspected too that later I would not be able to depend upon the professorships and public reading income with which other writers supplemented whatever their books earned. Nor did I necessarily expect to sell better than the American writers I admired most—Melville and Thoreau.

I had arrived in New York from humble origins. That is, I was a WASP with an Ivy League education and a lawyer for a father at a time (a decade or more after Bellow's debut) when it was important for a young writer in the city to be an "ethnic" whose father was a bartender and to have gone to City College. My prep school mate John McPhee and college classmate John Updike both needed to write twice as many books twice as well to gather an acclaim at all equivalent to what they would have won much more quickly if they had not been WASPs from the Ivy League.

Yet, of course, we'd benefited from our sumptuous educations. I'd enjoyed an uncannily balancing pair of writing teachers —Archibald MacLeish, who taught me how to be usefully sane, and John Berryman, who taught me how to be healthfully crazy. And though my father, lawyer-like, wrote to my first publisher's lawyer to try to stop my first novel from coming out, earlier he had traveled with me on a privileged vacation to western Canada, where in the mountains I experienced one of those visions of the work one hopes to do for years ahead such as Willa Cather describes in *The Professor's House.* Young professor St. Peter, "from the rose of dawn to the gold of sunset," lay on his back in a little boat skirting the south coast of Spain and saw the ranges of the Sierra Nevadas, "snow peak after snow peak, high beyond the flight of fancy, gleaming like crystal and topaz . . . and the design of his book unfolded in the air above him," just as did the mountain ranges. Ten years later I returned to Canada to write *Notes from the Century Before,* my first and favorite travel book.

My father grew up in Missouri with a paper route, a neighbor who kept pet coyotes, and the rest of it, working his way east in cattle cars and to Europe on a cattle boat. He was the first person of whom I endlessly asked the question that has been my stock in trade ever since: "What was it like back then?" Though he became an elegant citizen who seldom wanted to remove his tie, even on weekends, he retained that capacity to pile in the car and go and buy a couple of goats, stuff them in the back seat, and bring them home, into the house to show me, when I was sick in bed.

He gave me my first oysters at the University Club on Fifth Avenue when I was around seven, and I've always liked revisiting it or similar places because of my secret sense of still belonging. The money stopped when I was twenty-one, and for the next fifteen years I lived on an average of $3,000 annually; yet these memories of fancy clubs and summer resorts and suburban lawns manicured by gardeners named Alphonso or Brooks lent me a precious freedom from conflicting ambitions. Fame I did want as a writer, but money beyond financing the necessities meant much less to me. Choosing to be a writer, from my background, had involved surrendering the idea of money to begin with, and when I saw colleagues standing around shooting their cuffs at publishing parties, yearning for somebody to advance them the wherewithal to buy a house like the one I'd grown up in, I felt lucky.

My father was not a mover and shaker. He considered that a good lawyer never got his name in the papers. If a client ignored his advice and got into trouble, a gamecock-peacock attorney should be hired whose delight it was to wrangle out the matter in front of a judge. He was interested not in power for himself but in the smooth exercise of other people's power in an insulated world of adept phone calls and quiet meetings in high-up offices and on the golf course, where the arcane disciplines of the game —better than the pert procedures of a business lunch—prevented a prospective partner from concealing the full gamut of emotions beneath the surface of his face.

My father taught me, however, to betray less information and fewer opinions than I really had in asking questions and to cut my losses and not argue unduly if I made a mistake in a business arrangement, because most people are a mixed bag of honesty, dishonesty, charity, and meanness; they may turn around if they have done you dirt and do you a favor to make up for it. He taught me that the choice of whom to work with, more than the words in a contract, is what lubricates a professional agreement and that the chief considerations may never be stated. All good advice for an interviewer; but though he knew how to flatter individuals he wanted to talk to, I think he was too innocent to practice the ultimate flattery of putting himself at their mercy, as I have frequently done when far afield. He avoided confrontations, but as a lawyer shared the interest lawyers and essayists have in figuring out how to go against the grain of received opinion and attack "honorable men" occasionally. He would have approved of my going to school to Shakespeare's Antony for the purpose and beginning nearly any early controversial essay with some variety of "I come to bury Caesar, not to praise him."

My first long walks as a boy were with my father on the golf course. If he teed off before the crowd, we might see a fawn and doe, or a mink, mobbed by red-winged blackbirds, crossing the fairway with a nestling in its teeth. I could talk easily to dogs, goats, and pet alligators—though not to people—and so to the extent that stuttering directed my course as a writer, the choice for me all along may have been whether to become an essayist or to write about animals. After my first book, a circus novel called *Cat Man,* was published, several readers asked whether I didn't want to simplify things for myself and capitalize on my rapport with animals by setting out to wind up as Ernest Thompson Seton. Emphatically I didn't. My heroes were literary, and besides, I wanted to pour my heart out, which Ernest Thompson Seton never had.

The work of an essayist is, precisely, to pour out his heart. In fact, I recognized that one couldn't get to be as good a writer by writing about animals: first, because of the limits placed upon what a human being can observe of them; second, because to escape those limits and imagine one's way too deeply into the existence of an animal would remove the very itch that causes people to write books; and third, because of the limitations inherent in animals.

I was impatient, however, and remain so, of being patronized for writing about a primitive, eclipsed world, a child's world of folk figures. Somebody who writes much about animals now must deal with the death of whole constellations of creatures, perhaps half of Creation in a lifetime. And thus it turns out that the naturalist's path has converged with the novelist's or essayist's in the great, ungraspable, unspeakable (even fashionable) subject of the death of the earth, which has lately seized so many people's imaginations.

Still, I believe that we are here to thrive, not to die, or to "die" prematurely from timidity and discouragement. The evidence is everywhere, in the gaiety and speed of nature during the intense pursuits of getting food and lovemaking, and in our own sense of peace and ebullience when we feel attuned to where we are— reaching back again within ourselves for that natural man who smells the food on his fork before he eats. A writer's job is to pour out his heart, and whether his immediate concern is the death of whales and rhinos, or the death of civilization, there will be small chance for him not to.

The Anxious Fields of Play

RICHARD HUGO

Richard Hugo published nine collections of his poetry during his life, including his *Selected Poems* (1979). His collected poems will be published by W.W. Norton in the fall. Shortly before his death last year he was named a fellow of the Academy of American Poets.

By the mid-1930s, when I was ten or eleven, baseball had become such an obsession that I imagined ball parks everywhere. In the country, I visualized games in progress on the real grass cattle were eating. In the city as I rode down Fourth Avenue on the bus, the walls of warehouses became outfield fences with dramatic doubles and triples booming off them. Hitting was important in my fantasies. Pitching meant little except as a service necessary for some long drive far beyond the outfielders. I kept the parks small in my mind so home runs wouldn't be too difficult to hit.

The lot across the street from my grandparents' house was vacant and whenever I could get enough neighborhood friends to join me we'd have a game there. In center field a high board fence bounded the west side of the Noraines' backyard. It was about a hundred feet from the worn spot we called home plate. The right field fence, a good forty feet away at the imagined foul line, ran east and bordered the north side of the Brockermans' yard. "Over the fence," I yelled, "is a home run." "Over the fence," said Mr. Brockerman from his yard, hoping to keep his windows intact, "is out." "It's our game and we can make the rules, and besides, you can't even get a job," I yelled back. It was a cruel remark. The Depression was on and my grandfather was the only man in the neighborhood who had steady work. A few years later, when I was old enough to realize the hopeless state of things for men during the Depression, I wanted to apologize to Mr. Brockerman, but he had long since moved away. No left field fence. Just some trees and the ground of the Burns's yard, looking more trampled than the ferns and grass of the vacant lot.

One evening the men in the neighborhood joined us for a game. I was so excited, I bubbled. Growing up with my grandparents, I missed the vitality of a young father. I ran about the field, loudly picking all the men for my team. My hopes for a dynasty were shattered when a grownup explained that we might have a better game if we chose even sides. Days after, I trudged about the neighborhood asking the fathers if they would play ball again, but no luck.

When my grandparents had the basement put in, a concrete full-sized basement replacing the small dirt cave where Grandmother had kept her preserves, a pile of gravel was left on the north side of the house. Ours was the only house on that side of the block and in my mind the woods to the north became a baseball field. The rocks—smooth, round, averaging about the size of a quarter—were perfect for my purpose.

I fashioned a bat by carving a handle on a one-by-four and I played out entire nine-inning games, throwing the rocks up and swatting them into and over the trees. Third base was a willow tree. Second base was (I knew exactly in my mind) just beyond the honeysuckle and the giant hollow stump that usually held a pool of rainwater inside its slick mossed walls. Many times that pool reflected the world and my face back at me in solitary moments. First base, not really important because I seldom hit rocks that way, was vaguely a clump of alders.

I knew exactly how far a rock had to sail to be a home run. It had to clear the fence I dreamed beyond the woods. My games were always dramatic and ended with a home run, bases loaded, three runs down, two out, the count three and two, bottom of the ninth. How did I manage that? It was easy. I could control my hits well enough to hit three singles to load the bases, because my notion of what constituted a single was flexible. Then I'd select a rock whose size and shape indicated it might sail well, and clobber it. If, for some reason, it didn't sail far enough to be a home run, I simply tried again.

Inning after inning, I swatted rock outs, rock singles, rock doubles, rock triples, and rock home runs. I was the Yankees and also my opponents, the Giants. The only major league ball I heard was the World Series. It was carried on the radio and the Yankees were usually playing. The Yankees also had the most glamorous stars. Sometimes I played out the entire series, all seven games, letting the Giants win three. The score mounted. The lead changed hands. Then the last of the ninth, when Babe Ruth, Lou Gehrig, or Joe DiMaggio broke it up. I don't remember now if Ruth still played with New York when DiMaggio joined the team, but on my Yankees they were teammates.

One game, the dramatic situation in the ninth, a strong wind was blowing, as usual from the south. I tossed a flat round stone, perfect for sailing, and caught it just right. I still can see it climb and feel my disbelief. It soared out over the trees, turned over once, and started to climb like a determined bird. I couldn't have imagined I'd ever hit one that far. It was lovely. It rose and rose. I thought it might never stop riding that high wind north. It crossed the imaginary left field fence before its flight became an aesthetic matter, and it disappeared, a dot, still climbing, somewhere over Rossner's store on the corner of Sixteenth and Barton. I believe that rock traveled about two blocks. Why not? Joe Di-Maggio had hit it.

I couldn't see the neighborhood beyond the trees. I simply drove the rocks out over the woods and imagined the rest, though sometimes I heard doubles rattle off the sides and roof of the community hall in center field just beyond the woods. A few years later I realized how dangerous my Yankees had been, spraying stones about the neighborhood. During my absence in World War II, the woods were wiped out by new housing.

One Sunday I left the house to play off somewhere and so was gone when my uncle Lester from Tacoma showed up without warning to see if I wanted to go with him to watch the Seattle Indians play in the Pacific Coast League. When I got home and found I'd missed the chance, I wept bitterly and whined against the fates. I was still whining and sobbing when my uncle returned on his way back home. He must have been touched by my disappointment, because he returned the following Sunday and this time I was ready. It was kind of him. He saw that I was a bored, lonely boy. Grandfather had few passions outside of the house and the yard, and no interest in baseball.

When I was old enough and had some money, I went to the Sunday doubleheaders alone, catching a bus downtown and transferring to a trolley—an hour-long trip from White Center. I was there by ten o'clock, when the park opened, and waited for the players to arrive. I collected autographs, of course, and saw several stars on their way to the big leagues, including Ted Williams, who was hitting around .260 with San Diego. I took it all in—hitting practice, infield practice, then the two games. I went filled with anticipation, heart pounding, but I sat, untypically for someone my age, quietly in the stands watching the game. Recently my aunt Dol, Lester's widow, told me that in church I would sit so quietly for a small boy that people remarked on it. I can remember that despite my nervousness and anxiety, I also had moments when I was unusually patient and quiet. I could wait for hours with nothing to do. Given the drabness of life with my grandparents, I had developed ways of entertaining myself in my mind.

In 1936, I was a seventh grader and a substitute on the Highland Park softball team. That was something. Seldom did anyone but an eighth grader make the team, even as a sub. "You can beat eggs. You can beat cream. But you can't beat Highland Park's softball team." That was our yell, and the vowel repeat of "beat cream" intrigued me even then. The last game of that season, Mr. Fields, the coach, sent me in to pinch hit. I was twelve and had never been in a league game before. I was excited and frightened and people seemed to swirl—the other players, Mr. Fields, and Miss Shaefer, our other coach. My hero, Buss Mandin, our star pitcher, was watching. The world was watching. The pitcher was no longer another boy; he was a stranger from another universe. The ball came, surely too fast for any mortal to hit, yet as slow as if dreamed. I don't remember swinging. The bat seemed to swing itself and I saw the ball lining over the shortstop hole into left field, a clean single. Mandin, Fields, and Shaefer smiled approval from the sidelines as I held first. I had found a way of gaining the attention and approval of others, and I was not to let it go for nearly thirty years.

In the eighth grade next year, I was the softball team catcher. Ralph Lewin, a short thick powerful boy, was the pitcher. He was good. I was good too, and not afraid of the bat—a consideration at that age. I crouched quite close to the hitter and didn't flinch when he swung. Actually, the closer you squat to the batter, the easier catching is.

One night Ralph and I were at Betty Moore's house. She was the cutest girl in school and somehow I was supposed to be "with her." We were on a sun porch, the three of us, all thirteen years old. Betty's older brother and another boy his age had girls in the darkened front room and were necking. Ralph urged me to kiss Betty, but I was far too scared. He said to me, with disdain, "This is what you do," and he kissed her. I tried to keep my composure and I said, "Oh, is that it?" or something like that, and humiliation flooded my stomach. They went on necking. I had never seen a man kiss a woman before except in the movies, and I'm not putting anyone on when I say that I really thought people kissed only in films. I can never remember being kissed as a child, nor did I ever see any show of affection between my grandparents. I walked out, my face flushed with shame, through the dark living room, where one of the older boys yelled some insult at me, and finally, after years of groping, into the fresh air outside, free and alone. I walked the mile home, degraded and in anguish, and as I cried, my tears created a secondary glow around the street lights. I wanted to be like Ralph Lewin, like Betty Moore's brother, like anybody else. At home, my grandparents were already asleep, and I sat alone, as I did so many times in that still house, and stared into the solitary void I was certain would be my life.

But on the ball field, Ralph and I were social equals. One day we played the alumni, now freshmen and sophomores in high school, and I struck out, fooled badly on a change of pace. The fans laughed. Maybe I couldn't do anything about the humiliation I'd suffered in Betty Moore's house, but I could do something about it on the ball field. I promised myself no one would ever fool me again on a change of pace, and I kept my promise. I developed a technique of hitting late, of starting my swing at the last possible moment to avoid being tricked. Nearly all my hits for the next thirty years were to my off field, right field. Over the years, whenever players asked me why I hit to right and never pulled the ball,

I told them a half truth. I said I hit better to right field. That was true. When I hit to left, I tended to grind the ball into the dirt. But I never told them the real reason.

That final year in grammar school we won the championship of our league in an extra-inning game against E. C. Hughes. They had beaten us out of the soccer championship in an overtime game just a few months before and the softball win felt good. I looked to the city play-offs with confidence. In my small world, how could any team be better than ours? Our first play-off game, we were defeated by a team of seven Orientals, two blacks, and a tall Jewish short fielder, by the score of 14 to 0. Despite my working-class background, I was lucky to grow up knowing prejudice was wrong, but I remember thinking then that minority people possessed some sort of magic.

My hitting was my ticket to acceptance. That first summer out of grammar school I spent with my mother in Bremerton, and I joined a softball team. The opening game was played in a pasture, very like the pastures I'd imagined into ball fields years before, and I hit a single, a double, a triple, and two home runs. My standing with the other boys, strangers just a few days before, was insured. The summer was mine.

After that I turned to hardball for several years. In the Park League I began as a pitcher, but one day a shower of triples and home runs convinced me that either second base or the outfield was where I really belonged. The summer I was fourteen I played second base on the Boulevard Park Merchants. All the other players were adults except for my buddy, George Zimmerman, who lived in Boulevard Park and had me try out for the team. I played all the games and collected a lot of hits. I also made the American Legion Team in West Seattle and hit around .350 for the season.

Often a ball game gave me confidence I could find nowhere else. Once, playing center field in a Park League game when I was around fifteen, I memorized the lineup of the opposing team, and in the last inning, score 2 to 1 in our favor and the other team threatening with men on base and two out, I detected a player batting out of turn. The umpire checked and called the batter out.

In high school, though I made the squad all four years, I spent three of them on the bench. I knew the coach, Lloyd Doty, was reluctant not only to cut pitchers but even to try to distinguish between pitchers and players who called themselves pitchers. So I hung in there calling myself a pitcher and became a batting practice ace. Park League experience had taught me three things about my pitching. One, I had exceptional control for a boy; two, I was easy to hit; three, when I was hit, the ball went a hell of a long way. I was indispensable to the morale of the starting hitters. "Just throw your fast ball, Richard," Coach Doty said.

In my senior year, a starting outfielder was caught burglarizing a clothing store and was sent up for a year. I declared myself an outfielder and played every game in right field. I had a miserable season, made errors, failed to hit consistently. My desire for acceptance was so overwhelming in high school that out in the field or at bat I was dizzy with tension and fear of failing in front of the students. I remember I played better when we were away at other schools.

I played semipro ball in the city leagues after that and did well. Just after I turned nineteen, I was called into the service. In the army, the chances to play were few, and I seized them when they came. I remember playing second with some sharp players, one of them a professional, at Logan, Utah, where we held infield drills on the Utah State campus quadrangle. I put everything into it, whipping the final throw of each infield round from second to home in a taut rope that sang through the thin mountain air as the spectators gasped. I remember playing third base in a monastery courtyard at the Army Air Corps rest camp on Capri, while the monks and a Red Cross girl with gorgeous legs looked on. I did not relax on a ball field. I always played my best no matter how makeshift the game.

I was discharged in June of '45, and I immediately joined a semipro team in the city league. It was clear to me by then that I was fouled up sexually and I was drinking more and more. I even played a game drunk and hit a triple far over the right fielder's head. I ended up at third base gagging. The run had made me sick and the manager took me out.

I turned out for the University of Washington team in the spring of '46, and made the squad for a few weeks until I was caught playing intramural softball and cut. That summer I played on another semipro team, but was told to get out by the grim manager after the fourth game, when I made the mistake of trying to joke with him after we'd lost a close one. That hurt, the sudden hostile and permanent rejection when I was only trying to be friendly. I remember saying goodbye to one of the players, and though I barely knew him, I was close to tears. I felt I was losing something I loved, and with my life so void of satisfaction, the loss seemed monumental. The goodbye I was saying to whoever that player was seemed a big goodbye to many things.

I went to school, off and on, majoring in creative writing, but tiring badly after three or four quarters. Then I'd go out and find a menial job somewhere. I worked in warehouses and at a steel mill, then in California at an ammunition magazine. In the summer of '47, I went back to softball, to a team in West Seattle. Several members were old friends from high school, and they were good players. I came to the team after the season started and it took a while before I got into the lineup, but by the end of the season I was the catcher. It felt good, crouching close to the batter as Jimmy Gifford's pitches broke past the batter into my glove for the third strike, and I wheeled the ball down to Ed Schmidt at first base to start the infield throw around.

For the next thirteen years, I played softball in the West Seattle Class A League. The first year we lost the championship to a veteran team, the West Seattle Auto Dealers, in a play-off game. But we had the nucleus of a good team, as well as the camaraderie of young men who had known each other for several years, and in 1948 we became the power of league. By then, I had studied two quarters with Theodore Roethke and was working on poems at home in the evening, when I wasn't out drinking. I was still living with my grandparents, who were near-ing the end. With no sex life, there seemed little reason for me to move out. I was frozen, a perpetual fifteen, but after a bad two or three years, I was playing ball again and loving it. My appetite for acceptance, for the approval of others, was satisfied on the ball fields, if nowhere else.

Ken Gifford, Jim's brother, and one of my high school chums, played third base. John Popich, four or five years younger than Gifford and myself, played shortstop, and his cousin Walt, about my age, played second. Ed Schmidt, also a high school friend, played first. That was the nucleus of the team. When Jim Gifford went to Seattle University to play basketball and pitch softball, Mimo Campagnaro, a strange hypochondriac who threw best on those days he complained of a wrenched back or a devastating headache, became our pitcher. Stinkey Johnson, another high school friend, was the backup pitcher to Mimo. For years, it was as if we were still kids, or so it seemed to one of us.

The last scheduled game of the season in 1948, we found ourselves again playing the West Seattle Auto Dealers. We were tied in the standings for first place, so again the championship was on the line. With two out and the tying run on second in the last of the seventh, I drilled a single up the middle to send the game into extra innings. (Oh, Joe DiMaggio.) Ed Schmidt was managing, and though not a demonstrative man, he couldn't hide his delight in the first-base coaching box. We won in the bottom of the eighth.

I remained after the others went home. Dark clouds were moving in from the southwest. The field seemed lonely and forlorn, abandoned to the dusk. I luxuriated in the memory of the game just completed, and in some odd way I felt at one with the field deserted to the wind. Several times I visited ball fields in the fall and winter and sat alone in the car remembering some game I'd played there, as the rain fell or leaves blew across the empty grounds.

I cultivated a casual, joking attitude on the field to hide the seriousness with which I took each game. But I betrayed that seriousness by showing up earlier than the others and sitting around the park alone, waiting for the equipment to arrive. Whenever players were late, I kept an anxious lookout. (Two more and we'll have nine and won't have to forfeit.) I took that anxiety into the batter's box. I doubt that in those nearly thirty years of ball, I ever batted relaxed. Because hitting was so important, I developed ways of countering my anxiety. I managed to remove any idea of competition from my mind by ignoring the pitcher as a human being until he vanished and only the ball remained. If I was aware of the pitcher as a man, I was finished.

John Popich was just the opposite. He had to hate the opposition. "Let's beat these bastards," he would say without one touch of humor. The son of Yugoslavian immigrants, he grew up in

Riverside, where West Marginal Way parallels the Duwamish River, and life for him was an endless fight. Like most of those who grew up in Riverside, he had moved to middle-class West Seattle. I think he suffered conflicts that many children of immigrants do: the society pulling him one way, his loyalty to his heritage pulling him the other. He often spoke with fondness of Yugoslavian dishes his mother prepared. And he insisted, perhaps too much, on poking fun at the Italians on the team—Mimo and his brother Freddie; Robert Rimpini, an outfielder; and Morrie Capaloto, another outfielder, Italian-Jewish by background, who owned a small grocery in Alki. Popich's remarks usually implied the superiority of Yugoslavs. His cousin Walt, from the same area and circumstances, but emotionally far less complicated, suffered little conflict. When he spoke of Riverside, which he had left behind for good, it was usually as "those people."

Physically, John was easily the most gifted player on the team —fast, unusually strong, well coordinated. From his shortstop position, he fired accurate cannon shots at Schmidt, who took them easily in his cool, unhurried way as if they were easy tosses. Popich had one failing that prevented him from realizing his potential. He couldn't adjust his aggressive instincts to conditions. One game, he flew out every time up, trying to power the ball against a hopelessly stiff wind. With Schmidt's cool, he could have played professional baseball.

One game, at Alki Field, I was run over in a play at home. That was the one play I hated. It is always open season on the catcher, and later, during my last four or five years, I gave up blocking the plate and started tagging runners like a third baseman, flashing in once with my hands and getting out of there. This time, I made the mistake of taking Popich's streaking relay squatting on my haunches. The ball and the runner arrived at the same time and the runner, seeing how vulnerable I was, ran me down. His knee crashed into my head and I rolled back, green stars exploding. I remember lying there on the plate, holding the ball for a moment before my right hand involuntarily relaxed and the ball dribbled out. I was taken out, of course. I had double vision and my right arm ached from a stretched nerve trunk, a neuritis that stayed with me for three months. The run tied the game.

In the last of the seventh, Popich hit the longest home run I've seen in softball. The bases were loaded at the time, and the ball went far over the head of Jack Marshall, a fast young left fielder. It must have landed 150 feet beyond him as he ran back, and he had already been playing deep. I believe it would have cleared many left field fences in baseball parks. With my double vision, I saw two unbelievable drives sailing over two Jack Marshalls, and eight runners scoring.

Popich's home runs were raw power, shots that seemed to take less than a second in flight. Schmidt's were just the opposite. In one game, he unloaded two home runs, and with his classic swing the balls didn't seem hard hit at all. They soared slowly like lazy birds, beautiful to watch, like the rock I'd hit that day long before. Popich batted third, Schmidt fourth, and I followed, swinging the bat as if I was swatting off demons, driving the ball late into right field. Despite our hitting, we were primarily a defensive team. In a typical game, we would grab an early lead, then play flawless defensive ball. Once we got the lead, we seldom added to it. We concentrated on defense as if we considered the game already won. Usually, it was.

Most of the others were married and getting on with their lives. I took the scorebook home and computed averages. When I listened to professional games on the radio, I often lined out a score sheet on a piece of paper, using the blunt back edge of Grandmother's bread knife for a rule, and scored the entire game sitting alone at the table in the kitchen. I watched my dissolute life passing. Sometimes with anger and resentment that exploded into verbal abuse of friends when I was drunk and filled me with shame the next day, when, terrified I'd end up friendless and alone, I made embarrassed apologies. Sometimes with frustration when I refused to admit my defeat and sought out women, only to find myself unable to conquer my timidity. But mostly with sadness and the intense love of simple compensations like softball and fishing.

One day before a game at Lincoln Park, I had come early as usual, and was sitting in the grass near some boys in their middle teens. They were talking about girls and chewing the tender root ends of grass blades. "Sharon's easy," one of them said. "Jesus, she's easy." He was smiling. Ten years younger than I was, and already they knew more about life than I believed I ever would. I looked away through the trees at the sea. Somewhere out there beyond me was a life of normalcy and I was certain I would never be a part of it. It was farther than the islands I could see. It was beyond reach. It was a sad moment and I wanted the players to come and the game to begin.

Within a few years we had become a smooth, balanced team. Jim Gifford came back. He was now one of the best throwers in Seattle and could have pitched AA ball. Gordon Urquhart replaced Walt Popich at second base and we formed the best team I've ever played on. Urquhart and I managed the team, or rather I should say Urquhart managed the team on the field and I planned strategy with him over a beer at our sponsor's place, the Blew Eagle Café. The strange spelling had occurred during the Depression. Gino, the original owner, first named it the Blue Eagle Café, but when the Roosevelt administration launched the National Recovery Act in the early thirties, it adopted as its symbol a blue eagle. Every time a radio announcer said, "Look for the blue eagle," Gino got free advertising. The government insisted he comply with some law by changing the name, but Gino complied only by changing the spelling. The possibilities for obscenity were too good to pass up.

We went through the league undefeated, the first team to do it since the twenties, and that season I played in the most perfectly played game I can remember. Neither side made a mistake. Jim Gifford threw a no-hitter. The opposing pitcher threw a two-hitter. We won late in the game on a triple by our center fielder, Jim Burroughs, and an infield out. I remember it well because it again reflected the way I felt about things in general and my poems in particular. If something was good in itself, well done, it made no difference whether it was important or not, nor whether it had an audience. Here was a game in a Class A softball league at Alki Playfield in a city in the Far West, one of thousands of such games going on all over the country, with practically no one watching, and yet the game itself had been played with a perfection that to me made it important. I was constantly looking for perfection in my poems. It was a handicap really, because in my drive for perfection I rewrote poems completely out of existence. I was blind to all the mistakes I can see there now, but had I seen them then, I would have rewritten again and again until the mistake was gone. And while I didn't realize it then, the reason I had to rewrite so much was that making real changes was so difficult. Each rewrite was almost the same thing over, done with the hope something would change and that, in turn, would trigger other changes that would finally result in a perfect unit of sound. My perfectionism was really a symptom of my stagnation. No matter how I tried, my poems, like my life, were going nowhere. Later I tried to handle this theme in a long poem called "Duwamish Head." That's where the Duwamish is backed up by the sea and no longer seems to flow.

Gordon Urquhart was the most interesting person I played ball with. By lucky accident we found ourselves working together at Boeing and I got to know him well. He surmounted setbacks and adversity with a resiliency I found monumental and he had a great sense of humor. He had been a marine NCO in Korea in an outfit overrun by the Chinese. He found himself one night standing in the dark, firing wildly as Chinese soldiers in bewildering numbers rushed by all around him. He was hit in the leg and, typical of him, took charge of the survivors he could find the next morning and led them back to safety, hobbling on his wounded leg.

He loved his wife and she died, strangled in an asthmatic seizure while he held her, help on the way too late. I remember the voice over the intercom at work, telling him to call home, and his hurried departure. I offered my awkward condolences a few days later, when he returned. "Yes," he said, "it was a shock." He was most composed and his grief never surfaced, despite his emotional honesty. Later he remarried and went on his indestructible way. An alder. A catfish. Those are my two favorite private nicknames for masters of survival.

Gordon loathed the idea of privileged people, people on top. He used to say sarcastically, "What's happening to your precious Yankees?" when they were losing. He also hated Sugar Ray Robinson, and was outraged when Robinson got a championship fight against Bobo Olson, while Tiger Jones, who had beaten Robinson, was ignored. Of course, I loved Robinson and the Yankees because they had class, which, to paraphrase Henry Reed, in my case I had not got. Like my grandfather, who identified with Henry Ford, I appreciated the most successful, especially those who had what I thought of as style—those who won and looked good doing it. Urquhart was a winner who identified with the underprivileged, but only those who tried. (In my poems, I was on the side of the losers who lived their defeat.)

Urquhart's hatred of privilege was so intense, I think his own drive for success must have involved some conflict. I even imagine he may have disliked himself for it. The first time I met his father, he told me with undisguised bitterness that Roosevelt had broken him. I didn't get the story clear, but it seemed to involve large holdings of beef Mr. Urquhart had had in Montana in the thirties, a situation sure to profit him considerably until the federal government had made beef available at low prices or for free to the poor. Something like that, as I remember. This seemed to have ruined him for good, because he still dwelled on it with considerable anger despite the years that had gone by. I remember I was bewildered by it because my world was so small and immediate that to hate Roosevelt years after his death seemed a little like being pissed off at Xerxes.

Whatever Urquhart's relation was with his father, it must have involved intense attitudes about success and failure. When Robinson knocked out Gene Fullmer, I was delighted. Urquhart, of course, was furious and suggested at lunch the next day that New York money had bought Fullmer to take a dive. Fullmer was Urquhart: without style or grace, tough and aggressive, and probably most important, from a remote area where he could not benefit from the New York publicity centers. Urquhart had moved to Seattle from eastern Montana. Like Fullmer, he was a fighter from the moon. Urquhart was assailing Robinson, when I said, unexpectedly (even I didn't expect it and had I thought about it probably wouldn't have said it), "Isn't what you really don't like about him that he is a success?"

I might have accused him of murder. He was stunned and flashed into anger. I could have crawled away and died. I apologized later for the obvious hurt he had felt, but he was still angry and accepted my apology with something less than graciousness. Some people may think it odd that I would apologize when his anger demonstrated I was probably right. Let them. One of my favorite quotes is Valéry's: "I can't think of anything worse than being right."

Urquhart had little natural ability. He looked terrible in practice. He booted grounder after grounder. Made bad throws. He could never have made any team as good as ours, had we not known how good he was once the game started. I never remember Gordon making an error in a game, and although not a consistent hitter, he seldom failed when it counted. Unlike most softball players, he took his competitive instincts to his job, and I've heard he has risen quite high in the Boeing company. I dare say he did it on plenty of hard work and guts, clawing away, refusing to be beaten. He lacked the physical gifts of Popich, the fast reflexes of Ken Gifford, or the cool smoothness of Schmidt. Yet, more than anyone on the team, he was responsible for the best season we had. I find it hard to think of him in a high executive position. He was never good at hiding his feelings, an honesty not usually found in corporate executives. I can't imagine him as cold or manipulative, or anything really but a nice, tough, and resilient man. I remember him vividly because we played ball together. That was our link. We both loved playing, he with his honest intensity, and I with my intensity hidden behind my jokes because I knew if it surfaced it would ruin my ability to play.

Years after I was finally able to have sexual relations with women, I continued to play ball, both in the West Seattle League and in the Boeing League (employees only). Our West Seattle team got old, like that team we had first beaten out for the championship, and we found ourselves coming in second more often than first in the league. I published some painting poems in *Contact,* one of the best of the early West Coast magazines, and for the picture on the cover sent in a photo of myself in a Boeing All-Star softball shirt. I took a kind of perverse delight (still do) in not looking like a poet, and I enjoyed appearing on the cover looking like a jock alongside the pictures of the other contributors, some of them terribly affected shots (face half hidden by smoke in the coffeehouse gloom), when inside the magazine my poems, along with reproductions of the paintings that had triggered them, were by far the artiest items there.

Bob Peterson, the San Francisco poet and now a good friend, was poetry editor. He is also a baseball nut and, I think, entertains fantasies of himself as a star pitcher. When, for the contributors' notes, I sent in my Boeing League-leading batting average of .541, he reduced it to .400. "No one," he said, "would believe .541." "They would if they had seen the pitching," I wrote back. There were younger and much better players on our Boeing team, several of them top players in the city leagues, but they didn't take our games seriously and tried only to see how far they could hit the ball. I was still hitting as intensely as always to right field, no matter how absurd the score or weak the opposition.

A friend named Bill Daly pitched for that Boeing team. Bill made a remark one day to Dick Martin, the third baseman, that had a lot of wisdom: "Dick, I was thinking the other day how much time we've put into this game all these years. What if we'd put that time into work, making a living. We'd probably be rich." Bill also pitched against us in the West Seattle League, and though I knew his stuff well, he struck me out one game. He did it with a drop, not too much on it, that came in high and outside and dipped into the strike zone. I'd seen it all the way, saw it drop into my favorite spot, and I never pulled the trigger. (Goodbye, Joe.) I walked away, the message clear, remembering many times I'd slammed that pitch deep into the right center field gap, had seen the outfielders turned and running as I rounded first on my way to a triple or home run. My reflexes were going and I knew it as I sat down and waited for the inning to end. I didn't feel sad. I didn't feel any sense of loss. I didn't feel humiliated at striking out as I once would have, though I was still intensely trying to avoid it. More than just the reflexes had gone.

The only good sports poem I can remember reading was one called "Cobb Would Have Caught It" by Robert Fitzgerald. Whenever I tried to write about baseball or softball, I found myself thinking about the game itself, and the poem kept turning into a melodramatic sports story with the winning hit coming at the crucial moment. (Oh, Joe DiMaggio. Oh, beautiful rock sailing downwind high over Sixteenth and Barton.) I was interested in the score, not the words.

In the summer of '72, two of my students were playing softball in Missoula and I started going to the games. I foolishly put my name on the roster one night at the last minute to avoid a forfeit and before the season was over I played four games, a fat middle-aged man standing in the outfield, being eaten by mosquitoes and wishing he could lose twenty years for an hour and a half. My first time at bat in a serious game (serious because the pitcher was throwing hard), I lined a double over the right fielder's head. Anyone else would have had a home run. I hobbled into second, just as surprised as the spectators. The last game I played, I pulled off a running one-handed catch before a large crowd that went wild. I couldn't believe it when the ball, blurred by sweat and fear, hit my glove and stuck there as I ran full tilt toward the foul line. But now only luck was on my side and luck has a way of running out. I loved those late triumphs, but I could also laugh at them.

I took interest in the whole scene, not just the game. Except for those times I was obliged to play to prevent forfeits, I sat in the stands and took note of the spectators as well as the game, of the players' wives and children, of the players from teams not on the field. One night I watched a player's wife play with a small child. It was beautiful. *She* was beautiful, a full, warm woman who radiated affection. I imagined myself coming home to her from work tired and putting my head in her lap. Another wife kept score with intense dedication, marking each play in the book, always with the score, inning, and number of outs ready for anyone who would ask. Though she was in her thirties and the mother of three children, her flesh looked soft and virginal, like that of a high school girl.

The player-spectators who interested me were working people of the old cut, posturing, clowning, awkward, self-conscious, never quite accepting themselves, kidding the players in the field with loud, sometimes crude, always good-natured insults. They drank lots of beer. They also turned me through parts of my life I'd neglected for a long time and I suppose I loved them for that.

I thought again about those tiny worlds I'd lived in with far more desperation than I hoped any of them would ever know. I thought of Ingmar Bergman's film *The Naked Night* (sometimes called *Sawdust and Tinsel*), where the degraded protagonist and his wife have finally only each other with whom to face an arrogant, humiliating world. How the crutch we once needed to hobble through life remains in our closet long after our leg has healed. How Gordon Urquhart could fight through his setbacks and his complicated attitudes about life to a kind of success, while my best hope of avoiding defeat was to turn values around with words, to change loss into victory. How John Popich came to the field with his physical gifts, hoping in seven innings to win the battle he would probably never win. How failures are in many ways successes and how successful people, those who early in life accepted adult values and abandoned the harmless fields of play, are really failures because they never come to know the vital worth of human relationships, even if it takes the lines of a softball field to give them a frame. How, without play, many people sense too often and too immediately their impending doom. After nearly thirty years of writing, I was ready to try a softball poem.

Missoula Softball Tournament

This summer, most friends out of town
and no wind playing flash and dazzle
in the cottonwoods, music of the Clark Fork stale,
I've gone back to the old ways of defeat,
the softball field, familiar dust and thud,
pitcher winging drops and rises, and wives,
the beautiful wives in the stands, basic, used,
screeching runners home, infants unattended
in the dirt. A long triple sails into right center.
Two men on. Shouts from dugout: go, Ron, go.
Life is better run from. Distance to the fence,
both foul lines and dead center, is displayed.
I try to steal the tricky manager's signs.
Is hit-and-run the pulling of the ear?
The ump gives pitchers too much low inside.
Injustice? Fraud? Ancient problems focus
in the heat. Bad hop on routine grounder.
Close play missed by the team you want to win.
Players from the first game, high on beer,
ride players in the field. Their laughter
falls short of the wall. Under lights, the moths
are momentary stars, and wives, the beautiful wives
in the stands, now take the interest they once feigned,
oh, long ago, their marriage just begun, years
of helping husbands feel important just begun,
the scrimping, the anger brought home evenings
from degrading jobs. This poem goes out to them.
Is steal-of-home the touching of the heart?

Last pitch. A soft fly. A can of corn,
the players say. Routine, like mornings,
like the week. They shake hands on the mound.
Nice grab on that shot to left. Good game. Good game.
Dust rotates in their headlight beams.
The wives, the beautiful wives, are with their men.

It struck me as a crude poem and for a while I didn't like it.
It seems to be discussing its own meaning. But one day I came to
believe that the crudeness was right, at least for that poem.

The summer of '73 I returned again to watch a few games. It
was pleasant saying hello to a lot of nice people, most of whom
ask little from life or from others. A few inquired if I was going
to play again and I told them not a chance, but I felt a little
proud that they had asked. One night a big husky girl, who
played on one of the women's teams in town, brought a group of
handicapped young people to watch one of the men's games.
Some of them seemed retarded, others afflicted with physical and
neurological problems. From all I've written here, I should not
have to explain the following villanelle I finished a few months
ago.

The Freaks at Spurgin Road Field

The dim boy claps because the others clap.
The polite word, handicapped, is muttered in the stands.
Isn't it wrong, the way the mind moves back.

One whole day I sit, contrite, dirt, L.A.
Union Station '46, sweating through last night.
The dim boy claps because the others clap.

Score, 5 to 3. Pitcher fading badly in the heat.
Isn't it wrong to be or not be spastic?
Isn't it wrong, the way the mind moves back.

I'm laughing at a neighbor girl beaten to scream
by a savage father and I'm ashamed to look.
The dim boy claps because the others clap.

The score is always close, the rally always short.
I've left more wreckage than a quake.
Isn't it wrong, the way the mind moves back.

The afflicted never cheer in unison.
Isn't it wrong, the way the mind moves back
to stammering pastures where the picnic should have worked.
The dim boy claps because the others clap.

I think when I played softball I was telling the world and myself that futile as my life seemed, I still wanted to live.

The Chinese Girl

LEONARD MICHAELS

Leonard Michaels has published two collections of short shories and a novel, *The Men's Club*. He teaches at the University of California at Berkeley.

Writers are born, then discovered and variously judged. They feel adored or merely patronized. They feel ignored or misunderstood or maligned. They feel wonderful or dreadfully hurt. If they fall in love with themselves, or if they commit suicide, people suppose it was built into their vocation. In the South, it is said of a medical student, "He is going to make a doctor." For writers, there is no comparable expression, no diploma, no conclusive evidence that anything real has been made of himself or herself. Once born, they are doomed to the grotesque labors of being reborn, rediscovered, and then they are judged again and again. Naturally, they tend to smoke, drink, etc.

I have published stories and a novel, but I claim only to have had a career. Since I cannot talk about the value or the reality of my work, I'll talk about what might have influenced it.

The most immediate influence is my wife, especially her dreams. In the morning she wakes and tells them to me, even if I'm asleep, because she might forget them otherwise. Her voice goes in and out of my head, trailing a broken residue of strange events. This can be very irritating, but her dreams are sometimes so wonderful that I wake up and listen actively. I ask her to see more. See the whole dream. She speaks in a steady, neutral voice. The dream might be frightening, sad, funny, but her voice remains neutral. Thus, she tries to prevent it from interfering with what she sees. The more she speaks, the less present and accessible is her dream, but I listen hard. I have taken inventories of her dreams, as if they contained the goods and chattels of our communal property.

In less immediate ways, anything might influence my writing —weather, music, pain, politics. The least significant influence is the one easiest to talk about: the writing of other people. In my case, it is mostly long-dead Europeans, but among American moderns there are Saul Bellow and Wallace Stevens. They seem to me awesome and antithetical in their verbal imaginations. I often re-read them in the middle of the night when I am most anxious about matters in my life and work. I'm a slow reader. I read every word.

Bellow's novels, with their deep rhythms and paragraphs of dense, multitudinous apprehension, seem to me full of poems. Such a sentence as "Envying fallen sticks from his nearness to their state" is a poem in itself. Not even English, yet English must be proud to claim it. The word "nearness" gives the line a beautiful intimacy. If Bellow said "closeness," it would fail a little, but "nearness," with its slight pressure in the beat, releases the final three words and makes the motion, the gesture, the quality of feeling it intends. Indeed, to be near dead becomes, imaginably, worse than to be dead. The way Bellow puts this thrills me. I think I could write a book on his sentence—a chapter on its lyrical concision, another on the mournful Yiddish resonance in its simplicity.

Where Wallace Stevens describes the history of his mind as "tufted in straggling thunder and shattered sun," my enthusiasm and pleasure are less narcissistic. I know that Stevens's words are intrinsically good, but I don't then think I feel good because *I know that I know.* In his American English, I hear innumerable easy perfections forbidden to me. In Bellow, I hear something close.

The influence of these writers on my work is, finally, misdirection and frustration, but I am consoled by the knowledge that Keats wanted to be Milton, Kafka wanted to be Dickens, Lawrence and Hemingway wanted to be the King James Bible, and Beckett wants to be dead. Fortunately, since I have no choice, I don't really want to be anything or anyone else. Except maybe Chekhov. He is a European who I say, with all conceivable humility, influences me.

For example, his story "La Cigale." It is about a faithless wife. After she is faithless, her husband and his friend interrupt her when she tries to speak. They drown her out with loud singing, with peasant songs, so that, says Chekhov, "she will not tell any lies." The story is about more than this moment, but this moment, in this phrase, is seized with supernatural intelligence. I want everyone to stop trying to live and to hear me repeat the amazing thing Chekhov says: so she will not tell any lies.

Though my excitement is a species of self-congratulation— and will bring me shame—I must praise Chekhov. He is saved. The rest of us are going to hell. In such testimony there is an effect of influence. Exclusivistic. Extreme. I despise this excess in others, but I don't know how to speak otherwise.

Finally, the writer who influences me more than any other: Isaac Babel. I never talk about his work.

Here is a tentative approximation to the idea of influence:

It occurs obliquely or directly, but never through simple contact. You wouldn't say, "When I shoved him, he was influenced out the window." Influence, like gravity, is indicated when a thing acts upon another thing at a distance. The process, like the word, has liquidity in it as well as airy communication.

Vague, shallow, deep, it works by mysterious degrees. Hypnotism is influence. The Mafia is an influential organization. Money is an agency of influence. In literary form, influence is usually recognized as a negative manifestation, bespeaking some deficiency of original creative power. More largely considered, the ubiquitous and continuous operation of influence means only that we cannot conceive of anything absolutely discrete except God. To exemplify this large consideration, I will report an operation of influence that I once observed.

I was in a Buddhist temple, in a Hawaiian rain forest, at the edge of a sugar field. I was having a conversation with a Tibetan monk. He was called *Rimposhey,* which means teacher. We sat crosslegged on the floor, facing each other, in a large high-ceilinged room. The dominant color was bright red. I spoke in English. He spoke in Tibetan. A Chinese girl, fluent in both languages, sat beside us. She repeated whatever I said, speaking to me in different English words, then to the monk in Tibetan. Frequently, after I spoke, she would say, "Oh, yes. That is in the literature." To her, little I said was unique. To me, it was all unique and painful. The example of influence was in the connection between this girl and the monk.

I'd heard about her from a gifted linguist at a Western university, who was a member of this temple society. He said that he and the girl began studying Tibetan with the monk at the same time. She became fluent. He still struggled with primitive grammatical forms. In his view, the monk had chosen her to learn, though he did nothing to indicate his choice.

The linguist was resentful of her, but he was bitterly impressed by the monk, whom he admired very much. One learned from the monk if there was an authentic coincidence of the will to learn and the will to teach, as that was recognized by him. This is influence, maybe, in the aspect of love. It doesn't come from—but rather passes through—one to the other. As we used to say of love, in love, "It is bigger than both of us."

When I left the Buddhist temple, it was raining heavily. The forest was luscious, dark, and loud. Beyond the forest, along a narrow road through the field of tall thick sugar cane, I stopped for a moment to break a section off one of the canes. Then I gnawed at the juicy center. Perhaps I wanted to sink below the reach of any influence, into the sweet stringy fibers, with my teeth. I can imagine the monk laughing at me. How I stood amid the sugar canes, dripping and gnawing, all alone. When seized by inspiration, writers suffer this kind of foolish luxury.

The Lesson of the Master

CYNTHIA OZICK

Cynthia Ozick was born in New York City. She is the author of *Trust,* a novel, three collections of stories—*The Pagan Rabbi, Bloodshed,* and *Levitation*—and *Art and Ardor,* a forthcoming volume of essays. Nearly one hundred articles and essays have appeared in numerous periodicals and anthologies. She has twice won the O. Henry First Prize for the best short story, and is the recipient of the American Academy of Arts and Letters Award for Literature. She is married and the mother of a seventeen-year-old daughter.

There was a period in my life—to purloin a famous Jamesian title, "The Middle Years"—when I used to say, with as much ferocity as I could muster, "I hate Henry James and I wish he was dead."

I was not to have my disgruntled way. The dislike did not last and turned once again to adoration, ecstasy, and awe; and no one is more alive than Henry James, or more likely to sustain literary immortality. He is among the angels, as he meant to be.

But in earlier days I felt I had been betrayed by Henry James. I was like the youthful writer in "The Lesson of the Master" who believed in the Master's call to live immaculately, unspoiled by what we mean when we say "life"—relationship, family mess, distraction, exhaustion, anxiety, above all disappointment. Here is the Master, St. George, speaking to his young disciple, Paul Overt:

"One has no business to have any children," St. George placidly declared. "I mean, of course, if one wants to do anything good."

"But aren't they an inspiration—an incentive?"

"An incentive to damnation, artistically speaking."

And later Paul inquires:

"Is it deceptive that I find you living with every appearance of domestic felicity—blest with a devoted, accomplished wife, with children whose acquaintance I haven't yet had the pleasure of making, but who *must* be delightful young people, from what I know of their parents?"

St. George smiled as for the candour of his question. "It's all excellent, my dear fellow—heaven forbid I should deny it. . . . I've got a loaf on the shelf; I've got everything in fact but the great thing."

"And the great thing?" Paul kept echoing.

"The sense of having done the best—the sense which is the real life of the artist and the absence of which is his death, of having drawn from his intellectual instrument the finest music that nature had hidden in it, of having played it as it should be played. He either does that or he doesn't—and if he doesn't he isn't worth speaking of."

Paul pursues:

"Then what did you mean . . . by saying that children are a curse?"

"My dear youth, on what basis are we talking?" and St. George dropped upon the sofa at a short distance from him. . . . "On the supposition that a certain perfection's possible and even desirable—isn't it so? Well, all I say is that one's children interfere with perfection. One's wife interferes. Marriage interferes."

"You think, then, the artist shouldn't marry?"

"He does so at his peril—he does so at his cost."

Yet the Master who declares all this is himself profoundly, inextricably, married; and when his wife dies, he hastens to marry again, choosing Life over Art. Very properly James sees marriage as symbol and summary of the passion for ordinary human entanglement, as experience of the most commonplace, most fated kind.

But we are also given to understand, in the desolation of this comic tale, that the young artist, the Master's trusting disciple, is left both perplexed and bereft: the Master's second wife is the young artist's first love, and the Master has stolen away his disciple's chance for ordinary human entanglement.

So the Lesson of the Master is a double one: choose ordinary human entanglement, and live; or choose Art, and give up the vitality of life's passions and panics and endurances. What I am going to tell now is a stupidity, a misunderstanding, a great Jamesian life-mistake: an embarrassment and a life-shame. (Imagine that we are in one of those lavishly adorned Jamesian chambers where intimate confessions not accidentally but suspensefully take place.)

As I have said, I felt myself betrayed by a Jamesian trickery. Trusting in James, believing, like Paul Overt, in the overtness of the Jamesian lesson, I chose Art, and ended by blaming Henry James. It seemed to me James had left out the one important thing I ought to have known, even though he was saying it again and again. The trouble was that I was listening to the lesson of the Master at the wrong time, paying powerful and excessive attention at the wrong time; and this cost me my youth.

I suppose a case can be made that it is certainly inappropriate for anyone to moan about the loss of youth and how it is all Henry James's fault. All of us will lose our youth, and some of us, alas, have lost it already; but not all of us will pin the loss on Henry James.

I, however, do. I blame Henry James.

Never mind the sublime position of Henry James in American letters. Never mind the Jamesian prose style—never mind that it, too, is sublime, nuanced, imbricated with a thousand distinctions and observations (the reason H. G. Wells mocked it), and as idiosyncratically and ecstatically redolent of the spirals of past and future as a garlic clove. Set aside also the Jamesian impatience with idols, the moral seriousness active both in the work and in the life. (I am thinking, for example, of Edith Wharton's compliance in the face of their mutual friend Paul Bourget's anti-Semitism, and James's noble and definitive dissent.) Neglect all this, including every other beam that flies out from the stupendous Jamesian lantern to keep generations reading in rapture (which is all right), or else scribbling away at dissertation after dissertation (which is not so good). I myself, after all, committed a master's thesis, long ago, called "Parable in Henry James," in which I tried to catch up all of James in the net of a single idea. Before that, I lived many months in the black hole of a microfilm cell, transcribing every letter James ever wrote to Mr. Pinker, his London agent, for a professorial book; but the professor drank, and died, and after thirty years the letters still lie in the dark.

All that while I sat cramped in that black bleak microfilm cell, and all that while I was writing that thesis, James was sinking me and despoiling my youth, and I did not know it.

I want, parenthetically, to recommend to the Henry James Society—there is such an assemblage—that membership be limited; no one under age forty-two and three-quarters need apply. Proof of age via birth certificate should be mandatory; otherwise the consequences may be harsh and horrible. I offer myself as an Extreme and Hideous Example of Premature Exposure to Henry James. I was about seventeen, I recall, when my brother brought home from the public library a science fiction anthology, which, through an odd perspective that perplexes me still, included "The Beast in the Jungle." It was in this anthology, and at that age, that I first read James—fell, I should say, into the jaws of James. I had never heard of him before. I read "The Beast in the Jungle" and creepily thought: Here, here is my autobiography.

From that time forward, gradually but compellingly—and now I yield my scary confession—I became Henry James. Leaving graduate school at the age of twenty-two, disdaining the Ph.D. as an acquisition surely beneath the concerns of literary seriousness, I was already Henry James. When I say I "became" Henry James, you must understand this: though I was a nearsighted twenty-two-year-old young woman infected with the commonplace intention of writing a novel, I was *also* the elderly bald-headed Henry James. Even without close examination, you could see the light glancing off my pate; you could see my heavy chin, my watch chain, my walking stick, my tender paunch.

I had become Henry James, and for years and years I remained Henry James. There was no doubt about it: it was my own clear and faithful truth. Of course, there were some small differences: for one thing, I was not a genius. For another, even in my own insignificant scribbler class, I was not prolific. But I carried the Jamesian idea, I was of his cult, I was a worshiper of literature, literature was my single altar; I was, like the elderly bald-headed James, a priest at that altar; and that altar was all of my life. Like John Marcher in "The Beast in the Jungle," I let everything pass me by for the sake of waiting for the Beast to spring—but unlike John Marcher, I knew what the Beast was, I knew exactly, I even knew the Beast's name: the Beast was literature itself, the sinewy grand undulations of some unraveling fiction, meticulously dreamed out in a language of masterly resplendence, which was to pounce on me and turn me into an enchanted and glorious Being, as enchanted and glorious as the elderly bald-headed Henry James himself.

But though the years spent themselves extravagantly, that

ambush never occurred: the ambush of Sacred and Sublime Literature. The great shining Beast of Sacred and Sublime Literature did
not pounce. Instead, other beasts, lesser ones, unseemly and mis-
shapen, sprang out—all the beasts of ordinary life: sorrow, disease,
death, guilt, responsibility, envy, grievance, grief, disillusionment
—the beasts that are chained to human experience, and have nothing to do with Art except to interrupt and impede it, exactly according to the Lesson of the Master.

It was not until I read a certain vast and subtle book that I
understood what had happened to me. The book was not by Henry
James, but about him. Nowadays we give this sort of work a special
name: we call it a nonfiction novel. I am referring, of course, to
Leon Edel's ingenious and beautiful biography of Henry James,
which is as much the possession of Edel's imagination as it is of the
exhilaratingly reported facts of James's life. In Edel's rendering, I
learned what I had never before taken in—but the knowledge
came, in the Jamesian way, too late. What I learned was that Henry
James himself had not always been the elderly bald-headed Henry
James!—that he too had once been twenty-two years old.

This terrible and secret knowledge instantly set me against
James. From that point forward I was determined to eradicate him.
And for a long while I succeeded.

What had happened was this: in early young womanhood I
believed, with all the rigor and force and stunned ardor of religious
belief, in the old Henry James, in his scepter and his authority. I
believed that what *he* knew at sixty I was to encompass at twenty-
two; at twenty-two I lived like the elderly bald-headed Henry
James. I thought it was necessary—it was imperative, there was no
other path—to be, all at once, with no progression or evolution,
the author of the equivalent of *The Ambassadors* or *The Wings of the
Dove,* just as if "A Bundle of Letters," or "Four Meetings," or the
golden little *The Europeans* had never preceded the great late Master.

For me, the Lesson of the Master was a horror, a Jamesian tale
of a life of mishap and mistake and misconceiving. Though the
Master himself was saying, in *The Ambassadors,* in Gloriani's garden,
to Little Bilham, through the urgent cry of Strether, "Live, live!"
—and though the Master himself was saying, in "The Beast in the
Jungle," through May Bartram, how ghastly, how ghostly, it is to

eschew, to evade, to turn from, to miss absolutely and irrevocably what is all the time there for you to seize—I mistook him, I misheard him, I missed, absolutely and irrevocably, his essential note. What I heard instead was: *Become a Master.*

Now the truth is it could not have been done, even by a writer of genius; and what a pitiful flicker of the flame of high ambition for a writer who is no more than the ordinary article! No one—not even James himself—springs all at once in early youth into full Mastery, and no writer, whether robustly gifted, or only little and pale, should hope for this implausible fate.

All this, I suppose, is not at all a "secret" knowledge, as I have characterized it, but is, rather, as James named it in the very person of his naive young artist, most emphatically *overt*—so obvious that it is a mere access of foolishness even to talk about it. Still, I offer the implausible and preposterous model of myself to demonstrate the proposition that the Lesson of the Master is not a lesson about genius, or even about immense ambition; it is a lesson about misreading—about what happens when we misread the great voices of Art, and suppose that, because they speak of Art, they *mean* Art. The great voices of Art never mean *only* Art; they also mean Life, they always mean Life, and Henry James, when he evolved into the Master we revere, finally meant nothing else.

The true Lesson of the Master, then, is, simply, never to venerate what is complete, burnished, whole, in its grand organic flowering or finish—never to look toward the admirable and dazzling end; never to be ravished by the goal; never to worship ripe Art or the ripened artist; but instead to seek to be young while young, primitive while primitive, ungainly when ungainly—to look for crudeness and rudeness, to husband one's own stupidity or ungenius.

There *is* this mix-up most of us have between ourselves and what we admire or triumphantly cherish. We see this mix-up, this mishap, this mishmash, most often in writers: the writer of a new generation ravished by the genius writer of a classical generation, who begins to dream herself, or himself, as powerful, vigorous, and original—as if being filled up by the genius writer's images, scenes, and stratagems were the same as having the capacity to pull off the identical magic. To be any sort of competent writer, one must keep one's psychological distance from the supreme artists.

If I were twenty-two now, I would not undertake a cannibalistically ambitious Jamesian novel to begin with; I would look into the eyes of Henry James at twenty-two, and see the diffident hope, the uncertainty, the marveling tentativeness, the dream that is still only a dream; the young man still learning to fashion the Scene. Or I would go back still further, to the boy of seventeen, misplaced in a Swiss polytechnic school, who recalled in old age that "I so feared and abhorred mathematics that the simplest arithmetical operation had always found and kept me helpless and blank." It is not to the Master in his fullness I would give my awed, stricken, desperate fealty, but to the faltering, imperfect, dreaming youth.

If these words should happen to reach the ears of any young writer dumbstruck by the elderly bald-headed Henry James, one who has hungrily heard and ambitiously assimilated the voluptuous cathedral tones of the developed organmaster, I would say to her or him: Put out your lean and clumsy forefinger and strike your paltry, oafish, feeble, simple, skeletal, single note. Try for what Henry James at sixty would scorn—just as he scorned the work of his own earliness, and revised it and revised it in the manner of his later pen in that grand chastisement of youth known as the New York Edition. Trying, in youth, for what the Master in his mastery would condemn—that is the only road to modest mastery. Rapture and homage are not the way. Influence is perdition.

A Conversation with My Father

GRACE PALEY

Grace Paley lives in New York and Vermont, where she has been active in many radical causes of the past two decades. She teaches writing at Sarah Lawrence. Her two published collections of fiction are *The Little Disturbances of Man* and *Extraordinary Changes at the Last Minute*.

My father is eighty-six years old and in bed. His heart, that bloody motor, is equally old and will not do certain jobs anymore. It still floods his head with brainy light. But it won't let his legs carry the weight of his body around the house. Despite my metaphors, this muscle failure is not due to his old heart, he says, but to a potassium shortage. Sitting on one pillow, leaning on three, he offers last-minute advice and makes a request.

"I would like you to write a simple story just once more," he says, "the kind de Maupassant wrote, or Chekhov, the kind you used to write. Just recognizable people, and then write down what happened to them next."

I say, "Yes, why not? That's possible." I want to please him, though I don't remember writing that way. I *would* like to try to tell such a story, if he means the kind that begins: "There was a woman . . ." followed by plot, the absolute line between two points which I've always despised. Not for literary reasons, but because it takes all hope away. Everyone, real or invented, deserves the open destiny of life.

Finally I thought of a story that had been happening for a couple of years right across the street. I wrote it down, then read it aloud. "Pa," I said, "how about this? Do you mean something like this?"

Once in my time there was a woman and she had a son. They lived nicely, in a small apartment in Manhattan. This boy at about fifteen became a junkie, which is not unusual in our neighborhood. In order to maintain her close friendship with him, she became a junkie too. She said it was part of the youth culture, with which she felt very much at home. After a while, for a number of reasons, the boy gave it all up and left the city and his mother in disgust. Hopeless and alone, she grieved. We all visit her.

"O.K., Pa, that's it," I said, "an unadorned and miserable tale."

"But that's not what I mean," my father said. "You misunderstood me on purpose. You know there's a lot more to it. You know that. You left everything out. Turgenev wouldn't do that. Chekhov wouldn't do that. There are in fact Russian writers you never heard of, you don't have an inkling of, as good as anyone, who can write a plain ordinary story, who would not leave out what you have left out. I object not to facts, but to people sitting in trees talking senselessly, voices from who knows where. . . ."

"Forget that one, Pa; what have I left out now? In this one?"

"Her looks, for instance."

"Oh. Quite handsome, I think. Yes."

"Her hair?"

"Dark, with heavy braids, as though she were a girl or a foreigner."

"What were her parents like, her stock? That she became such a person. It's interesting, you know."

"From out of town. Professional people. The first to be divorced in their county. How's that? Enough?" I asked.

"With you, it's all a joke," he said. "What about the boy's father? Why didn't you mention him? Who was he? Or was the boy born out of wedlock?"

"Yes," I said. "He was born out of wedlock."

"For Godsakes, doesn't anyone in your stories get married? Doesn't anyone have the time to run down to City Hall before they jump into bed?"

"No," I said. "In real life, yes. But in my stories, no."

"Why do you answer me like that?"

"Oh, Pa, this is a simple story about a smart woman who came

to N.Y.C. full of interest love trust excitement very uptodate and
about her son, what a hard time she had in this world. Married or
not, it's of small consequence."

"It is of great consequence," he said.

"O.K.," I said.

"O.K. O.K. yourself," he said, "but listen. I believe you that
she's good-looking, but I don't think she was so smart."

"That's true," I said. "Actually that's the trouble with stories.
People start out fantastic. You think they're extraordinary, but it
turns out, as the work goes along, they're just average with a good
education, sometimes the other way around, the person's a kind of
dumb innocent, but he outwits you and you can't even think of an
ending good enough."

"What do you do then?" he asked. He had been a doctor for
a couple of decades and then an artist for a couple of decades and
he's still interested in details, craft, technique.

"Well, you just have to let the story lie around till some agreement can be reached between you and the stubborn hero."

"Aren't you talking silly now?" he asked. "Start again," he
said. "It so happens I'm not going out this evening. Tell the story
again. See what you can do this time."

"O.K.," I said. "But it's not a five-minute job." Second attempt:

Once, across the street from us, there was a fine handsome woman, our
neighbor. She had a son whom she loved because she'd known him since
birth (in helpless chubby infancy, and in the wrestling, hugging ages,
seven to ten, as well as earlier and later). This boy when he fell into the
fist of adolescence became a junkie. He was not a hopeless one. He was
in fact hopeful, an ideologue, and a successful converter. With his busy
brilliance, he wrote persuasive articles for his high school newspaper.
Seeking a wider audience, using important connections, he drummed
into lower Manhattan newsstand distribution a periodical called *Oh!
Golden Horse!*

In order to keep him from feeling guilty (because guilt is the stony
heart of nine-tenths of all clinically diagnosed cancers in America today,
she said), and because she had always believed in giving bad habits
room at home where one could keep an eye on them, she too became
a junkie. Her kitchen was famous for a while—a center for intellectual
addicts who knew what they were doing. A few felt artistic like Cole-

ridge and others were scientific and revolutionary like Leary. Although she was often high herself, certain good mothering reflexes remained, and she saw to it that there was lots of orange juice around and honey and milk and vitamin pills. However she never cooked anything but chili, and that no more than once a week. She explained, when we talked to her, seriously, with neighborly concern, that it was her part in the youth culture and she would rather be with the young, it was an honor, than with her own generation.

One week, while nodding through an Antonioni film, this boy was severely jabbed by the elbow of a stern and proselytizing girl, sitting beside him. She offered immediate apricots and nuts for his sugar level, spoke to him sharply, and took him home.

She had heard of him and his work and she herself published, edited, and wrote a competitive journal called *Man Does Live by Bread Alone.* In the organic heat of her continuous presence he could not help but become interested once more in his muscles, his arteries and nerve connections. In fact he began to love them, treasure them, praise them with funny little songs in *Man Does Live* . . .

> the fingers of my flesh transcend
> my transcendental soul
> the tightness in my shoulders end
> my teeth have made me whole

To the mouth of his head (that glory of will and determination) he brought hard apples, nuts, wheat germ, and soybean oil. He said to his old friends: From now on, I guess I'll keep my wits about me. I'm going on the natch. He said he was about to begin a spiritual deep-breathing journey. How about you too, Mom? he asked kindly.

His conversion was so radiant, splendid, that neighborhood kids his age began to say that he had never been a real addict at all, only a journalist along for the smell of the story. The mother tried several times to give up what had become without her son and his friends a lonely habit. This effort only brought it to supportable levels. The boy and his girl took their electronic mimeograph and moved to the bushy edge of another borough. They were very strict. They said they would not see her again until she had been off drugs for sixty days.

At home alone in the evening, weeping, the mother read and reread the seven issues of *Oh! Golden Horse!* They seemed to her as truthful as ever. We often crossed the street to visit and console. But if we mentioned any of our children who were at college or in the hospital or dropouts at home, she would cry out, My baby! My baby! and burst into terrible, face-scarring, time-consuming tears. The end.

First my father was silent, then he said, "Number one: You have a nice sense of humor. Number two: I see you can't tell a plain story. So don't waste time." Then he said, sadly, "Number three: I suppose that means she was alone, she was left like that, his mother. Alone. Probably sick?"

I said, "Yes."

"Poor woman. Poor girl, to be born in a time of fools, to live among fools. The end. The end. You were right to put that down. The end."

I didn't want to argue, but I had to say, "Well, it's not necessarily the end, Pa."

"Yes," he said, "what a tragedy. The end of a person."

"No, Pa," I begged him. "It doesn't have to be. She's only about forty. She could be a hundred different things in this world as time goes on. A teacher or a social worker. An ex-junkie! Sometimes it's better than having a master's in education."

"Jokes," he said. "As a writer that's your main trouble. You don't want to recognize it. Tragedy! Plain tragedy! Historical tragedy! No hope. The end."

"Oh, Pa," I said. "She could change."

"In your own life, too, you have to look it in the face." He took a couple of nitroglycerin. "Turn to five," he said, pointing to the dial on the oxygen tank. He inserted the tubes into his nostrils and breathed deep. He closed his eyes and said, "No."

I had promised the family to always let him have the last word when arguing, but in this case I had a different responsibility. That woman lives across the street. She's my knowledge and my invention. I'm sorry for her. I'm not going to leave her there in that house crying. (Actually, neither would Life, which unlike me has no pity.)

Therefore: She did change. Of course her son never came home again. But right now, she's the receptionist in a storefront community clinic in the East Village. Most of the customers are young people, some old friends. The head doctor has said to her, "If we only had three people in this clinic with your experiences . . ."

"The doctor said that?" My father took the oxygen tubes out of his nostrils and said, "Jokes. Jokes again."

"No, Pa, it could really happen that way; it's a funny world nowadays."

"No," he said. "Truth first. She will slide back. A person must have character. She does not."

"No, Pa," I said. "That's it. She's got a job. Forget it. She's in that storefront, working."

"How long will it be?" he asked. "Tragedy! You too. When will you look it in the face?"

For Ernest Hemingway

REYNOLDS PRICE

Reynolds Price published his first novel, *A Long and Happy Life,* in 1962. His fifth, *The Source of Light,* was published in 1981. In those two decades, he has published also volumes of short stories, essays, translations from the Bible, and a play. His first volume of poems, *Vital Provisions,* appeared in 1982. His books have appeared in fourteen languages. He is James B. Duke Professor of English at Duke University.

If I had been conscious of caring enough, as late as the spring of 1970, to check the state of my own feelings about the work of Hemingway (nine years after his death and at least five since I'd read more of him than an occasional story for teaching purposes), I'd probably have come up with a reading close to the postmortem consensus—that once one has abandoned illusions of his being a novelist and has set aside, as thoroughly as any spectator can, the decades of increasingly public descent into artistic senility (dosing those memories with the sad and sterile revelations of Carlos Baker's biography), then one can honor him as "a minor romantic poet"* who wrote a lovely early novel, *The Sun Also Rises,* and a handful of early stories of the north woods, the first war, postwar Americans in Europe, which are likely to remain readable and, despite their truculent preciosity, leanly but steadily rewarding. But I don't remember caring enough to come up with even that grudging an estimate.

Why? Partly a participation in the understandable, if unlikable, international sigh of relief at the flattening of one more Sitting Bull, especially one who had made strenuous attempts to publicize

*Patrick Cruttwell, "Fiction Chronicle," *Hudson Review* XXIV (Spring 1971), p. 180.

his own worst nature; partly an attenuation of my lines to the work itself; partly a response to the discovery that in my first three years of teaching, *A Farewell to Arms* had dissolved with alarming ease, under the corrosive of prolonged scrutiny, into its soft components (narcissism and blindness) when a superficially softer-looking book like *The Great Gatsby* proved diamond; but mostly the two common responses to any family death: forgetfulness and ingratitude.

. Then two reminding signals. In the summer of '70, I visited Key West and wandered with a friend one morning down Whitehead to the Hemingway house, tall, square, and iron-galleried, with high airy rooms on ample grounds thick with tropic green, still privately owned (though not by his heirs) and casually open, once you've paid your dollar, for the sort of slow unattended poking around all but universally forbidden in other American shrines. His bed, his tile bath, his war souvenirs (all distinctly small-town Southern, human-sized; middle-class careless well-to-do—the surroundings of, say, a taciturn literate doctor and his tanned leggy wife just gone for two weeks with their kin in Charleston or to Asheville, cool and golfy; and you inexplicably permitted to hang spectral in their momentarily cast shell). But more—the large room over the yard house in which Hemingway wrote a good part of his work between 1931 and 1939 (six books) at a small round table, dark brown and unsteady; the small swimming pool beneath, prowled by the dozens of deformed multi-toed cats descended from a Hemingway pair of the thirties. Green shade, hustling surly old Key West silent behind walls, a rising scent of sadness—that Eden survived, not destroyed at all but here and reachable, though not by its intended inhabitants, who are barred by the simple choices of their lives and, now, by death (Hemingway lost the house in 1939 at his second divorce). The rising sense that I am surrounded, accompanied by more than my friend—

> I am moved by fancies that are curled
> Around these images, and cling:
> The notion of some infinitely gentle
> Infinitely suffering thing.

The center of my strong and unexpected response began to clarify when I discovered, at home, that I had recalled Eliot's first adjective as *delicate*—"some infinitely delicate/Infinitely suffering thing." What thing?

In October, the second signal. *Islands in the Stream* was published and received, with one or two enthusiastic notices, a few sane ones (Irving Howe, John Aldridge), and a number of tantrums of the beat-it-to-death, scatter-the-ashes sort. In fact, the kinds of notices calculated to rush serious readers to a bookstore (such response being a fairly sure sign that a book is alive and scary, capable of harm); and no doubt I'd have read the book eventually, but a combination of my fresh memories of Key West and a natural surge of sympathy after such a press sent me out to buy it, a ten-dollar vote of—what? *Thanks,* I suddenly knew, to Hemingway.

For what? For being a strong force in both my own early awareness of a need to write and my early sense of how to write. Maybe the strongest. A fact I'd handily forgot but was firmly returned to now, by *Islands in the Stream.*

A long novel—466 pages—it threatens for nearly half its length to be his best. And the first of its three parts—"Bimini," two hundred pages—is his finest sustained fiction, itself an independent novella. Finest, I think, for a number of reasons that will be self-evident to anyone who can bury his conditioned responses to the Hemingway of post-1940, but chiefly because in it Hemingway deals for the first time substantially, masterfully, and to crushing effect with the only one of the four possible human relations which he had previously avoided—parental devotion, filial return. (The other three relations—with God, with the earth, with a female or male lover or friend—he had worked from the start, failing almost always with the first, puzzlingly often with the third, succeeding as richly as anyone with the second.)

It would violate the apparent loose-handedness of those two hundred pages to pick in them for exhibits. Hemingway, unlike Faulkner, is always badly served by spot quotation, as anyone will know who turns from critical discussions of him (with their repertoire of a dozen Great Paragraphs) back to the works themselves. Faulkner, so often short-winded, can be flattered by brief citation, shown at the stunning moment of triumph. But Hemingway's power, despite his continued fame for "style," is always built upon *breath,* long breath, even in the shortest piece—upon a sustained legato of quiet pleading which acts on a willing reader in almost exactly the same way as the opening phrase of Handel's *"Care selve"* or *"Ombra mai fù."* What the words are ostensibly saying in both Hemingway and Handel is less true, less complete, than the slow arc of their total movement throughout their length. Therefore any excerpt is likely to emphasize momentary weakness—artificiality of pose, frailty of emotion—which may well dissolve in the context of their intended whole. The words of *"Ombra mai fù"* translate literally as "Never was the shade of my dear and lovable vegetable so soothing"; and any three lines from say, the beautifully built trout-fishing pages of *The Sun Also Rises* are likely to read as equally simple-minded, dangerously vapid—

He was a good trout, and I banged his head against the timber so that he quivered out straight, and then slipped him into my bag.

So may this from Part I of *Islands in the Stream*—

The boys slept on cots on the screened porch and it is much less lonely sleeping when you can hear children breathing when you wake in the night.

But in the last novel, the love among Thomas Hudson, a good marine painter, and his three sons is created—compelled in the reader—by a slow lateral and spiral movement of episodes (lateral and spiral because no episode reaches a clear climax or peaks the others in revelation). All the episodes are built not on "style" or charged moments, though there are lovely moments, or on the ground-bass hum of a cerebral dynamo like Conrad's or Mann's, but on simple *threat*—potentially serious physical or psychic damage avoided: the middle son's encounter with a shark while spear fishing, the same boy's six-hour battle to bloody near-collapse with a giant marlin who escapes at the last moment (the only passage outside *The Old Man and the Sea* where I'm seduced into brief comprehension of his love of hunting), the boys' joint participation in a funny but sinister practical joke at a local bar (they convincingly pretend to be juvenile alcoholics, to the alarm of tourists). Threats which delay their action for the short interim of the visit with their father but prove at the end of the section to have been dire warnings or prophecies (warnings imply a chance of escape)—the two younger boys are killed with their mother in a car wreck, shortly after their return to France. Only when we—and

Thomas Hudson—are possessed of that news can the helix of episodes deliver, decode, its appalling message, to us and to him. The lovely-seeming lazy days were white with the effort to speak their knowledge. *Avoid dependence, contingency.* The rest of the novel (a little more than half) tries to face those injunctions (restated in further calamities) and seems to me to fail, for reasons I'll guess at later; but the first part stands, firm and independent, simultaneously a populated accurate picture and an elaborate unanswerable statement about that picture. Or scenes with music.

For in that first two hundred pages, the junction of love and threat, encountered for the first time in Hemingway within a family of blood kin, exact from him a prose which, despite my claims of its unexcerptibility, is as patient and attentive to the forms of life which pass before it (shark, marlin, men) and as richly elliptical as any he wrote, requiring our rendezvous with him in the job—and all that as late as the early 1950s, just after the debacle of *Across the River and Into the Trees.* Take these lines of the son David after his ordeal with the marlin—

"Thank you very much, Mr. Davis, for what you said when I first lost him," David said with his eyes still shut.

Thomas Hudson never knew what it was that Roger had said to him.

Or this between Hudson and young Tom, his eldest—

"Can you remember Christmas there?"

"No. Just you and snow and our dog Schnautz and my nurse. She was beautiful. And I remember mother on skis and how beautiful she was. I can remember seeing you and mother coming down skiing through an orchard. I don't know where it was. But I can remember the Jardin du Luxembourg well. I can remember afternoons with the boats on the lake by the fountain in the big garden with trees."

(That last sentence, incidentally, reestablishes Hemingway's mastery of one of the most treacherous but potentially revealing components of narrative—the preposition, a genuine cadenza of prepositions set naturally in the mouth of a boy, not for exhibit but as a function of a vision based as profoundly as Cézanne's on the *stance* of objects in relation to one another: a child, late light, boats on water near shore, flowers, shade.)

Such prose, recognizable yet renewed within the old forms by

the fertility of its new impetus—family love—is only the first indi-
cation, coming as late as it does, of how terribly Hemingway
maimed himself as an artist by generally banishing such passionate
tenderness and emotional reciprocity from the previous thirty
years of his work (it is clear enough from *A Moveable Feast*, the
Baker biography, and private anecdotes from some of his more
credible friends that such responses and returns were an important
component of his daily life). The remaining 260 pages suggest—
in their attempt to chart Hudson's strategies for dealing with external and internal calamity, his final almost glad acceptance of solitude and bareness—an even more melancholy possibility: that the
years of avoiding permanent emotional relations in his work left
him at the end unable to define his profoundest subject, prevented
his even seeing that after the initial energy of his north-woods-and-
war youth had spent itself (by 1933), he began to fail as artist and
man not because of exhaustion of limited resource but because he
could not or would not proceed from that first worked vein on into
a richer, maybe endless vein, darker, heavier, more inaccessible
but of proportionately greater value to him and his readers; a vein
that might have fueled him through a long yielding life with his
truest subject (because his truest need).

Wasn't his lifelong subject *saintliness*? Wasn't it generally as
secret from him (a lapsing but never quite lost Christian) as from
his readers? And doesn't that refusal, or inability, to identify and
then attempt understanding of his central concern constitute the
forced end of his work—and our failure as his readers, collusive in
blindness? Hasn't the enormous and repetitive critical literature
devoted to dissecting his obsession with codes and rituals, which
may permit brief happiness in a meaningless world, discovered
only a small (and unrealistic, intellectually jejune) portion of his
long search? But doesn't he discover at last—and tell us in *Islands
in the Stream*—that his search was not for survival and the tech-
niques of survival but for goodness, thus victory?

What kind of goodness? Granted that a depressing amount of
the work till 1940 (till *For Whom the Bell Tolls*) is so obsessed with
codes of behavior as to come perilously close to comprising another of those deadest of all ducks—etiquettes: Castiglione, Elyot,
Post (and anyone reared in middle-class America in the past forty
years has known at least one Youth, generally aging, who was using

Hemingway thus—a use which his own public person and need for disciples persistently encouraged). Yet beneath the thirty years of posturing, his serious readers detected, and honored, great pain and the groping for unspecific, often brutal anodynes—pain whose precise nature and origin he did not begin to face until the last pages of *For Whom the Bell Tolls* and which, though he can diagnose in *Islands in the Stream,* he could not adequately dramatize: the polar agonies of love, need, contingency, and of solitude, hate, freedom.

What seems to me strange and sad now is that few of his admirers and none of his abusers appear to have sighted what surfaces so often in his last three novels and in *A Moveable Feast*— the signs that the old quest for manly skills (of necessity, temporary skills) became a quest for virtue. The quest for skills was clearly related to *danger*—danger of damage to the self by Nada, Chance or Frederic Henry's "They": "They threw you in and told you the rules and the first time they caught you off base they killed you." But the quest of Col. Cantwell in *Across the River* (which metamorphoses from obsession with narcotic rituals for living well to the study of how to die), the unconscious quest of Santiago in *The Old Man and the Sea* (too heavily and obscurely underscored by crucifixion imagery), the clear fact that the subject of *A Moveable Feast* is Hemingway's own early failure as a man (husband, father, friend), and the fully altered quest of Thomas Hudson in *Islands in the Stream* (from good father and comrade in life to good solitary animal in death)—all are related not so much to danger as to mystery. No longer the easy late-Victorian "They" or the sophomore's Nada (both no more adequate responses to human experience than the tub-thumping of Henley's "Invictus") but something that might approximately be described as God, Order, the Source of Vaguely Discernible Law. The attempt not so much to "understand" apparent Order and Law as to detect its outlines (as by Braille in darkness), to strain to hear and obey some of its demands.

What demands did he hear? Most clearly, I think, the demand to survive the end of pleasure (and to end bad, useless pleasures). That is obviously a demand most often heard by the aged or middle-aged, droning through the deaths of friends, lovers, family, their own fading faculties. But Hemingway's characters from the first have heard it, and early in their lives—Nick Adams faced on all sides with disintegrated hopes, Jake Barnes deprived of genitals, Frederic Henry of Catherine and their son, the Italian major of his family in "In Another Country," Marie Morgan of her Harry, and on and on. Those early characters generally face deprivation with a common answer—activity. And it is surprising how often the activity is artistic. Nick Adams becomes a writer after the war (the author of his own stories); Jake Barnes is a journalist with ambitions (and, not at all incidentally, a good Catholic); Frederic Henry, without love, becomes the man who dictates to us *A Farewell to Arms;* Robert Jordan hopes to return, once the Spanish Civil War is over, to his university teaching in Missoula, Montana, and to write a good book. But whatever its nature, activity remains their aim and their only hope of survival intact—activity as waiting tactic (waiting for the end, total death), as gyrostabilizer, narcotic. In the last novels, however—most explicitly in *Islands in the Stream*—deprivation is met by *duty,* what the last heroes see as the performance of duty (there are earlier heroes with notions of duty—Nick, Jake—but their duty is more nearly chivalry, a self-consciously graceful *noblesse oblige*).

The duty is not to survive or to grace the lives of their waiting companions but to do their work—lonely fishing, lonely soldiering, lonely painting and submarine hunting. For whom? Not for family (wives, sons) or lovers (there are none; Cantwell knows his teenage contessa is a moment's dream). Well, for one's human witnesses then. Why? Cantwell goes on apparently, and a little incredibly, because any form of stop would diminish the vitality of his men, his friend the headwaiter, his girl—their grip upon the rims of their own abysses. Santiago endures his ordeal largely for the boy Manolin, that he not be ashamed of his aging friend and withdraw love and care. Thomas Hudson asks himself in a crucial passage in Part III (when he has, disastrously for his soul, stopped painting after the deaths of his three sons and gone to chasing Nazi subs off Cuba)—

Well, it keeps your mind off things. What things? There aren't any things any more. Oh yes, there are. There is this ship and the people on her and the sea and the bastards you are hunting. Afterwards you will see your animals and go into town and get drunk as you can and your ashes dragged and then get ready to go out and do it again.

Hudson deals a few lines later with the fact that his present work
is literally murder, that he does it "Because we are all murderers";
and he never really faces up to the tragedy of having permitted
family sorrow to derail his true work—his rudder, his *use* to God
and men as maker of ordered reflection—but those few lines,
which out of context sound like a dozen Stoic monologues in the
earlier work, actually bring Hudson nearer than any other Hemingway hero toward an explicit statement of that yearning for
goodness which I suspect in all the work, from the very start—the
generally suppressed intimation that *happiness* for all the young
sufferers, or at least *rest,* would lie at the pole opposite their present position, the pole of pure solitude, detachment from the love
of other created beings (in the words of John of the Cross), and
only then in work for the two remaining witnesses: one's self and
the inhuman universe. "There is this ship and the people on her
and the sea and the bastards you are hunting"—brothers, the
Mother, enemies: all the categories of created things. Hudson, and
Hemingway, halt one step short of defining the traditional goal of
virtue—the heart of God. And two pages before the end, when
Hudson has taken fatal wounds from a wrecked sub crew, he struggles to stay alive by thinking—

Think about the war and when you will paint again. . . . You can paint
the sea better than anyone now if you will do it and not get mixed up in
other things. Hang on good now to how you truly want to do it. You must
hold hard to life to do it. But life is a cheap thing beside a man's work.
The only thing is that you need it. Hold it tight. Now is the true time you
make your play. Make it now without hope of anything. You always
coagulated well and you can make one more real play. We are not the
lumpenproletariat. We are the best and we do it for free.

But again, do it for whom? Most of Hudson's prewar pictures have been described as intended for this or that person—he
paints for his middle son the lost giant marlin, Caribbean wa-
terspouts for his bartender, a portrait of his loved-and-lost first
wife (which he later gives her). Intended then as gifts, *from* love
and *for* love, like most gifts. But now, in death, the reverbera-
tions threaten to deepen—Thomas Hudson's paintings (and by
intimation, the clenched dignity of Nick Adams and Jake Barnes,
Robert Jordan's inconsistent but passionate hunger for justice,

Cantwell's tidy death, Santiago's mad endurance—most of Hemingway's work) seem intended to enhance, even to create if necessary, the love of creation in its witnesses and thereby to confirm an approach by the worker toward goodness, literal virtue, the manly performance of the will of God. *Saintliness,* I've called it (*goodness* if you'd rather, though *saintliness* suggests at least the fierce need, its desperation)—a saint being, by one definition, a life which shows God lovable.

Any God is seldom mentioned (never seriously by Hudson, though Jake Barnes is a quiet Catholic, Santiago a rainy-day one —and though Hemingway himself nursed an intense if sporadic relation with the Church, from his mid-twenties on, saying in 1955, "I like to think I am [a Catholic] insofar as I can be" and in 1958 that he "believed in belief").* Isn't that the most damaging lack of all, in the life and the work?—from the beginning but most desperate toward the end, as the body and its satellites dissolved in age and the abuse of decades? I mean the simple fact that neither Hemingway nor any of his heroes (except maybe Santiago and, long before, the young priest from the Abruzzi who lingers in the mind, with Count Greffi, as one of the two polar heroes of *A Farewell to Arms*) could make the leap from an enduring love of creatures to a usable love of a Creator, a leap which (barring prevenient grace, some personal experience of the supernal) would have been the wildest, most dangerous act of all. Maybe, though, the *saving* one—leap into a still, or stiller, harbor from which (with the strengths of his life's vision about him, none canceled or denied but their natural arcs now permitted completion) he could have made further and final works, good for him and us. That he didn't (not necessarily *couldn't,* though of modern novelists maybe only Tolstoy, Dostoevsky, and Bernanos have given us sustained great work from such a choice) has become the single most famous fact of his life—its end: blind, baffled.

But he wrote a good deal, not one of the Monster Oeuvres yet much more than one might guess who followed the news reports of his leisure; and there remain apparently hundreds of pages of unpublished manuscript. What does it come to?—what does it tell us; do to us, for us, against us?

*Carlos Baker, *Ernest Hemingway, A Life Story* (Scribner's, 1969), pp. 530, 543.

I've mentioned the low present standing of his stock, among critics and reviewers and older readers. Young people don't seem to read him. My university students—the youngest of whom were nine when he died—seem to have no special relations with him. What seemed to us cool grace seems to many of them huffery-puffery. But then, as is famous, a depressing majority of students have special relations with only the feyest available books. (Will Hemingway prove to be the last Classic Author upon whom a generation modeled its lives?—for *classic* read *good.*) Even his two earliest, most enthusiastic, and most careful academic critics have lately beat sad retreat. Carlos Baker's long love visibly disintegrates as he tallies each breath of the sixty-two years; and Philip Young nears the end of the revised edition of his influential "trauma" study (which caused Hemingway such pain) with this—

Hemingway wrote two very good early novels, several very good stories and a few great ones . . . and an excellent if quite small book of reminiscence. That's all it takes. This is such stuff as immortalities are made on.

The hope is that the good books will survive a depression inevitable after so many years of inflation (Eliot is presently suffering as badly; Faulkner, after decades of neglect, has swollen and will probably assuage until we see him again as a very deep but narrow trench, not the Great Meteor Crater he now seems to many)—and that we may even, as Young wagers gingerly, come to see some of the repugnant late work in the light of Hemingway's own puzzling claim that in it he had gone beyond mathematics into the calculus (differential calculus is defined, for instance, as "the branch of higher mathematics that deals with the relations of differentials to the constant on which they depend"—isn't his constant clarifying now, whatever his reluctance to search it out, his failures to dramatize its demands?).

But since no reader can wait for the verdict of years, what can one feel now? What do I feel?—an American novelist, age thirty-eight (the age at which Hemingway published his eighth book, *To Have and Have Not;* his collected stories appeared a year later), whose work would appear to have slim relations, in matter or manner, with the work of Hemingway and whose life might well have had his scorn? (he was healthily inconsistent with his scorn).

I have to return to my intense responses of a year ago—to the powerful presence of a profoundly attractive and needy man still residing in the Key West house and to the reception of his final novel. I've hinted that these responses were in the nature of neglected long-due debts, payment offered too late to be of any likely use to the lender. All the same—what debts?

To go back some years short of the start—in the summer of 1961, I was twenty-eight years old and had been writing seriously for six years. I had completed a novel but had only published stories, and those in England. Still, the novel was in proof at Atheneum—*A Long and Happy Life*—and was scheduled for publication in the fall. I had taken a year's leave from teaching and was heading to England for steady writing—and to be out of reach on publication day. On my way in mid-July I stopped in New York and met my publishers. They had asked me to list the names of literary people who might be interested enough in my book to help it; and I had listed the writers who had previously been helpful. But as we speculated that July (no one on the list had then replied)—and as we brushed over the death of Hemingway ten days before—Michael Bessie startled me by saying that he had seen Hemingway in April, had given him a copy of the proofs of *A Long and Happy Life,* and had (on the basis of past kindnesses Hemingway had done for young writers) half hoped for a comment. None had come. But I boarded my ship with three feelings. One was a response to Bessie's reply to my asking "How did you feel about Hemingway when you saw him?"—"That he was a wounded animal who should be allowed to go off and die as he chose." The second was my own obvious curiosity—had Hemingway read my novel? what had he thought? was there a sentence about it, somewhere, in his hand or had he, as seemed likely, been far beyond reading and responding? The third was more than a little self-protective and was an index to the degree to which I'd suppressed my debts to Hemingway— what had possessed Bessie in thinking that Hemingway might conceivably have liked my novel, the story of a twenty-year-old North Carolina farm girl with elaborate emotional hesitations and scruples? My feelings, close on a death as they were, were so near to baffled revulsion that I can only attribute them to two sources. First, the success of Hemingway's public relations in the forties and fifties. He had managed to displace the unassailable core of the work itself from my memory and replace it with the coarse useless icon of Self which he planted, or permitted, in dozens of issues of *Life* and *Look,* gossip columns, *Photoplay*—an icon which the apparent sclerosis of the later work had till then, for me at least, not made human. Second, emotions of which I was unconscious—filial envy, the need of most young writers to believe in their own utter newness, the suppression of my own early bonds with Hemingway. In short, and awfully, I had come close to accepting his last verdict on himself—forgetting that he laid the death sentence on his life, not the work.

Yet, a month later, I received a statement which Stephen Spender had written, knowing nothing of the recent distant pass with Hemingway. It said, in part, that I was a "kinetic" writer of a kind that recalled certain pages of Hemingway, and Joyce. I was pleased, of course, especially by Joyce's name ("The Dead" having long seemed to me about as great as narrative prose gets—certain pages of the Bible excepted); but again I was surprised by the presence of Hemingway. Spender had known my work since 1957. He was the first editor to publish a story of mine, in *Encounter;* and in his own *World Within World,* he had written briefly but with great freshness of his own acquaintance with Hemingway in Spain during the civil war (one of the first memoirs to counter the received image of Loud Fist). So I might well have paused in my elation to think out whatever resemblance Spender saw. But I was deep in a second book—and in the heady impetus toward publication of the first—and a sober rereading of Hemingway (or a reading; I'd read by no means half his work) was low on my list of priorities.

It should have been high; for if I had attempted to trace and understand Hemingway's help in my own work, I'd have been much better equipped for dealing with (in my own head at least) a comment that greeted *A Long and Happy Life* from almost all quarters, even the most sympathetic—that it sprang from the side of Faulkner. It didn't; but in my resentment at being looped into the long and crowded cow chain that stretched behind a writer for whom I felt admiration but no attraction, I expended a fair amount of energy in denials and in the offering of alternative masters—the Bible, Milton, Tolstoy, Eudora Welty. If I had been able to follow the lead offered by Bessie and Spender, I could have offered a still more accurate, more revealing name.

So it was ten years before my morning in the house in Key

West and my admiration for *Islands in the Stream* reminded me that, for me as a high school student in Raleigh in the early fifties and as an undergraduate at Duke, the most visible model of Novelist was Hemingway (*artist* of any sort, except maybe Picasso, with whom Hemingway shared many external attributes but whose central faculty—continuous intellectual imagination, a mind like a frightening infallible engine endowed with the power of growth—he lacked). For how many writers born in the twenties and thirties can Hemingway not have been a breathing Mount Rushmore?—though his presence and pressure seem to have taken a far heavier toll on the older generation, who not only read Hemingway but took him to war as well. Not only most visible but, oddly, most universally *certified.* Even our public school teachers admired him, when they had been so clearly pained by Faulkner's Nobel—the author of *Sanctuary* and other sex books. In fact, when I reconstruct the chronology of my introduction to Hemingway, I discover that I must have encountered the work first, at a distant remove, in movies of the forties—*The Short Happy Life of Francis Macomber, For Whom the Bell Tolls.* It was apparently not until the tenth or eleventh grade—age fifteen or sixteen—that I read any of him. As the first thing, I remember "Old Man at the Bridge" in a textbook. And then, for an "oral book report" in the eleventh grade, *A Farewell to Arms.* (I remember standing on my feet before forty healthy adolescents—it was only 1949—and saying that Hemingway had shown me that illicit love could be pure and worth having. I don't remember remarking that, like water, it could also kill you—or your Juliet—but I must have acquired, subliminally at least, the welcome news that it made Frederic Henry, a would-be architect, into a highly skilled novelist.)

It was not till my freshman year in college, however, that the effect began to show (in high school, like everyone else, I'd been a poet). My first serious pieces of prose narrative have a kind of grave faith in the eyes, the gaze of the narrator at the moving objects who are his study—a narrowed gaze, through lashes that screen eighty percent of "detail" from the language and the helpless reader, which seems now surely helped onward, if not grounded in, early Hemingway. Here, for example, is the end of the first "theme" I remember writing in freshman English, a five-hundred-word memory of the death of my aunt's dog Mick—

It was still hot for late afternoon, but I kept walking. Mick must have been getting tired; but she bounced along, doing her best to look about as pert as a race horse. My head was down, and I was thinking that I would turn around and head home as soon as I could tear that auction sale sign off the telephone pole down the road. A car passed. It sounded as if it threw a rock up under the fender. I looked up at the highway. Mick was lying there. The car did not stop. I went over and picked her up. I carried her to the shoulder of the road and laid her down in the dry, gray dust. She was hardly bleeding, but her side was split open like a ripe grape, and the skin underneath was as white and waxy as soap. I was really sorry that it had happened to Mick. I really was. I sat down in the dust, and Mick was in front of me. I just sat there for a long time thinking, and then I got up and went home. It was almost supper time.

The fact that I'd read *The Catcher in the Rye* a couple of months earlier may account for the *about* in the second sentence and the *I really was,* though they are normal in the context; but it would be hard to maintain now, in the face of the elaborate syntax required by my later work, that this early sketch wasn't actually a piece of ventriloquism—the lips of my memory worked by Hemingway, or by my notion of Hemingway. This was remarked on, and mildly lamented, by my instructor, an otherwise helpful man who would probably have been better advised to wonder: Why is this boy, visibly so polar to Hemingway or Hemingway's apparent heroes, nonetheless needful of lessons from him, and lessons in vision not behavior? (Strangely, the man shot himself three years later.) Maybe it's as well that he didn't. I suspect now that I was responding, at the butt end of an adolescence perceived as monstrously lonely and rejected, to the siren song in the little Hemingway I'd read and that I heard it this way—"If you can tell what you know about pain and loss (physical and spiritual damage, incomprehension, bad love) and tell it in language so magically bare in its bones, so lean and irresistible in its threnody, as to be instantly audible to any passerby, then by your clarity and skill, the depth and validity of your own precarious experience, you will compel large amounts of good love from those same passers, who'll restore your losses or repair them." And if I'd been conscious of the degree of self-pity involved in that first exchange, I might have been revolted and turned from narrative (as I'd turned, two years before, from drawing and painting). But I was only warned that I "sounded like

Hemingway"; and since I knew perfectly well that everyone in America sounded like Hemingway, that was no obstacle. So I had written several sketches and my first real story, "Michael Egerton" —all under the tutelage of Hemingway's voice and stance—before I had read more than one or two of his stories and *A Farewell to Arms*. An "influence" can be exerted by the blinking of an eye, the literal movement of a hand from here to there, five words spoken in a memorable voice; and the almost universal sterility of academ-ic-journalistic influence-hunting has followed from a refusal to go beyond merely symptomatic surface likenesses toward causes and the necessary question "Why was this writer hungry for this; what lack or taste was nourished by this?"

I did go on. One of the exciting nights of my life was spent in early September 1952, reading *The Old Man and the Sea* in *Life* magazine, straight through by a naked light bulb, in the bed in which I was born (reread now, after years of accepting secondhand opinions on its weakness, it again seems fresh and dangerous, and though a little rigid, one of the great long stories). I remember reading, admiring, and—better—feeling affection for *The Sun Also Rises* during a course at Harvard in the summer of 1954; and I still have my old Modern Library edition of the first forty-nine stories, with neat stern notes to less than half the stories in my college senior's hand—the notes of a technician, and as knowing and disapproving as only a young technician can be, but so unnaturally attentive as to signal clearly that some sort of unspoken love was involved, exchanged in fact—the exchange I began to define above, and to which I'll return. But oddly, that was it—after 1955, I don't recall reading any more Hemingway till 1963, *A Moveable Feast*, well after I'd written two books of my own—and then not again till 1971, when I reread all I'd covered and the two-thirds I hadn't.

Why? Not *why was I rereading?* but why had I read him in the first place, more than twenty years ago; and why had he helped so powerfully that I felt last summer—and still—this strong rush of gratitude? And why did I put him down so soon? Maybe another piece of Spender's comment will crack the door. He suggested that *A Long and Happy Life* advanced the chief discovery of Joyce and Hemingway, "which was to involve the reader, as with his blood and muscles, in the texture of the intensely observed and vividly imagistic writing." Assuming what I hope is true—that I needn't drown in self-contemplation if I think that out a little, and that I'm not pressing to death a comment made in kindness—what can Spender have meant? I remember, at the time, being especially pleased by his calling the prose "kinetic," which I took to mean concerned with and productive of movement. I don't recall telling Spender, but it had been my premise or faith before beginning *A Long and Happy Life* that by describing fully and accurately every physical gesture of three widely separated days in the lives of two people, I could convey the people—literally deliver them—to you, your room, your senses (I considered *thought* a physical gesture, which it is, though often invisible to the ordinary spectator). That faith, consciously held, guided the book through two years of writing and seems to me still the motive force of its claim on readers.

Isn't it also Hemingway's faith, in every line he wrote? Isn't it Tolstoy's, Flaubert's? Doesn't it provide the terrible force of the greatest narratives of the Bible?—Genesis 22, John 21. I'd read those as well, long before my discovery of Hemingway; and from the ninth grade, after *Anna Karenina,* I'd had my answer to the question "Who's best?" But as a tyro, I clearly took light from Hemingway. He was there, alive in Cuba, nine hundred miles from the desk in my bedroom, still writing—ergo, *writing was possible.* The texture of his work, his method, was apparently more lucid than Tolstoy's, unquestionably more human than Flaubert's (at least as I knew them in translation); and everything was briefer and thus more readily usable. But far more important—again I don't remember thinking about it—was what lay beneath that apparent lucidity. He said more than once that a good writer could omit anything from a story—knowingly, purposely—and the reader would respond to its presence with an intensity beyond mere understanding. There are striking examples—the famous one of "Big Two-Hearted River," which is utterly silent about its subject, and now *Islands in the Stream,* which has a huge secret embedded in its heart, its claim against love, against life (as terrible as Tolstoy's in *The Kreutzer Sonata* or Céline's, though entirely personal and, like theirs, not dramatized). But what I discovered, detected with the sensing devices no one possesses after, say, sixteen, was both more general and more nourishingly specific—the knowledge that Hemingway had begun to write, and continued, for the reasons that were rapidly gathering behind me as my nearly terminal case of adolescence was beginning to relent: write or choke in self-loathing; write to comprehend and control fear. Loathing and fear of what? Anyone who has read my early fiction will probably know (they are not rare fears), and in the only way that might conceivably matter to anyone but me; nor is it wise-guy reductive to say that any sympathetic reader of Hemingway has possessed that knowledge of him since *In Our Time*—and that such knowledge is precisely what Hemingway intended, knowledge acquired from the work, not directly from the life. But the magnetic fields of fear in both cases—or so I felt, and feel—are located in simultaneous desperate love and dread of parents, imagined and actual abandonment by one's earliest peers, the early discovery that the certified emotions (affection, love, loyalty) are as likely to produce waste, pain, and damage to the animal self as are hate, solitude, freedom—perhaps more likely.

But Hemingway's work, at least, is complete and no damage can be done him or it by one more consideration of his technical procedures and their engines, their impetus (harm to a dead writer could only be the destruction of all copies of his work). And oddly, in all that I know of the vast body of Hemingway criticism, there is almost no close attention to the bones of language, of the illuminating sort which Proust, for instance, gave to Flaubert. This despite the fact that most of his readers have always acknowledged that he gave as passionate a care to word and rhythm as Mallarmé. The most interesting discussion of his method is in fact by a writer —Frank O'Connor in his study of the short story, *The Lonely Voice* —and though it is finally destructive in its wrongheadedness and envy, it is near enough to insight to be worth a look. O'Connor feels that Hemingway studied and understood Joyce's early method and then proceeded to set up shop with Joyce's tools— "and a handsome little business he made of it." And regardless of the justice of that (it's at least a refreshing alternative to the usual references to Gertrude Stein and Sherwood Anderson), it is in O'Connor's description of the Joyce of *Dubliners* that he casts indirect light on Hemingway—

It is a style that originated with Walter Pater but was then modeled very closely on that of Flaubert. It is a highly pictorial style; one intended to exclude the reader from the action and instead to present him with a series of images of the events described, which he may accept or reject but cannot modify to suit his own mood or environment.

The following, however, is as far as he goes toward an attempt at understanding the motive for such procedure, in either Joyce or Hemingway—

By the repetition of key words and key phrases . . . it slows down the whole conversational movement of prose, the casual, sinuous, evocative quality that distinguishes it from poetry and is intended to link author and reader in a common perception of the object, and replaces it by a series of verbal rituals which are intended to evoke the object as it may be supposed to be. At an extreme point it attempts to substitute the image for the reality. It is a rhetorician's dream.

And finally—

in neither of these passages [from Joyce and Hemingway] is there what you could call a human voice speaking, nobody resembling yourself who is trying to persuade you to share in an experience of his own, and whom you can imagine yourself questioning about its nature—nothing but an old magician sitting over his crystal ball, or a hypnotist waving his hands gently before your eyes and muttering, "You are falling asleep; you are falling asleep; slowly, slowly your eyes are beginning to close; your eyelids are growing heavy; you are—falling—asleep."

Despite the fact that *I* feel strong bonds with the voice in early Hemingway at least, the core of that seems roughly true of both writers—Joyce in the cold dexterity of *A Portrait of the Artist* and Hemingway all his life, though in an entirely different way. Why true? Surely the motives are different and infinitely complex in each case (though one might suspect, especially after Ellman's biography, that Joyce's production of such a distancing method was only one more cast skin of an essentially reptilian nature). If I attempt my own description of Hemingway's procedure (a description largely coincident with what I *felt* as a student and what drew me to him as I began to write), then I can guess more legitimately at motives.

Hemingway's attempt, in all his fiction, is *not* to work magic spells on a reader, locking him into a rigid instrument of vision (in fact, into a movie) which controls not only what he sees but what he feels. The always remarked absence of qualifiers (adjectives, adverbs) is the simplest and surest sign here. Such an attempt— and one does feel and resent it often, in Flaubert and Joyce—is essentially the dream of achieving perfect empathic response, of making the reader become the story, or the story's emotional center at any given moment: Emma Bovary, Gabriel Conroy. And it is the dream not only of a few geniuses but of a large percentage of readers of fiction—the hunger for literally substitute life. Doomed of course, for the sane at least. But while Hemingway attempts as unremittingly as anyone to control his reader—to station him precisely in relation to both the visible and the invisible actions of the story and to the author himself, and finally to trigger in him the desired response (again, to both story and author)—his strategy is entirely his own, and is in fact his great invention (the pure language itself being older than literature). Look at the famous opening of *A Farewell to Arms*—

In the late summer of that year we lived in a house in a village that looked across the river and the plain to the mountains. In the bed of the river there were pebbles and boulders, dry and white in the sun, and the water was clear and swiftly moving and blue in the channels.

As classical as Horace—in the sense of generalized, delocalized, deprived of native texture. What size house and what color, built how and of what? What village, arranged how around what brand of inhabitants, who do what to live? What river, how wide and deep? What kind of plain, growing what; and what mountains? Later—considerably later—he will tell you a little more, but very little. If you have never traveled in northern Italy in late summer —or seen the film of the book—you'll have no certainty of knowing how the earth looks above and beneath the action, in this or any other of his works. Or in fact, how anything or anyone else *looks*. But by the audacity of its filterings, it demands that you lean forward toward the voice which is quietly offering the story—only then will it begin to yield, to give you what it intends. And the gift will be what you *hear*—the voices of imagined characters speaking a dialect which purports to be your own (and has now convinced two generations of its accuracy). His early strategy is always, at its most calculated, an oral strategy. If we hear it read, it seems the convincing speaking voice of this sensibility. Only on the silent

page do we discover that it is as unidiomatic, as ruthlessly intentional, as any *tirade* of Racine's. For behind and beneath all the
voices of actors (themselves as few in number as in Sophocles)
rides the one real voice—the maker's. And what it says, early and
late, is always this—"This is what I see with my clean keen equipment. Work to see it after me." What it does not say but implies
is more important—"For you I have narrowed and filtered my
gaze. I am screening my vision so you will not see all. Why? Because you must enact this story for yourself; cast it, dress it, set it.
Notice the chances I've left for you: no noun or verb is colored by
me. I require your senses." What is most important of all—and
what I think is the central motive—is this, which is concealed and
of which the voice itself may be unconscious: "I tell you this, in this
voice, because you must share—*must* because I require your presence, your company in my vision. I beg you to certify my knowledge and experience, my goodness and worthiness. I mostly speak
as *I*. What I need from you is not empathy, identity, but patient
approving witness—loving. License my life. Believe me." (If that
many-staged plea is heard only intermittently in Hemingway's
work after 1940—broken then by stretches of "confidence"—I'd
guess that the cause would be the sclerosis consequent upon his
success, the success of the voice which *won* him love, worship, a
carte blanche he lacked the power to use well. Goethe said, "Beware
of what you want when young; you'll get it when old." And the
memory of the famished face of the deathbound Hemingway,
quilted with adoration and money, is among the saddest and most
instructive memories of Americans over twenty-five; his last gift to
us.)

I've suggested that a final intention of Hemingway's method
is the production of belief in the reader—belief in his total being
and vision. Remember that he always spoke of the heavy role of the
Bible in his literary education. The role has been generally misunderstood; seen as a superficial matter of King James rhythms, the
frequent use of *and,* narrative "simplicity." But look at a brief
though complete story from Genesis 32—

In the night Jacob rose, took his two wives, the two slave girls, and his
eleven sons, and crossed the ford of Jabbok. When he had carried them

all across, he sent his belongings. Then Jacob was alone, and some man wrestled with him there till daybreak. When he saw that he could not pin Jacob, he struck him in the pit of his thigh so that Jacob's hip unsocketed as they wrestled. Then he said, "Let me go; it is daybreak."

Jacob said, "I will not let go till you bless me."

The man said, "What is your name?"

He said, "Jacob."

The man said, "You are Jacob no more but Israel—you have fought gods and men and lasted."

Jacob said, "Tell me your name, please."

He said "Why ask my name?" and departed.

So Jacob called the place *Penuel,* face of God, "For I have seen God's face and endured"; and the sun struck him as he passed Penuel, limping.*

—and then at Erich Auerbach's description of Old Testament narrative:

the externalization of only so much of the phenomena as is necessary for the purpose of the narrative, all else left in obscurity; the decisive points of the narrative alone are emphasized, what lies between is nonexistent; time and place are undefined and call for interpretation; thoughts and feelings remain unexpressed, are only suggested by the silence and the fragmentary speeches; the whole, permeated with the most unrelieved suspense and directed toward a single goal . . . remains mysterious and "fraught with background."†

There is, give or take an idiom, a profound likeness between the account of Jacob's struggle and any scene in Hemingway; and Auerbach might well be describing Hemingway, not the Bible. I have already implied the nature of the likeness, the specific hunger in Hemingway which was met by biblical method. Both require our strenuous participation, in the hope of compelling our allegiance, our belief. Here are three passages chosen at random from a continuous supply—the opening of "A Very Short Story":

One hot evening in Padua they carried him up onto the roof and he could look out over the top of the town. There were chimney swifts in the sky. After a while it got dark and the searchlights came out. The others went down and took the bottles with them. He and Luz could hear them below

*Translation by Reynolds Price.
†Erich Auerbach, *Mimesis* (Doubleday Anchor Books, 1957), p. 9.

on the balcony. Luz sat on the bed. She was cool and fresh in the hot night.

a moment from Thomas Hudson's Nazi hunt in the Cuban keys:

They called to the shack and a woman came out. She was dark as a sea Indian and was barefooted and her long hair hung down almost to her waist. While she talked, another woman came out. She was dark, too, and long-haired and she carried a baby. As soon as she finished speaking, Ara and Antonio shook hands with the two women and came back to the dinghy. They shoved off and started the motor and came out.

and—curiously analogous to Jacob's ordeal with "some man"— the almost intolerably charged and delicate exchange between Frederic Henry and his friend the young Italian priest who has visited him in hospital with a gift of vermouth:

> "You were very good to come, father. Will you drink a glass of vermouth?"
> "Thank you. You keep it. It's for you."
> "No, drink a glass."
> "All right. I will bring you more then."
> The orderly brought the glasses and opened the bottle. He broke off the cork and the end had to be shoved down into the bottle. I could see the priest was disappointed but he said, "That's all right. It's no matter."
> "Here's to your health, father."
> "To your better health."

Given the basic narrative strategies of the Old Testament and Hemingway, only the tone of the motives is different—and in the third-person Old Testament the voice is plain command; in Hemingway, a dignified pleading: *Believe!* and *Please believe.* Believe what? *The thing I know.* What do you know? In one case, the presence of the hidden hand of God; in the other, that his life is good and deserving of your witness, will even help your life. Then why believe? In one case, simply and awfully, so that God be served; in the other, so that the voice—and the man behind it—may proceed through his life. That is the sense in which both styles are almost irresistibly kinetic. And the reason why they have been two of the most successful styles in the history of literature.

Why did it fail him then?—his work, the literal words in their order on the page. In one sense, it succeeded too brilliantly—

won him millions of readers willing to exert the energy and certify the life, some of them willing even to alter their own lives in
obedience to what they, understandably though ludicrously, took
to be injunctions of the work (there are certainly injunctions,
though not to noise and bluster). But for nothing—or too little.
In the only sense that can have mattered to him, his vision and its
language failed him appallingly. It won him neither the relatively
serene middle working years of a Conrad or a Mann nor the transcendent old age of a Tolstoy, a James, Proust's precocious mastery of a silly life. Nor did it, with all its success in the world, allay
even half his daily weight of fear. Immense time and energy were
thrown elsewhere in flagging hope—sport, love, companions,
drink, all of which took dreadful cuts of their own. Maybe it's
permissible to *ask* why the words failed him; but to dabble in
answers if one did not at least share a long stretch of his daily life
and witness the desperate efforts in their long mysterious complexity is only a game, though a solemn game which can be
played more or less responsibly and one which can no longer
harm him or the work.

I've indulged already in the early pages of this with a guess,
from the gathering evidence of his last four books, about his sub-
merged subject which he found and attempted to float too late,
when the search itself—or flight from the search—had dangerously
depleted his senses and, worse, prevented the intellectual growth
which might have compensated. But the words themselves? and
the vision and needs which literally pressed words from him? Were
they doomed from the start to kill him? A language fatally obsessed
with defending the self and the few natural objects which the self
both loves and trusts? A vision narrowed, crouched in apprehension of the world's design to maul, humiliate? Insufficiently surrendered to that design? Whatever the answers (and I'd guess that
each is a mysterious Yes), it's clear that he was never capable of the
calm firm-footed gaze of the godlike Tolstoy, who at twenty-six was
producing from his own military experience, in a story called "The
Wood-Felling," narrative so sure of its power as to be a near-lethal
radiation—

The wounded man lay at the bottom of the cart holding on to the sides
with both hands. His broad healthy face had completely changed during

those few moments; he seemed to have grown thinner and years older, his lips were thin and pale and pressed together with an evident strain. The hasty and dull expression of his glance was replaced by a kind of bright clear radiance, and on the bloody forehead and nose already lay the impress of death. Though the least movement caused him excruciating pain, he nevertheless asked to have a small *chérez* with money taken from his left leg.

The sight of his bare, white, healthy leg, when his jack-boot had been taken off and the purse untied, produced on me a terribly sad feeling.*

Or even of the constitutionally hectic D. H. Lawrence, who in fragments from an unfinished novel could see and speak in a language of open trust in man and nature which promises the stamina of his death—

Quickly the light was withdrawn. Down where the water was, all grew shadow. The girl came tramping back into the open space, and stood before the holly tree. She was a slim, light thing of about eighteen. Her dress was of weathered blue, her kerchief crimson. She went up to the little tree, reached up, fingering the twigs. The shadow was creeping uphill. It went over her unnoticed. She was still pulling down the twigs to see which had the thickest bunch of berries. All the clearing died and went cold. Suddenly the whistling stopped. She stood to listen. Then she snapped off the twig she had chosen and stood a moment admiring it.

A man's voice, strong and cheerful, shouted: "Bill—Bill—Bi-ill!"
The donkey lifted its head, listened, then went on eating.
"Go on!" said the girl, waving her twig of holly at it. The donkey walked stolidly two paces from her, then took no notice.

All the hillside was dark. There was a tender flush in the east. Away among the darkening blue and green over the west, a faint star appeared. There came from far off a small jangling of bells—one two three—one two three four five! The valley was all twilight, yet near at hand things seemed to stand in day.

"Bill—Bill!" came the man's voice from a distance.
"He's here!" shrilled the girl.
"Wheer?" came the man's shout, nearer, after a moment.
"Here!" shrilled the girl.
She looked at the donkey that was bundled in its cloth.

*Leo Tolstoy, *Tales of Army Life*, translated by Louise and Aylmer Maude (Oxford, 1935), p. 66.

"Why don't ye go, dummy!" she said.

"Wheer is 'e?" said the man's voice, near at hand.

"Here!"

In a moment a youth strode through the bushes.

"Bill, tha chump!" he said.

The donkey walked serenely towards him. He was a big boned, limber youth of twenty. His trousers were belted very low, so that his loins remained flexible under the shirt. He wore a black felt hat, from under which his brown eyes gazed at the girl.

"Was it you as shouted?" he said.

"I knowed it was you," she replied, tapping her skirt with the richly berried holly sprig.*

Yet Hemingway's work—its damaged tentative voice, for all its large failures, its small ignorances and meannesses—did a great deal, for him and us. Beyond carrying him through an after all long life and conveying an extraordinary, apparently usable portion of that life's texture of pleasure and pain to millions of contemporary strangers, it has left live remains—a body of fourteen volumes which, in my guess, will winnow to eight and then stand as an achievement so far unexcelled in American letters, certainly by no one in his own century.† For what? For the intensity of their gaze, however screening, at a range of men and dangers which, with the inevitable allowances for private obsession, are as broadly and deeply representative as any but the great masters' (we don't yet possess one); for the stamina of their search, however veiled, through four decades for the demands and conditions and duties of human goodness in relation to other men, beasts and objects, and finally God; and then (strongest but most unprovable, most primitive and mysterious) for the language in which the search externalized itself, his optics and shield, weapon and gift. Gift to whom?

Me, as I've said, who have responded over twenty-five years to what I took to be an asking voice with what I now see was apprenticeship, neither exclusive nor conscious and quickly renegade, but clearly the gravest homage I can offer. Useless to him but

*The surviving fragments are printed in Edward Nehls, ed., *D. H. Lawrence, A Composite Biography,* I (University of Michigan, 1957), pp. 184–95.

†My own list, now, would be: *The Collected Stories, The Sun Also Rises, A Farewell to Arms, Green Hills of Africa, For Whom the Bell Tolls, The Old Man and the Sea, A Moveable Feast, Islands in the Stream.*

profound nonetheless. The profoundest—for I also see that I loved his voice and studied its shapes, not for its often balked and raging message but because I, balked and enraged, shared the motives at which I've guessed and, stranger, its two subjects: freedom and virtue. Polar heights, inaccessible maybe to climbers more intent on self-protection (footholds, handholds) than on the climb itself, the route and destination.

Gift also to all other living American writers as obsessed as he with defense of what the self is and what it knows, any one of whom seems to me more nearly brother to him—in need and diet, dream and fulfillment, vision and blindness—than to any other artist in our history, or anyone else's (and, oddly, our avatar of Byron, the proto-American artist). Like it or not, our emblem and master whose lessons wait, patient and terrible.

Gift especially to the young. For it is almost certainly with them that his life now lies. It is easy enough to patronize Children's Classics—Omar, Mrs. Browning, Wolfe, lately Hesse—but any writer's useful survival is in heavy danger when the young abandon him entirely; it is only on them that he stands a chance of inflicting permanent damage (are Milton and Dante effectively alive? can they yet be saved in some form they'd have agreed to?—not by schools, apparently). In all Hemingway's work, until *The Old Man and the Sea* and *Islands in the Stream,* the warnings, if not the pleas, are for them; the lessons of one master, diffidently but desperately offered—*Prepare, strip, divest for life that awaits you; learn solitude and work; see how little is lovely but love that.*

Half the lesson of the desert fathers, and given in language of the desert, bleached, leached to essence. The other half—an answer to *Why?*—is withheld until the last, and then only muttered. Surely there are young people now, readers and writers—children when he died—to whom he is speaking his dark secret language of caution and love, help and beggary, in the lean voice of an infinitely delicate, infinitely suffering thing. No shield, no help at all, of course, to him or us (he never said it would be); yet more—a diamond point that drills through time and pain, a single voice which moves through pain toward rest and presses forward shyly with its greeting and offer, its crushing plea, like that of the hermit Paul when St. Antony had tracked him through beasts and desert and begged for instruction:

Behold, thou lookest on a man that is soon to be dust. Yet because love endureth all things, tell me, I pray thee, how fares the human race: if new roofs be risen in the ancient cities, whose empire is it that now sways the world; and if any still survive, snared in the error of the demons.*

1971

*St. Jerome, "The Life of St. Paul the First Hermit," in Helen Waddell, ed. and trans., *The Desert Fathers* (Henry Holt, 1936), pp. 47-48.

An Honest Tub

All art is the disengaging of a soul
from place and history . . .
        W. B. Yeats

DAVE SMITH

Dave Smith was born in Portsmouth, Virginia. He taught high school English and coached football at Poquoson High School (Virginia), served in
the U.S. Air Force, and has taught at numerous colleges. His books include
a novel, *Onliness,* an edition of essays on James Wright, *The Pure Clear Word:
Essays on the Poetry of James Wright,* and a seventh collection of poems, *In the
House of the Judge* (Harper & Row, 1983).

It was Christmas day. A rare snow had fallen, maybe three inches,
and had covered the hundred or so workboats berthed in the small
harbor. We had shoveled and scraped it off the *Peter Liss.* Now,
piled in Billy Carmines' Volkswagen, we headed home. We were
sweaty and loose, sipping a communal bottle. Billy was lying about
vicious cheaters who ran buy-boats. I, who knew nothing about
watermen and their boats, listened like a child, though already I
saw Billy had slipped into the lie. Just the night before, I had
caught him, drunk as I had been, in a story about a winter so bad
that his uncle Luke had got ice on his washboards thick enough
that he'd taken out his prick to hammer it away. Now Billy swore
that his father, Peter Liss, who sat glum and small between bottle
and windshield, had once put a wish on one particularly unscrupu-
lous son of a bitch, whose buy-boat had immediately sunk.

"Oh, shit," I said in the back seat.

Peter Liss swiveled his turtle head around the edge of the seat
and said, "You go to college too?"

Sometimes late at night, reading, I think about Peter Liss, especially when I read the Anglo-Saxon poems I love. "The Wanderer" says:

The forms of his kinsmen	take shape in the silence;
In rapture he greets them;	in gladness he scans
Old comrades remembered.	But they melt into air
With no word of greeting	to gladden his heart.

What lasts? The answers to that are about all any writer's words try to tell him. His books are the answers he allows the reader to overhear. The Wanderer tells us that "All the foundation of earth   shall fail!" But later in his poem, to buck up his courage, he says, "Good man is he   who guardeth his faith." A writer is after knowing faith in what. Or who. Joseph Conrad found faith in wretched Kurtz, who had an idea, who was an idea to T. S. Eliot—one gone wrongly out of the world when the hollow men marched in. Eliot and Conrad, like the Wanderer, knew Kurtz's idea made him one of those who were "men enough to face the darkness." His idea, or illusion, gave him character enough to hope for dignity, for life beyond mere survival. Kurtz and his writers got this illusion from a people and a place. The illusion was an obligation, to the dead and the living, a responsibility for the life and the place that continues after us. Flannery O'Connor says about place that "The writer operates at a peculiar crossroads where time and place and eternity somehow meet. His problem is to find that location." The writer who imaginatively claims a place as the foundation for vision knows something about the illusions by which it is both possible and necessary to live. That knowledge isn't so easy to come by, but when the writer has it, he has, it appears, his obligation, his subject, his influence.

My first poems, and in some ways all I have ever written, are about the watermen from Poquoson, Virginia, a people and a town of which I was entirely ignorant until they hired me as a high school teacher of French and a coach of football. I was then twenty-two years old. My first, self-published, chapbook of poems was called *Bull Island,* the native name for Poquoson. In the world of my mind, the lower Virginia waterman has become indistinguishable from the Anglo-Saxon wanderer. I regard him as mythic brother, father, and silent poet. Of him I know two things clearly: I will never understand him precisely and I cannot resign from trying to understand him. Yet, for me, he is not a type but a man and his son, two without whom I doubt I would ever have written at all. Were I to attempt this meandering speculation about their lives, their place, and art, both Billy Carmines and his father, Peter Liss, would, with vile and crusty affection, ridicule me for my fancy *idears.* How I love saying their word and hearing the *endearment* so unconsciously built into its corrupted form! Plain men and halves of one whole to me, they liked to think they had no idears, but they are the one idear that has got into me and that I have been trying to communicate since the day we buried the boat.

Peter Lisle Carmines was dead, that was the main thing. He had been dead for two weeks, had been duly and properly put in the Methodist ground. The church accountants marked his ticket paid. I stood at the dock with his sons Billy and George, still unaware I was about to be part of something that would change my life. We were preparing to bury Peter Liss's boat. The sun was yet low ahead of us but the heat was intense, the humidity like invisible plaster. When you grow up in this climate you learn to move slowly. Breathing sometimes feels like whispering with your head in a bucket. But we moved even more gravely than the heat required.

I was an ignorant teacher in the high school where Billy's wife taught, where he had gone to school and had also taught. We partied together. They had already introduced me to the woman I would marry. I knew brother George, but not much. Billy was a junior high school principal now, a keeper of discipline, and George was what his problems grew up to be, a half-ass bar brawler and drifter. Both had been off and on watermen, like their father, but neither could stand up to the grinding labor, loneliness, and sad wages, unlike their father. If George hadn't happened to be unemployed again, he would have been in Florida.

"Hot as shit," Billy said. We'd climbed aboard the *Peter Liss.* Billy knelt at the engine and tried to make a rusted cable fast to a car battery he had lugged along. Both brothers were grieving, though neither ever much got on with their father. There was none of the usual chatter about bluefish, booze, pussy, boats, or what one had forgotten more of than the other would ever learn.

I sat on the flat sheet of plywood nailed to the twenty-footer's stern, the cull board on which a waterman culls oysters from empty shells. I looked south at Langley Air Force Base, across Back River, where a morning mist floated as pretty as you please. George, arms crossed, surly, leaned against the port washboard. The cigarette hanging from his lips made him look like James Dean. We all wore white T-shirts and faded jeans. Billy and George wore the waterman's tall rubber boots that had a red trim just at the knee. These were hard to find, but you could get them at Rooster Smith's general store. Rooster kept decades of insults and credit in his head. He raised his son, Clyde Russell, with that credit in his head too, and the names of families and histories to go along. I had on white Converse low-cuts.

Billy worked at the engine until his shirt grayed with sweat. Finally the Lathrop sputtered and caught. I watched him adjust this, open that, close the other, working in a patient sequence. If he needed help, he didn't ask for it. George never offered any. There were bleaching crab fins all over the deck, without smell now, and a pair of pliers rusted to the wood. This boat hadn't sailed in some time.

The Lathrop died. Billy repeated the sequence and got it going. It never did, as a bad novel might say, roar to life. Slowly, reluctantly, belching and farting, dying down to be goosed into yet another shudder, it sounded about like the clunker that Humphrey Bogart so memorably nursed in *The African Queen.* We eased away from the pier.

The sun was now turning everything the color of lemon, even the stacked crab pots that look as if they are made of chicken wire but are not. To starboard, the tower on which the first American astronauts had trained stood high over Langley, for all the world a child's giant Erector set abandoned in a backyard. Lyndon Johnson, quite objectively, it was said, had thought the astronauts would do better in Houston, which is Texas. Local people said they had been screwed out of their future, meaning their payrolls. Peter Liss and the other watermen had said nothing. Maybe they hadn't noticed.

One day Peter Liss had sailed up this river to fish his crab pots. A crabber sets out maybe eighty pots over a mile of water. Each pot is daily baited, sunk to the bottom, marked by a rope and a Clorox bottle float, and then returned to daily so the crabber can

lift the forty-pound pots one by one and take off his catch. Sometimes he'll sell crabs to a warehouse; sometimes he'll eat them.
Ordinarily crabbers work deep channels. Peter Liss worked this
river because he was old and it was safe water. He worked it also
because he had done just that for more than fifty years. This day
he was stopped before the first pot. The coast guard man said
nobody could fish. Lyndon Johnson was visiting Langley. Lyndon
Johnson was a man even Peter Liss had to notice.

Lyndon Johnson didn't know, Liss may have told us but probably did not, that the goddamn crabs would drown and rot in the
cage; or that these crabs were all he and Miss Homer, his wife of
more than fifty years, would have to eat that day. He probably
didn't say that Johnson and his frigging moonmen had got flat in
the way of a life that he hadn't known to be interrupted even by
the German U-boats that used to surface at midnight and send in
the bodies of dead American seamen, a way of life that existed
before the first white man heard of the Pedernales. But I remember
Liss telling about the coast guard pistol easing down on him because he had said *something.* Of course, as Liss noted, that wasn't
the first time. Now I watched that tower, eerie, dead as Lyndon
Johnson. Dead as Liss, too.

We headed at the sun, toward the Chesapeake Bay. Off to the
right was Hampton, Buckroe Beach, and Phoebus, the setting for
William Styron's *Lie Down in Darkness.* I had read about Peyton
Loftis and the Warwick Country Club while in college. It had
seemed very real. We began to swing west around Plum Tree
Island. The air force used Plum Tree as a bombing range. Sometimes they'd made little mistakes. I remembered Peter Liss describing kin that had been blown out of the water. He fished the same
spot next day. We started across Egg Island Bar.

Liss had told Billy where to take the boat. By car it was only
ten minutes from his house, but we were riding in a forty-six-year-
old heavy-bellied lady that took ten minutes to go fifty yards, if she
felt like it and didn't quit. She quit just onto the bar. And kept on
quitting. She stalled better than Proust. I almost believed she was
resisting. Patiently, Billy coaxed her ahead. For the first time I
began to understand he was, truly, a waterman. I knew he was what
was called, locally, a wild hair. He was the only man I'd ever known
who had commanded a coast guard cutter and who, on his last

active-duty day, had run her full tilt into the guard headquarters dock at Portsmouth, shattering every window for three floors. The secretaries applauded him. I've bounced through gales in rowboats with Billy, my fingernails sunk into the pine planks, running wide open for no reason. I've gone with him up winding canals full of sunken hulls, skimming at almost fifty miles per hour with only a slice of moonlight on his teeth. He scared the shit out of me and I don't think he knew I was even there. Only himself against the night, the water, and himself. As I watched him fool with that engine, I could see Liss doing the same thing year after year.

Billy has read William Warner's Pulitzer Prize–winning *Beautiful Swimmers: Watermen, Crabs, and the Chesapeake Bay.* Very few watermen have. Billy knows how beautiful that book is, how close to righteous Warner is. He also knows that Warner has only written about the upper bay. *Swimmers* doesn't touch the watermen from Hampton, Yorktown, Poquoson, or Gloucester—all less than fifteen miles apart, men who think themselves entirely different according to their place. Well, they aren't very different. They make a living from crabs, oysters, fish, clams, whatever they can take. They love their boats like a cowboy loves his horse, only they wouldn't say so. They don't talk about it. They become it, are connected to the water and to a heritage by that workboat. Billy sent me a letter some years ago in which he describes what I didn't know that burial day about a waterman, his boat, and his idears:

Boat

His boat was a reflection of his personality. She was always shabby but well painted & coppered. She was built of bull pine planks that were two inches thick. She was always cluttered with oyster tongs, rope, crab traps, patent dips, old lunch bags (with biscuits—he wouldn't eat loaf bread). She had a small cabin that always smelled of mildew with old clothes, sou'wester, rusty wrenches lying everywhere. Her bow was always covered with rope, never coiled, never neat. Her bow was lower than her stern when afloat because of the weight of her engine forward. She was slow & solid with, in later years, a Lathrop 64 horse power. During the 30ies and 40ies he used Model "A" engines but they wouldn't last over a couple of years. I was surprised to see how high & proud her bow was when she was on the railway. She was a good sailor in bad weather, wet & able. (Once Vernon Page & myself went with him because the weather was so bad—blowing a gale southwest. We got so wet in her cabin that we had to put on oil clothes & get on the stern.)

She had no name but everyone called her the "Peter Liss." She was built with the bottom lines of the old sail boats (Skipjack, Bugeye). So she never performed too well. With an engine. No matter how much power you used she would not plane only suck down at the stern and carry a tremendous wave from bow & stern.

He put a 40 gal. gas tank on the port side (the side he worked his tongs on) and kept it filled so she always listed to port thus the man working the starboard side had to raise his tongs higher & always looked like he was getting beat (not catching as many oysters as the other man). (Competition was always keen between the men in the same boat & between boats as to size of catch. If you wanted to say a man was a better oysterman you say he could turn the boat over on him—catch so many more oysters that the boat would list to your side.) He was an excellent oysterman worked longer than anyone else but left the dock later. He was never an early-bird. His epitaph should have been "he was a hard working man made many a dollar gave an honest tub."

The *Peter Liss* coughed, pitched, and pooped out on the western edge of Egg Island Bar. This time she seemed gone for good. We drifted over white sand marked by patches of dark weed, moving silently, not disturbing fish and crabs beneath us. I had spent weekends here treading clams as Billy had showed me: feeling them under my bare feet, diving for them, gathering them in the bucket that trailed behind me on a rope. While Billy had both hands working at the scorched engine, I watched for the black lid of clouds and the manic storms that often came up too fast for a workboat to beat it to a safe cove, but it was early morning and I knew storms came in the afternoon. The water was, as watermen say, "slick kam," and the sky a wide blue. Billy got her going again just as a blowfly bloodied my neck.

He pushed the stick forward and we bobbed back toward shore. Most workboats have a waist-high stick fixed to the washboard and connected by rope to the rudder. A steering wheel would be easier, but they use sticks. Some say it leaves your arms free to lift pots, nets, or tongs. Others say it's just the way it always has been. These workboats, like the watermen they ferry, resist change the way they resist order. They aren't tidy, spare, or shipshape. They belong to no navy. Their only heritage is steady, single-minded work. Their "cabin" will hold no more than two small, crouching men, as if they figure God's weather is all a man needs. I've heard them called the Lord's ugliest vessel. But not by watermen and not before watermen. They are repeatedly painted but rarely sanded, scraped, or prepared. They have thick skins and look a little like a painter's truck. Perhaps it's no wonder that garden clubs and the like complain they litter the creeks and coves. Maybe they do turn off tourists who have somehow wandered away from the phony streets of Williamsburg or the Revolutionary redoubts at Yorktown—which my brother-in-law bulldozed up for a nice piece of change. But you won't hear watermen complain, and they have to navigate around the dead boats. Sometimes outsiders come to do feature stories on the watermen and their boats. The watermen grin a lot.

I had come to Bull Island as an outsider. Now I was aboard the *Peter Liss* and moving into a faint breeze tinged with the smell of pine and deep water. I was thinking how I had got where I was. I hadn't yet thought about what I was. Somehow I was now an insider, or else I would be having no part in burying a man's boat.

Maybe any beginning is arbitrary when you start having a sense that the events of your life are and have been inevitable. This morning had started two weeks earlier when I stood on the boat dock at Langley Air Force Yacht Club. I had been invited aboard a forty-foot Hatteras for a day of trolling in the Chesapeake Bay. I was carrying gear on board when a small boat roared up to the next dock some thirty or so feet away. It was what watermen call a bateau. A man was shouting for help as he let the bateau die against the pier. People gathered quickly and I went for more gear. Later I saw a master sergeant bent over the body of a man on the dock. He seemed to kiss the body, then pounded its chest. At one point he leaned over the water to spit out somebody's vomit. A few feet away, back to this scene, a man dangled his legs from the dock. He rolled his waders down to mid-calf. Then he rolled them up. Then back down.

A Hatteras yacht moves like a Cadillac. I sipped my banana daiquiri as we glided into open water. I never imagined that man on the dock was Peter Liss, or that Peter Liss could die. I would have said, anyway, that Peter Liss didn't sail on Saturdays, not at age sixty-eight. But it was him, and he had sailed. For one thing, he and Miss Homer needed something to eat. For another, George was home and maybe he meant to come on the water at last. But the most of it was that a waterman can't stand not working on a bright day, can't stand the roof overhead. This is why he won't have a union—though he knows very well the buyers are killing him: because he can't stand the idea of someone saying he can't work. Liss had sucked himself up and sailed. George said they were pulling crab pots and his daddy leaned over the hot motor to check weed in the wheel (propeller). Then he lay down on the motor and didn't flinch. Dr. Cecil Evans, kin to almost everybody in Bull Island, said "his heart plain give out."

It seems to me now that I saw every instant of that day unfold, as if I, not George, had gone with Liss. But I was miles out in the bay, into daiquiris. I did not see much more of subsequent events than of Liss's death, but I have them in my head as if I had invented them. There was a wake, three days of it, with Peter Liss dressed in somebody's suit. He lay in the bed where he had got himself eight children. There was an abundance of good food, none take-out, brought by wrinkled women who spoke briefly with Miss Homer, sat in the living room a spell, and left quietly in sun that hurt their eyes. There was, as Liss would have said, "a right smart of drinking" by men who did not remember not knowing him. Watermen mostly, they wore what looked like somebody's suit. They lied a lot about what a fine man Liss had been. On the third night, behind that house jacked up on blocks against floods, its three rooms jammed, there came a clutch of black men to stand mute until Miss Homer passed them a pie out the screen door. Except for some white hair and a little shining, they were part of the black night.

"What the hell them niggers doing round here?" Somebody said. The room slammed silent and Somebody left. The lying backed into the old days. Liss had sailed with blacks. The watermen kept their boats on the James River then, nearly fourteen miles south. They walked over on Sunday night, worked all week on the boat, then walked back on Friday night. There weren't men enough willing to do that, so they'd taken blacks on. A full third share given. The names of black men, old or dead, darted through the air. But only Miss Homer spoke through the screen to those who had come to pay respects to a man who had been part of their history, as they were part of his.

Bull Island is as racist a place as I have ever known. It is home
to no blacks. There are some families who are, technically, black,
but they grow lighter-skinned and bluer-eyed every generation.
The blacks were gerrymandered when the town formed, put in
their place—which was just outside the town line. The year Peter
Liss died, 1969, the town had maybe five thousand people. It has
more than doubled because of all the white souls from Hampton,
Newport News, and Warwick who say they dream of living on the
water. Few blacks seem to have this dream. No Bull Islander was
ever a greater bigot than Peter Lisle Carmines. That is what Billy
has always said, at any rate. Yet here were the faces of black men
on that white ground, what the Wanderer might have called "old
comrades." How did they know Liss had died? Why did they care?
Why had these bigots not stopped that nigger-hating Somebody
from taking a hasty, tactful leave? Why, when these blacks began
a low, moaning spiritual, were so many dabbing at their eyes? How
is it possible to know the *idears* at the soul of such a place?

Peter Liss went into the ground pretty much the way everyone
he had ever known had gone. Hymns. Prayers. The summer sun
steamed through stained glass. Rows of ladies' hats bobbed; bald
heads gleamed. Then they went home. They probably told more
lies about the old days, about the fine men they all were. Little said,
I suppose, about the blacks. Life went on as it must for watermen,
a life of habit and work that they can't get enough of and don't
understand. Most didn't ask what it all meant. Most didn't think
about or hope for change. There wouldn't be any, except for the
Peter Liss.

I don't know where Liss left the scrawled, illegible note that
was his will, but Billy had it, as he had the duty to bury his father's
boat in the place and the manner Liss prescribed. It sounded
simple enough: take her one last time around the point, over the
bar, and at the appointed hump of marsh run her aground. The
hole he'd knock in her bottom would leave her to the slow re-
possession of water and weather and time. He knew the place. As
a boy sailing out with his father, he'd seen the boats mount up
there. They had been sailed by men who could not remember not
knowing Liss, four or five of them stove up on each other, mostly
underwater, broken casually, looking for all the world like children
who'd raced to a point and bumped heads. This was what man-

hood, a life, had come to. A body had gone into the ground, but this was where Peter Liss would spend eternity, with the marsh, the water, and friends. He had ordered it.

I would be a long time knowing these were more than dead boats. Some men, I knew, kept their father's boat or sold it. Or traded it for a fiberglass fishing skiff. Billy never said why the *Peter Liss* had to be buried. But he stalled. He meant to do it when the wake was over, meant to. He waited a long two weeks. He drank hard. Liss had been a prodigious drinker. George drank. He called and harangued Billy. Billy harangued his wife, me, anybody near him.

The telephone woke me before dawn that Saturday. Billy had been up all night drinking, though he could not get drunk. He had gone to bed, but woke terrified he was having a heart attack. He sat through the hours in his small knotty-pine den, stared at the framed photographs of the *Peter Liss* and the others like her, and he knew. It wouldn't speak but it was there, punching him in the chest even through the mildewed Bible he clutched against it. He drank hard to shake himself free of his father's ghost, but he knew. I was less literary then and did not think, when he told me this, of Hamlet's father on the battlement. I think about it now. When Billy could stand it no more, he called me to meet him at the dock by dawn. He didn't ask if I wanted to. I didn't say.

George ignored me, but he didn't like me being there. I wasn't even a lost cousin. But Billy was the oldest son and he had decided. If George meant to bitch, he'd done it when Billy called him. I knew Billy had called him first. Somehow I knew that. I still couldn't help feeling I didn't belong any more than the bateau roped to and bobbing at our stern. I don't think I even knew why the bateau was there.

By now the sun beat in my head like a gong. I had not worn my waterman's cap, the baseball cap that farmers wear—except instead of a tractor's name it has a leaping swordfish above the brim. Billy and George wore them. When workboats pass, these caps are dipped ever so slightly in salute, unless there's been an insult in the preceding hundred years.

I knew the cove but not its name. It was shaped like a Mateus wine bottle and we were in its neck. Parachutes of jellyfish like small angels hung in the water. Along the shore were newly built docks to starboard, empty marsh to port. At the docks were sleek, expensive speedboats. Beyond pine trees there would be brick ranchers, barbecue pits, and garden clubbers. All white. I also knew this land had once been hunted by Powhatan's subtribes.

Ahead of the bow, three-quarters of a mile off, the tin roof of Bennett's Crab Wholesalers flashed high above the stilts it stood on. All over the cove, stobs, sapling trees pruned of limbs, rose from the green water; workboats tied to them faced us. The tide was coming in. A hundred yards more and Billy tried to idle the *Peter Liss.* She died. Now I could see where we had been heading, where the *Peter Liss* had been heading for forty-six years. Suddenly, there was no breeze. The crabhouse stank. Heat and humidity greased us. Gnats, mosquitoes, blowflies swarmed at us. I slapped. Billy knelt placidly at the engine. George smoked. Oddly, there were no voices drifting from the ranchers, no boats moving out yet.

The place where we would put her was marsh grass about waist-high. A foot or so at the edge would be black mud festered by the holes of fiddler crabs. As a boy I had dreamed these holes were doors to a magic city underground. I could see the remains of a few boats canted in the sun. A wheelhouse with glass windows still unbroken, no vandalism here. This had been a dredge boat. The outlines of several washboards. Workboats. They seemed to me whole, not broken, just resting in the shallow water. Maybe that's what is in my mind now. They seemed to be grateful for the sun. They seemed to be waiting, full of themselves.

Once again Billy eased her forward, already turning her into position. He told George he meant to run her over *Jumps.* He didn't say "the *Jumps,*" for he made no distinction between the man named Jumps and the boat the man had left. Nor did that man and his boat belong to some dateless history. They were a being forever, there, waiting. I don't know what it means to be an American, a Southerner. I'm a Bull Islander. If I wasn't anything before that moment, I became a Bull Islander. No pledge of allegiance, no flag or card to be carried, merely the obligation to a sleepy, forgotten place. The obligation to be a man among men, maybe.

Billy and I climbed into the bateau. He got her running, told me where to take her, then went back aboard the idling *Peter Liss.* When I tried to back this mufflerless bitch, I saw she had no throttle. But I wasn't going to ask for help. I sweated. Impatient now, Billy called at my back that I should use the valve on the carburetor. I looked over my shoulder to see George sitting in my place on the cull board. He had an ax resting on his shoulder. I drifted with the tide away from them.

A workboat's ugliness may be exceeded only by its steady dependability. In this it is like a good mule. Jury-built, ad hoc, its spark plugs apt to be rusted to its cylinders, these boats work— though God knows why. She had died on us all morning, but now the *Peter Liss* gave Billy her best, hard rpms.

He backed her lightly, like a car stuck in snow, then shoved the throttle. She did not leap or surge. She simply dug through the water. Almost, I think now, almost she did plane. I am certain she tried and, almost, I see a gap of light between her severe bow and the water. Not quickly, but with heavyweight dignity, she rode up over *Jumps*. I think I heard those belabored, weak planks groan in recognition. Then the little cove rocked everywhere with a spreading wake. Even the workboats tied to stobs swayed gracefully, like nodding tufts of white hair. It was over, I thought.

Billy came aft and unplugged the *Peter Liss*'s seacock. George went forward and made three feeble swipes with his ax, the flash of sunlight on the blade becoming, as it does in James Dickey's poem "At Darien Bridge," seagulls in flight.

"Goddammit, George, don't do that," Billy screamed. Fifty yards away, he was clear over the racket of the outboard under my arm. He grabbed the ax from George and threw it in the water. I watched them jaw at each other. Then Billy turned and waved me to take them off the back-filling *Peter Liss*.

I reached my right arm back for the throttle valve, holding the metal brace on the front of the motor with my left. This was what Peter Liss had steered with. The valve wouldn't budge. Mosquitoes were all over me.

"Push it, goddammit," Billy shouted.

I pushed hard, ashamed, failing my part. The valve stayed stuck. Then it didn't. Instantly the motor was wide open, the bateau lifted like a bike doing wheelies. Ahead of me, when I looked, was nothing but greasy bateau bottom. I was about to mount the *Peter Liss.*

"Turn the motherfucker. Turn the motherfucker," George screamed. I'd heard this anger in his voice once when he'd come to borrow Billy's coast guard .45 after hearing some assholes were oystering the underwater beds that Peter Liss had rented from the state of Virginia for ninety-nine years. There was no fear in that voice, only outrage.

I hauled on the crossbrace and felt the bateau heave sickeningly. It dug around. I felt as if I was riding a banana. Between trying to force the valve back and screaming out my problem, I kept leaning out too far to see what stob, boat, bank, or pier I was going to die on. I hauled, compensated, overcompensated, and hauled again. I knew I was spinning in an oblique circle when I started to bounce and skid over my own wake. At times I lifted free of the water, as if I had sailed somehow out of time.

I don't know how I got that valve unstuck. All at once, it was awesomely still and I was putting forward. My wakes were lapping audibly, like a mocking applause. Blood pounded from my ears to my tennis shoes.

"You stupid college-educated son of a bitch," somebody said. I'm sure I heard that. Billy, who was turned toward the marsh, swears he did not speak. George faced me. He had said nothing. Peter Liss, who had often enough said this to Billy, was dead. Maybe it does not matter who said it. But why did I feel so worthless, so ashamed? What illusion had done this to me? How can I apologize and for what?

When Billy and George had settled in the bateau, I crammed myself so far into the narrow vee of the bow that I pinched bruises on my thighs. I faced forward while Billy took us rapidly back where we had begun. I knew his eyes under his cap were black and hard as a seahawk's. In less than half an hour we sat shoulder to shoulder in George's battered 1956 Chevy pickup truck. We faced Back River and for a long time did not speak. Drained, hungry, we watched a line of fat Hatterases ghost out of Langley's yacht basin. Beyond them Lyndon Johnson's tower cast a long shadow like a dead hand toward Bull Island. The fifth of Early Times that George pulled out was hot, but we drank it. I didn't rub the bottle's mouth on my sleeve and neither did they. All I could think of was it felt right to be in that place in that time, connected with these two to something so huge I could feel it but not think it. With the second bottle, Billy's, George spoke.

"Got to go back. Gone have to knock a hole in her."

"Know it," Billy said. "Got to take her wheel off first, else somebody will."

"Motherfuckers," George said.

But they did not knock a hole in her, as Peter Liss would have done, when a week later they did go back. They took off her pitiful little brass and left her. Billy thought, so he said, she was in safe enough. That Fall a nor'easter floated her free and the *Peter Liss* does not rest where she was buried. No one knows where or in how many places she may be. If she had broken up in that cove the low tides would have found her. Maybe she found a way into the deep water of the bay. Maybe she's nestled against Egg Island Bar somewhere. It's even possible she might have made it into the Back River channel. All that is certain is that she doesn't lie where Peter Liss wanted her. And that is because of a failure of love, because Billy loved his father and his father's boat too much, and because he was human enough that he paid too little attention to the history of his place. It's a subject he broods upon and is unwilling to discuss. It's why he wakes abruptly, convinced he is having heart attacks. But this is only part of how that day ended.

I remember that, at least to my way of thinking, there was an ample willingness in that truck to rehearse, inflate, and lie about the details of my part. We drank the second bottle slowly, beginning to laugh. George, I think, brought up the matter of any man's having *some* common sense—enough to work an outboard, I believe is how he put it. Billy agreed, though he did point out that "she were a bad-rusted piece" for the reason that she had at least twice gone to the bottom, once when George tied her too close to the dock before a high tide and once when Peter Liss, drinking some, had forgotten to bolt her onto the transom. Most of what we said after this has grown as murky as the water over Egg Island Bar, water that watermen will tell you now leaves oil on your body. But all of it remains with me like a grand illusion. In that illusion, I am convinced, are a few *idears* of crucial importance. I may have expressed an awareness of them, but probably I have not made a clear communication of them. I mean to try one more time, for it is by *idears* that men must live if they have any hope of living with purpose. I have not heard watermen speak of obligations to bury boats or anything else so tribal as that, certainly not the abiding spirits of the dead, to which we must be responsible. Billy would say that you only bury a boat when she is dangerously rotten. Watermen squirm in the presence of idears.

We buried that boat ceremoniously because we were witnessing what it means to be a man. We did it to be watermen, because we couldn't resign from what we already were, good or bad, because we were acted *upon* by ideas that made us know a man has obligations in and to the world. He has to *do* and to *know* what he does. Burying a boat, a man witnesses his history, the intersection of forces that make him what he is. Like a writer, he puts the boat where he can keep it in sight, a little alive, testifying to the character he must keep alive in order to keep himself alive. As long as men pass on that water they will pass the shape of their character, what they have made and been. What they must keep faith with. I do not mean they are required, even by the dead, to meditate or worship. A waterman would not know what, if anything, this meant. But he knows, he feels, in that passing that some things durably *are,* just are, and these seem to say to him you are "one of us." In the spiraling dark of time you shall feel you are connected to the greatness of the world for a moment, and even forever.

Sometimes I think the luckiest thing that ever happened to me was to get slowly drunk, exhilarated, full of joy and lies at what must sure to God be the end of the world. I may have agreed we had buried a boat only because a numb-nutted old man wanted his way and because his boat wasn't worth any trouble to keep it. O.K. It doesn't matter what lies we tell ourselves so long as they help us know we are indivisibly part of something, are a self and a part. For many of us, when the text or the critic or the professor whines that we are the hollow men, merely entries, we are obliged to whisper, *Bullshit.* We are still ourselves, Somebody or not; we are the dead who live because idears live us, and in us, like genes. Sometimes we feel very good because we have been faithful. We have given our honest tubs and earned some kind of right to say fuck fate. This sustains us as we sustain the dead and their place. My life as a writer, which seems to me to begin in the ceremony I have described, consists in my obligation to become aware and to communicate the place where I know life is, just is.

I was drunk again the night before I left Bull Island to go to graduate school. I had already begun to publish poems in maga-

zines, poems that were vaguely focused because I didn't know what
they were about. They were about ideas and illusions I didn't
recognize or even know I had. With my wife and Billy and his wife,
I sat up most of the night. I don't remember what our ugly black
quarreling chewed over except that I was leaving and Billy didn't
want me to go. I swayed in the door the way the *Peter Liss* had as
it settled over the *Jumps.* Billy screamed at the night beyond me:
"You son of a bitch, don't you know people are the same everywhere? Why the fuck do you want to go?" Then, almost tenderly,
he said, "Will you ever come back?"

My words keep saying yes. And no. They are my obligation,
my crossroads, my faith. I send Billy a copy of everything I write.
I do not know if he reads my words, but he knows what they are
about. They are stove up on his bookshelves, piled together like
friends, where he passes in and out every day. I hope they gladden
his heart as the writing of them has gladdened mine.

A Few Good Voices
in Your Head

TED SOLOTAROFF

Ted Solotaroff was born in Elizabeth, New Jersey, served in the U.S. Navy after World War II, and was educated at Michigan and Chicago. Since 1960 he has worked as an editor in New York. His literary pieces from the 1960s are collected in *The Red Hot Vacuum* and he is presently putting together a collection that deals with the 1970s.

Some years ago, probably around 1971, a young writer came to see me. He wanted to write an essay for *American Review* about the sudden decline of the Counterculture, and we talked about that for a while. He seemed both jaunty and troubled, as many young people were in that fading era of fresh alternatives, but he didn't seem to have much of a grip on his subject. I suggested that instead of talking, he might do better to sit down and write and see what he really wanted to say. He said that that was the other thing he wanted to talk to me about. He had been having trouble writing lately and he thought that writing for *American Review* might get him going. "I don't know who to write for anymore," he said.

Who had he written for in the past? Well, he'd started out as an English major at Yale and written mostly for his professors. "I came on as a sort of young Northrop Frye." After college he landed a job at *Time* and became a staff writer, which was a welcome change from fancy literary jargon, and he did it happily for a couple of years. But then, "I got tired of the *Time* style, of having to come up with clever locutions like *sluburb* and *peacemonger.*" Also, as he said, "My politics were changing and most of my friends were writing for *The Village Voice* or *Rolling Stone.*" So he began to moonlight for the underground press, and after a while he left *Time* and traveled around the country, writing reportage about the new street communities, communes, and so forth.

Why, then, didn't he write this piece for, say, *Rolling Stone?* He explained that writing for the youth culture had become like the flip side of writing for *Time:* you were just "enthusiastic and snotty about the opposite things." Also you had to deal with another standardized style—words like *downer,* and *heavy,* and *hassle,* and spelling America with a *k.* That's why, he said, "I'd like to write for *AR*—you don't have any one style, any one point of view, and that grabs me. On the other hand, it's hard to know what you're looking for."

He was watching me carefully, as though I might reveal the secret requirement. I said that *AR* attracted so many good manuscripts that I found myself selecting only the ones I couldn't stand to put back in the envelope. Usually they were the ones that seemed necessary for the writer to have written, which is why I suggested he try to find out what he really needed to say. He nodded but pressed on. "O.K., but look—you write yourself, right? Who do you write for?" I thought for a moment and said, "I guess I write for a few good voices in my head." At which point he suddenly smiled, relaxed, looked at me in a companionly way, and said, "A few good voices in your head—far out!"

Well, I've been thinking about that idea off and on ever since. I don't think it's as far out as the young writer found it. I think it's the way people start out writing—or painting, or composing or doing scientific research: for one or two powerfully meaningful figures in their lives. And I think that those who continue as artists remain in touch with complementary and internalized versions of those early good voices. Needless to say, there are also bad voices in one's head—voices of doubt and despair and intimidation, particularly intimidation, which can also have a powerful effect early in one's career, and late as well. Harry Stack Sullivan calls these voices "supervisory presences" or "personifications of the self." These monitors are evident in daily behavior; they prepare our faces for the faces that we meet, put us at ease or turn on the anxiety, tell us to be gentle or firm, or to keep quiet, or to cut out the crap. And so with writing. Sullivan describes his own writing supervisor as a "charming pill, bitterly paranoid, a very brilliant thinker and a wrongheaded imbecile, whose harassment in the name of an impossible clarity is all but entirely responsible for the fact that I almost never publish anything."

But to return to the benign voices. Literary scholarship, at least the more conventional kind, looks for another kind of supervisory presences, which it calls "influences." Thus scholars say that Hemingway was deeply influenced by Gertrude Stein and find the main import of this in Hemingway's sparse idiom, his use of repetition, his short sentence rhythms, his impassive point of view, etc. But such studies of stylistic influence or even of borrowings of content, of concepts, seem to me the signs of what is really a deeper process, that has less to do with imitation than with validation. Perhaps what Hemingway got most from Gertrude Stein was confirmation—that his way of being a writer was all right, or rather that this way, one of several possibilities for him, was the right way because it brought out the precarious best in him. In other words, I'd like to talk about these matters in the spirit of Gorky's statement about Tolstoy: "As long as this man is alive, I am not alone in the world."

Actually, Tolstoy's role in Gorky's sense of self and vocation, his encouraging and confirming presence, probably came relatively late in Gorky's development, and was preceded by other good voices, good supervisory presences, beginning with his loving, storytelling grandmother, the main redemptive figure in that disaster area of poverty, brutality, and uprootedness that was Gorky's childhood. The reason a writer needs such presences is that they minister to the ongoing identity conflict, sometimes acute, sometimes dormant, but probably never resolved, that is, as we're often told, characteristic of the literary vocation itself. A writer's identity, to paraphrase Erik Erikson, often begins to be formed in late adolescence, and points to the individual's unique core, and its intimate relation to his own group's inner tradition. As Erikson puts it, "the young individual must learn to be most himself when he means most to others, the others being those who mean most to him." A writer's "identity," then, involves a mutual relation, between what earlier ages would have called one's spirit or soul and a persistent ability to share it with others. Thus the problem of my young visitor, who was trying to tell me he no longer knew who he was as a writer, so dependent had his identity become on a succession of immediate, receptive, but transient audiences, so removed had he become, in trying to accommodate them, from this unique core.

The young writer is typically beset on both sides of the issue —of "being most himself" and of "meaning most to others." On the one hand, he is likely to be just emerging from the adolescent warfare in which his creative self has been under attack from his conforming, socialized self for being freakish, timid, unpopular. On the other hand, he is also beginning the process, likely as not, of challenging the values of his home and community, which are felt to be inimical to a literary career but which are also connected to the "inner tradition" that he sooner or later finds he abandons at his peril.

Hence the importance of the right literary role model. "As long as this man is alive, I am not alone in the world." Such a figure nurtures the young writer in the estranged and divided state that William James calls being "twice born." Part authority figure, part ally, whether real or imagined, the right older writer confers upon the enterprise of writing a more powerful and refined version of your way of feeling, your sense of truth. His durable presence instills within you a hopefulness that you can somehow, someday, embody—not imitate but embody—the same felt values that this higher kindred spirit does. By being there, if only in your imagination, he prevents you from being an orphan as a writer—merely your parents' son, on the one hand, and your dubiously sensitive side, on the other. From this influence can come the beginnings of a style, because as you fall under the spell of the writer, you try to make the bond a little tighter and more intimate by being adopted, as it were, by his voice. But the durable influence, I say, is from the kindred but refined attitudes and values behind the voice, which center and inspire you by evoking the new but "persistent sameness of self." It's not so very different from finding a best friend or a good psychotherapist who brings out our better nature, as we say, who prompts our calmest, most personal, most truthful voice. It's also not so very different from prayer.

Not all influences, as I've said, are centering and enabling ones. Erikson observes that the twice-born are particularly vulnerable to new ideologies that provide answers to those pressing questions that come with a new identity and also offer a way of repudiating the past life which nourished and frustrated the self. At the time, for example, that I was starting to think of myself as a writer, there was a prevailing literary ideology, known as the New Criticism. Its principal canon was that literature was best read hermetically and hermeneutically. The true meaning and emotion of a poem or story or a novel were to be found in the text itself, especially between the lines, where the deeper content was hidden away from common view in the form of ambiguity, irony, paradox. Literature was the great tradition of sacrosanct texts, and a literary vocation was like a priestly one, in which you first mastered these texts and the mode of interpretation before you were really entitled to practice the rites. There was even a recondite, mysterious language—"sacramental vision," "social anagogic," "the heresy of unintelligence," and so forth—which bespoke the hieratic aspiration. The New Criticism and its favorite texts and authors were suffused in a Catholic or Anglo-Catholic aura or an American Protestant one, and even had room in them for the anti-Semitism of Eliot and Pound. All of which I was caught up in by the time I was a junior at Michigan, and I was carried away until my coarse, practical, middle-class Jewish background and its heavyhearted liberal moralism were all but out of sight, much less reach.

Erikson observes that the twice-born does not necessarily solve his identity problem by adopting a new ideology; in doing so, he may well be creating a kind of pseudo-self and a subsequent crisis at the point when he "half-realizes that he is fatally overcommitted to what he is not." This was to be the story of my next five years: a pretentious literary self with fetishistic notions of detachment and purity of style and covertly placed meanings. Mostly I wrote stories over and over again, modeled on the austere surfaces of Joyce's *Dubliners* or Flaubert's *"Un Coeur Simple,"* beneath which lay a circuitry that was switched on only at the end by an epiphany that was supposed to cast a subtle retrospective light. Or something like that. A full account of this dead end is in an essay called "Silence, Exile, and Cunning" (*New American Review* 8).

Fortunately, life did not leave my pseudo-self alone. While I was still at Michigan I wrote a review for the *Daily* of the stories of William Carlos Williams. Since he, too, was part of the modernist pantheon, I assumed that his stories were much more complex than they seemed and I gave them the exegetical treatment, as

though Williams were Kafka, ambiguities and paradoxes everywhere; whereas his stories were really much more like those of his
fellow physician Chekhov, all eyes and heart. The review was rejected as being too "obscure." At first this didn't dismay me. What
would a newspaper editor know about symbolic meaning? Looking
for vindication, I showed my review to my favorite English professor. He said that my writing style had certainly changed a lot since
the last time he'd read it. He also said that reading my review made
him feel as if he'd been hung up by his suspenders.

His name was Herbert Barrows. He wasn't a New Critic either,
but I took his response hard. He was the most civilized man I had
yet met, a Boston bachelor who might have stepped out of the
pages of a Henry James novel, one of those discreet tutelary figures
like Ralph Touchet or Lambert Strether, who say little but understand everything. That Barrows had thought well of my writing had
been my first and abiding incentive to become a writer. I'd also
hung around him because he made me feel interesting to myself;
there was a Jamesian encounter going on between us—between
Cambridge, Massachusetts, and Elizabeth, New Jersey, as well as
between a seasoned literary mind and a green one. I particularly
loved his sense of humor, its wryness, freshness, accuracy—which
was his way of relating to life while keeping his retiring distance.
I once asked him, for example, if he'd been at Michigan when
Auden was. No, he'd come there shortly after. "But you could
pretty well follow his doings by the trail of sulfur he left." Barrows
had no literary method to teach me, other than to read a writer
until you'd gotten "the hang" of his work. He seemed to have the
hang of everyone from Henry Adams to Henry Miller. For what he
had to teach me was more primary than method: it was literary
taste, which he communicated with his whole being. For being
alone and rather reclusive, he was sustained by the arts and treated
their works accordingly, as nutritive and pleasurable or not. Hence
his judgments were unaffected by fashions and conventions and
pretensions and came directly from his character. He said that a
good style was like a simple, expensive black dress that you could
then make expressive in your own way: a bad style was like a gaudy
dress from Woolworth's that you couldn't do anything with. Perhaps he told me that on the day I sat in his office with my William
Carlos Williams review and realized I was becoming not a little

screwed up. He said that he was going to try a course in something called "practical criticism" and suggested that it might be helpful to me.

And so it was.

It was a swell course, or better, group; that is to say a course that became a kind of little community that assembled three times a week, so we could all learn from each other. The first thing Barrows did, for a while, was to read us a story or a poem and ask us to jot down what struck us as significant about it. The first few times I was left at the post in a kind of panic. I could barely make out the lines on this one reading; how was I supposed to read between them? But this, of course, was the point of the exercise, which had to do not with ingenuity but with a kind of basic responsiveness known as paying attention, and with letting an impression grow inside you, and with articulating it. Clearly I had a lot to learn, beginning with the distinction between having an impression and making one. The pretender-critic, same root as pretentious, in myself didn't have impressions, for that was to be impressionistic, which was the last thing a New Critic could afford to be in his pursuit of order and complexity. But someone with my name had better begin to have some impressions, if I was to stop handing in my desperate gibberish.

I had a lot of help from Barrows and from the group itself. There was one student who regularly came up with an amazingly sharp and interesting response. He seemed older than most of us, and he wore a hearing aid, which at first I thought might be really a miniature tape recorder, by which he would play back to himself what the rest of us had heard only once and were stumbling to remember. But as I began to see, his secret advantage lay elsewhere. Instead of groping about to describe or judge the poem or story—this poem is about X, what I like about it is Y, and so forth —he would find an image, which as he deftly developed it characterized the work and stated its appeal in such a way that it came back from his mind as freshly and distinctively as it had entered. I remember him speaking about a Yeats poem as being like a patch of ocean where two mighty warships had just fought and gone down, leaving a single empty lifeboat circling on the surface.

So I began to see that practical criticism was not only trusting your own impressions but also using your imagination to take the measure of a work, to turn it this way and that so as to locate it in the world of your own experience. As time went on and I got "the hang," it was like being let off a leash; my mind could nose around in a work, looking for its real interests, and respond with its natural energy. Criticism stopped being the ponderous, anxious school of lifting up the lines and sentences to see if you could find the structural grid underneath, or of injecting an image or a detail with added significance so that the work became like a chicken shot full of artificial hormones; instead criticism became more like play: i.e., making a piece of the world your own object, letting your response and the writer's work meet each other halfway.

Toward the end of Barrows's course, I wrote a review of e.e. cummings's collection *Xaipe,* which began:

cummings is back again at his old stand, working this time out of a satchel with this cryptic Greek word pasted on its side. . . . Again one can watch adjectives dance into adverbs and participles put on weight and sit down as nouns, while the commas plummet and the clauses disappear and the parenthetical expressions get sawn in half. Whole mountains are again given the chance to dance and city pavements to grow flowers. The individual is sung back to significance and the social outcast to humanity.

I remember writing this for Barrows with a kind of "Look, Mom" élan. According to the English psychoanalyst A. W. Winnecott, who has a great deal to teach about these matters, that's how creativity begins: exploring, self-expressive play under the auspices of a mother who frees the child of anxiety; who is, in effect, one's first and determining audience. To Winnecott, psychotherapy is or should be a mode of play in this sense and so are those other inventive activities that take place on the interface between one's inner and outer worlds. As the sort of "holding" figure Winnecott speaks of, Barrows enabled me to relax, to open up, to trust my imagination, and to stop pretending, which is really a form of compliance bred by anxiety. By his kindness and probity toward me as well as by his example, he helped me to see that I had to find some way to be literary and still be myself. But he could not lead me to my "inner tradition." A different figure was needed for that.

His name was Isaac Rosenfeld. I first met him through a story published in a *Partisan Review* anthology. This was in 1954, a few years after I had left college and was living in Greenwich Village, working occasionally as a waiter to support myself in my state of "alienation." Though I was where I was supposed to be, existentially speaking—that is, 180 degrees from the middle class—I was still writing stories so self-consciously posed they couldn't live. I was trying to be like the Joyce of *Dubliners* without his confidence or charm. Rosenfeld's story was called "The Hand That Fed Me" and tells of a young writer named Joseph Feigenbaum. It is set back in the early 1940s, where he has reached bottom. The WPA Writers Project has folded up, the war effort has passed him by, the last six women he has approached have turned him down. He receives a Christmas card from a Russian girl who flirted with him one day three years before, took him home for lunch, and then dropped him. Touched and wounded, hopeful and bitter, he writes one letter after another, none of which she answers. He becomes more desperate, even calls at her home, and is turned away by her brother. Finally, Feigenbaum comes to rest in his yearning and humiliation:

For after all, what is humiliation? It does not endure forever. And when it has led us underground to our last comfort, look, it has served its purpose and is gone. Who knows when newer heights may not appear? I believe some men are capable of rising out of their own lives. They stand on the same ground as their brothers, but they are, somehow, transcendental, while their brothers are underground. Their only secret is a tremendous willingness—they do not struggle with themselves!

Here was Dostoevski's underground man—but with an American Jewish voice that I could immediately relate to. And not just his voice. Here I was, running around New York in a fake tuxedo looking for work as a temporary waiter. I whose motto was Stephen Dedalus's *"Non serviam!"* Like Feigenbaum I was pretty confused, and like him I could no more stop struggling with myself than I could fly. But I had found someone who understood me, who knew better than I where I was coming from and what I was looking for. As Feigenbaum says to his beautiful, heedless *shiksa:*

Be gentle to the unfullfilled, be good to it. We are accustomed to sing the joys of the happy, the fulfilled men. Let us also sings the joys of the desolate, the empty men. Theirs is the necessity without fulfillment, but it is possible that even to them—who knows—some joy may come.

    This heart-flooded story that somehow managed to soar at the
end—at least in my lofty mind, busy with its unwanted offerings
and compromises—was the first thing that fastened me to Rosenfeld. A couple of years later, when I decided to try graduate school,
I chose Chicago, partly because I'd heard he was teaching there.
He died before I met him, but that made him even more of a
shining presence to me. I'd slip away, now and then, from the
scholarly grind in the library stacks to hunt up his pieces in *Partisan
Review, New Republic, Commentary,* et al. He had much to teach me,
not the least of which had to do with my false consciousness of
"alienation." One of his essays dealt with Sartre and the underground and began with the thought that modern writers like to
believe they stand at a necessary remove from society, resisting, if
passively, its disorder, amorality, and so forth.

This has put a high value on confessions, disclosures of the private life
and its feelings, usually revulsions, which earlier ages have found neither
interesting nor tolerable. The tone of very much modern writing is,
accordingly, one of malaise. But we are so accustomed to it, we are
seldom aware of it as such; and when we do take this malaise into direct
account, we readily mistake it for what it is not—a report from the underground.

    The burden of this passage—as relevant today as it was
thirty years ago—is that writers have no more right to their disaf-
fection than anyone else, particularly in view of the self-preening
uses to which it is put. This was a good thing for me to hear; it
was also exhilarating to see Rosenfeld arraign Sartre for taking
the view from the café—"its contactlessness, the emptiness and
superfluity of existence, the sexual miseries and perversions, violence and self-destruction"—as the leading truths of existence.
Sartre, after all, was the leading intellectual in the West at the
time and existentialism was everywhere in vogue. Yet here was
Rosenfeld, in his calm, clear way, exercising his right, as he
would say elsewhere, to "take a good look" at the attitude with
which Sartre approached experience and to weigh it on a firm,
moral scale.

    This was not like the New Criticism at all. Rosenfeld's criti-
cism was full of immediate encounter and judgment ("I should
like to say what I must about Jean Malaquais' war diary with the

humility owing to a man who has been through hell"), yet was lucid and even-tempered and steady. I knew in my Jewish bones, well before Matthew Arnold confirmed it, that literature was first and last a criticism of life, and now I had found a voice that embodied this viewpoint in a warm, masculine, somehow familiar way. It was less like discovering a writer than like finding a terrific older brother.

The first significant essay I wrote was done under his spell. The *TLS* was planning a special supplement on the American imagination and asked Philip Roth to write an essay on the Jewish role in American letters. He said that he didn't know much about it, but he had this friend in Chicago who did. What little I knew about it I'd already exhausted in a review of *Good-bye, Columbus,* which compared him to Bellow and Malamud as, not surprisingly, Jewish moralists. But there were professors of mine at Chicago who would have killed to get a letter to the editor into the *TLS,* and I was being asked to contribute three thousand words. As I say, I didn't really know very much about the subject. But I knew my way around a library by then (I was doing a dissertation on Henry James), so I got a new bundle of three-by-five cards and camped out in the stacks. I read Rosenfeld's colleagues at *Partisan Review* and *Commentary* and *Midstream,* and as much as I could about the historical background of Jewish writing in America. I had six weeks, and in dutiful graduate student fashion, I gave myself five weeks to do the research and one week to write. And then toward the very end, just as I was beginning to do the writing, I was playing first base for a local tavern and broke my finger. I couldn't type very well, which was the way I wrote, and the whole project, still shaky at best, began to collapse. I didn't know what I was talking about; so how was I supposed to be as truthful as I could?

I sat there thinking: Here's your big chance and it's all going down the drain. In despair, I picked up a posthumous essay of Rosenfeld's which had just come out in the *Chicago Review.* At one point, he talks about himself as being "uncertain, alone, and much of the time afraid," which was exactly how I felt, and about the importance of the attitude with which you approached experience. About the only thing I was sure of about Jewish writing was my attitude, which was one of tremendous enthusiasm for the contribution that so many novelists, playwrights, poets, and critics were making to American letters. Until now, I'd avoided Jewish chauvinism like the plague, but there was no getting around my discovery, amplified by my research, that the contemporary writers who interested and inspired me were Jewish—whether overtly so like Singer or Howe or Malamud, or more indirectly so like Trilling or Arthur Miller or Stanley Kunitz. What I could trust, then, was my own excitement that the Jewish sensibility, however broadly defined, had suddenly come into its own, that there was what Leslie Fiedler had called "the breakthrough."

That word, "breakthrough," began to resonate in my mind. I sat down again, with my broken finger, and my heart in my mouth, and wrote a passionate essay in real trembling—"our doubt is our passion," as Henry James said. I sent it off, thinking it would be rejected summarily as being the babblings of an enthusiast. But it wasn't; it was published and was even well received. In fact, it got me a job at *Commentary;* Norman Podhoretz read it, and said that he could tell the writer didn't know what he was talking about, but had guessed right ninety percent of the time, and hence would make a good editor.

I went to New York, became an editor of and contributor to *Commentary,* and a new nephew in what Podhoretz was to call the "Family." After a few months I met William Phillips, who asked me to write a piece for *Partisan Review.* If the *TLS* was august at that time, *Partisan Review* was out of sight for a young critic of my background. *PR* was the Castle. So I'd arrived. Or so I thought.

The truth is that virtually every piece I've written since has meant starting out again. At a certain point, the enterprise invariably breaks down and I don't see how I can write this review or essay; in fact, I shouldn't write anymore at all. Because I continue to lose confidence, including the confidence that may have accrued from seeing the last piece in print: the reasonably clear, clean product of all that disarray. It's the ongoing identity crisis I mentioned earlier: this constant struggle, this manual and psychic labor we perform against our doubts and misgivings and sense of unworthiness, in which we do rely, at times quite desperately, on those good voices in our heads. I know this to be so because each time the crisis hits full force again—when I say I must abandon this, it's just too painful to go on, I'm too ignorant, too superficial,

I don't have enough time, I can't write anyway—I'll open a book of literary pieces, *An Age of Enormity* by Isaac Rosenfeld, read a page or two, quiet down, gather myself, and say: Well, that's what it's all about, he's just telling the truth as best he can, get on with it.

Genetic Coding

GILBERT SORRENTINO

"I was born in Brooklyn, New York, in 1929 and educated in the New York
public school system. I studied English literature and classics at Brooklyn
College. I was a soldier for two years and have held many different kinds
of jobs. I began to write in 1949, am married, and have three children, all
grown. It is almost inconceivable to me that the decayed, superficial, and
'boosterish' city in which I live is the same shining, glamorous, and magical
New York in which I was raised."

Anyone who has read my fiction can isolate, with a greater or lesser
degree of accuracy, the writers who have influenced me, or, more
precisely, can see, to use Butor's terms, my fiction as the particular
"knot" formed within the "cultural texture" from which I have
emerged. With Butor, and other writers, I do not believe in Origi-
nality, but consider writers a kind of "collaborative" band, each
adding a stratum to the work done by others, each stratum possible
only because of that work. My novel *Mulligan Stew* is not truly
intelligible unless it is seen as dependent on the work of Joyce and
Flann O'Brien, as well as on the shiftings and permutations of the
Zeitgeist of the past half century, its rubbish and ephemera. The
novel is, or was meant to be, the end of that process we call
modernism, and its ultimate roots are in *Bouvard and Pécuchet*.
Edward Sapir, in his brilliant 1931 paper "Fashion," notes that "a
specific fashion is utterly unintelligible if lifted out of its place in
a sequence of forms." If I substitute "literary work" for "fashion,"
I might say, then, that *Mulligan Stew* is *only* intelligible when in
place in the sequence of forms known as the modernist movement.

But this is by the way. It interests me only insofar as it allows me to ask a question of myself: Why these particular influences? What I am trying to get at is this: Does a writer choose his influences, or are they, so to speak, lying in wait for him, so that when encountered they are seen to be destined for him? I think this must be the case, and if it is, it means that one's influences are deeper than the "merely" literary; are, indeed, at the core of one's life.

My mother was Irish on her mother's side and Welsh-Irish on her father's. My maternal grandmother was Roman Catholic, my maternal grandfather "Church of Ireland"—an Orangeman. My father's father was born in Salerno, my father's mother in Sciacca, Sicily, as was he. That side of my family is wholly Roman Catholic. This is a common mixture of blood among many people of my generation and class in the large industrial cities of the North, but none the less remarkable because of its ordinariness. Neapolitans are extroverted, demonstrative, masters of bravura, and expert in the niceties of social intercourse; Sicilians are withdrawn, proud, "Byzantine" and convoluted in their mental processes, and equally expert in the niceties of social intercourse. The Irish are a people who suffer from what Vivian Mercier calls "life-hatred"; from this comes their incredible sense of the comic futility of human existence, especially as it relates to the great mysteries of sex and death. To the Irish, there is nothing to be done about them, and hence they are ruthlessly mocked.

Both the Italians and the Irish have an understanding of the essential idiocy of living, the former possessing the Mediterranean tragic sense of life in a pure state, and the latter cloaking their despair under violent, savage, and heartless comedy, comedy that is grounded in what Beckett calls the "mirthless laugh . . . the laugh of laughs, the *risus purus,* the laugh laughing at the laugh." Both have a cynical contempt for authority beyond the family and "clan" and are, to put a nice face on it, bemused as well as amused by it. As far as their art goes, well, now we may begin to see something of that toward which I am, as best I can, digging. In brief, their art is complexly unrealistic: life is not enough for it.

Italian art is, generally speaking, the art of layering: one adds and adds and then adds some more, until the initial impetus, the base upon which the work rests, is almost unrecognizable. We see this in Dante, Cavalcanti, Pirandello, Calvino, Fellini; in the statues of saints in New York churches; in cuisine and pastry; in the elaborate rituals of manners played out by Italians who are introduced to strangers. It is a conscious gilding of the poor thing offered up as "reality." And Irish art is so far removed from nature that the latter is grotesquely distorted in it: in the Book of Kells, Swift, Sterne, Shaw, Wilde, Joyce, Synge, Yeats, O'Brien, we see a withdrawal from the representational.

The Italians and the Irish hold reality cheap, and the brilliance of the art produced by these peoples is, by and large, the brilliance of formal invention used to break to pieces that which is recognizable to the quotidian eye. (That the objects that we think we see in the real world are the result of interactions between outer wave patterns and mental wave patterns—i.e., that we do not "see" the same world as the fish does, or the cockroach, or the eagle, but "see" a world that reflects the human mind—is the suggestion, perhaps not coincidentally, of Vasco Ronchi of the National Institute of Optics in Arcetri.) The hallmark of the art of both these peoples is a relentless investigation into the possibilities of form, a retreat from nature, a dearth of content. This is art made out of Yeats's "mouthful of air"; in the modern parlance, it is not "sincere," that is, it is interested in how to say it, and not in what is said. "In the long run the truth does not matter," Wallace Stevens writes. It never has for either the Italians or the Irish, which may be why Italian rodomontade and verbal pyrotechnics are often thought of as transparent flattery or "charm," and why Irish stories are called blarney or bunk—as if the speakers were not fully conscious of themselves in the act of invention!

It is from this background that I come, and it is this background that allowed me to recognize those influences that were "mine" when I encountered them, that allowed me to use them: they were, indeed, "lying in wait" for me. They spoke to my genetic memories, and permitted me to see my possibilities as an artist. And it was amazing to recognize that these two background streams were so much alike, so that Fellini, for instance, crammed with dreams, fantasies, mockery of modern life and sexual contretemps, grotesques and cripples, and over all, ever-present death, is oddly Irish; and Joyce, with his "unnecessary" swirls, his "self-indulgent" games, his strata of baroque decoration, his false clues and exaggerations, is almost Italian.

This is my "cultural texture," out of which the "knot" of my work, such as it is, emerges. I am, most helplessly, an American writer, but my formal concerns are rooted in my hereditary makeup, so that my Americanism is one of the materials to hand. Or, to put it another way, I am sure that had I been born and raised in France or Germany, I would have used *their* cultural and national materials in the same way that I use the American ones—i.e., I am closer to Laurence Sterne than I am to Henry Thoreau, and I "understand" Italo Calvino better than I do John Cheever.

So then. The writers who influenced me did so because of the deeper influence of genetic coding. They agreed with my own artistic necessities, which are: an obsessive concern with formal structure, a dislike of the replication of experience, a love of digression and embroidery, a great pleasure in false or ambiguous information, a desire to invent problems that only the invention of new forms can solve, and a joy in making mountains out of molehills.

I end with two stories, which may be read as glosses on this piece. The first concerns a man who goes into an Italian cobbler's shop with a pair of shoes to be heeled. He makes it clear that he must have the shoes that same evening, and that if the cobbler can't do the job, he won't leave the shoes. The cobbler swears that the shoes will be ready. That evening, the man returns to find that the shoes are not ready, and, exasperated, he asks the cobbler why he swore to him that they would be. The cobbler replies: "Telling you that they'd be ready, even when I knew they wouldn't, made you happy all day."

The second is the joke about the Irishman who comes home to his wife drunk every night. A priest tells her that she should throw a good scare into her husband to cure him, and that night, when he arrives at the door, his wife appears in a sheet, and screams at him: "I am the devil, come to take you to hell!" The drunk looks at this figure, and after a moment, says: "I'm pleased to meet you. . . . I married your sister!" That this latter touches on the strange Irish affinity for the heresy of Manichaeism is another story.

Some Secrets

GERALD STERN

Gerald Stern was born in Pittsburgh, Pa., on February 22, 1925. He did his undergraduate work at the University of Pittsburgh and earned his M.A. at Columbia University in 1949. He is the author of *Rejoicings, The Pineys, The Naming of Beasts, Lucky Life,* and *The Red Coal. Lucky Life* won the Lamont Award in 1977 and *The Red Coal* the Melville Cane Award in 1982. A recent dramatic poem, *Father Guzman,* won the Bernard F. Connors Prize, given by the *Paris Review.* He is married to Patricia Stern, and his children are Rachel and David.

I

I have always admired the relationship between younger artists and older ones, and when I read about the schools and the dear lofts and the desperate sofas where the one held the other's hand or pressed a cold washrag to his head, I have a certain envy that I was never one of them, neither the young taker nor, later, the giver. It's even a source of embarrassment to me—at interviews, for example—when I am questioned about my *origins* and find myself stammering or overelaborating, trying desperately to account for myself, longing to be a branch of some tree, a leaf somewhere with clear veins and a regular shape. It may be that I am just being taken in by the silly morphologists, who after all make a living from branches, and other poets have also walked around without masters, holding their own disembodied heads against their chests like weird creatures out of Bosch, but when I remember *The Lives* I remember, case after case, two faces bowed over a text, two hearts watching a river together, or a dirty sunset. Of course, now that I've come through it all unscathed, or with very few scars showing, I am a little proud of my terrible isolation and even delight a little in its mystery, as if it were the result of some master plan, and certainly my poetry has resulted from it, but it would have been nice, I realize now, to have had a little help, to have had a sense of some nourishment somewhere, however tenuous or even symbolic it was.

I make it sound as if I suddenly emerged like an unknown blossom in some incredible Alp, or burst full-grown out of the head or thigh of some Eskimo god, biting my own way through the great caul. After all, I did have school and books and friends and family and place and identifiable decade. Probably my "separateness," if I can call it that, had a great deal to do with my own biology and my own history, with a certain shyness and a certain secrecy, coupled with a kind of arrogance, although that isn't exactly the right word, that made me unwilling to submit at the same time as I was too distant, too modest even, to do so. I think this is accurate, though it sounds terribly like mutterings from a couch. And I guess it's no accident that I use the word "submit" to describe my connection with the nonexistent master. Certainly it wouldn't be that word that Hart Crane would use as he thought of his dear Walt or his dearer Arthur, and if it was submission that Robert Lowell was engaged in on Allen Tate's front lawn, or Allen Ginsberg on W.C.W.'s side porch, or Pound in the Provençal room or Whitman in the Emerson room, or Rimbaud behind the smoking revolver, there were no apologies and no agonies. It may be that for me the issue is simply that I did not have one great influence, one master, but a number, even an endless number, and that's what's causing my confusion, and certainly, like everyone else, I did have a great number of influences, but I don't think that's the case. Rather I think it's the case that I'm not accountable as the result of my apparent influences, except in the most obvious ways. The Left, for example, has been an influence on me, as it's been an influence on dozens of other writers, from Williams to Auden to Rukeyser to God knows whom. Each has used it in his or her poetry, or been used by it, in a particular way. But to identify my connection with the Left, mostly tenuous, even sometimes a little sentimental and nostalgic, does not identify in any significant way my poetry. It identifies my sentiment, it shows a little the nature of my loyalty, it says something about my history—and these are important things—but it is not a critical element in my writing. Likewise, Judaism has been an influence on me. But there, too, my connection has been a little tenuous and sometimes nostalgic. That is, the connection with my writing. Although, in that case, the historical *idea* of the Jew as an eternally stubborn, hopeful, and dreaming creature has been an influence, as have been some of the mystical texts, albeit I use those texts as a kind of midwife and secret metaphor for my own inclinations, and use the Jewish texts, as opposed to, say, Buddhist ones, as much out of loyalty as out of belief.

If I were to explore other apparent, even "obvious," influences on me, I think I might arrive at the same conclusion. Perhaps I am saying that I want to discount ideological or formal influences and find the "true" ones in my own personal, accidental history: the city I happened to live in, or being the victim of anti-Semitic slurs and physical abuse all during my early childhood—until we moved into a Jewish neighborhood when I was ten—or living during the Great Depression but not suffering directly from it, at least financially, or being left-handed in the days of organized hatred of the *sinister,* or living for years in the same house with an Orthodox grandmother and a black maid, or wandering alone for hours through a large city woods across the street from my house. But I don't think these fully account either. Maybe my sister's death, when she was nine and I was eight, is the one exception. This was important for me not only insofar as it generated a direct response from me, but also because it affected my parents so strongly and thus changed their behavior toward me, causing them, among other things, to overprotect and overnourish me—the one child left—and at the same time, in a subtle way, to reject me and even "accuse" me, crazy as it sounds, because I was the survivor in that visit of death. This experience is encapsulated for me in the sad Saturday nights I spent with my mother while my father was working late. She took me to bed with her and held me while she wept, crying "Sylvia, Sylvia, Sylvia" over and over again while I tried to console her. It may have happened only once or twice, but I remember it as a ritual occurrence. Clearly I was being both loved and rejected. Clearly I was helpless and uncomfortable and living in two places at once, with two debts to bear, my mother's and my own. If anything came close to being a direct influence over me it was this, and it caused me the most pain and confusion, although I still don't fully understand its connection with my writing.

I know little—really I know nothing—about the psychology of masterhood. I don't know if one is more, or less, inclined to seek out a master if one has a weak, or a strong, father. Maybe it has nothing to do with the father but rather with the mother, or with an older brother—or sister. Maybe, like baldness, it has to do with the maternal grandfather. So many things conspired in my case to provide a world without authority, if I may put it that way. For one thing, neither parent ever "interfered" with my education, and I had no older brother, and no teacher in my early years, or later for that matter, ever took an interest. I think I discovered college itself by sheer accident—I mean even the buildings. I happened to be passing by the University of Pittsburgh one day in the early fall and I wandered in and found myself registering for classes. It was during the war, so I had no trouble getting in. We had no advisers in those days. And a few years later, when I began writing, I had no one to turn to, although by that time I knew it was a good idea to have someone. I gave some poems, I remember, to an English professor I was taking a course in the essay from, and after holding them for about two months, he advised me to read Kafka. I still don't know why. The poems were unmarked, possibly unread. There were no poets coming by giving readings then, there were only a few magazines in the libraries, there were no workshops, no small presses. We lived in darkness. Moreover, I wasn't an English major and I had no friends who wrote. I don't think I knew what a bohemian was. I did carry a little notebook around with me in which I wrote my poems, mostly sonnets in a kind of Edwardian style. I also carried a little book of Untermeyer's in my coat pocket. I wore white shirts, ties, wing-tip shoes, double-breasted suits. I was on the football team, then the debate team. I played nine-ball. I didn't know one was or could be an actual poet. It wasn't until I was in the army, in 1946, and went to New Orleans and Washington and Baltimore, and started wandering through the bookstores and libraries, that I began to realize that writing was an occupation, and it wasn't until then that there began to stir in me that sweet idea of one day becoming a writer. But there still wasn't anyone I looked up to or even got signals from, except, maybe a little, Thomas Wolfe, whose novels I began to read. But there were no poets for me, not yet. The idea of going to a school and studying under a poet never occurred to me. I didn't know yet who the poets were, and later, when I did, I had no idea where they worked—or that they did work—and I didn't know you could study poetry, say at Princeton or Iowa or Columbia, or that one even visited and talked to living poets. There wasn't one other soul in the world I could talk to about the books I read or show a poem or story to. But I was very happy and was not bitter and was not in longing. I lived and studied without direction, and if anything was going to be a permanent influence on me it was that.

II

By 1948, even as early as 1947, I was moving from shelf to shelf, devouring the major poets, putting together the odd history, listening carefully to the music. I read with no real logic, Spenser one week, Swinburne another, and like a threadbare angel, a poor naïf, I was moved all by myself as I encountered the great speeches, the breathtaking lines, the vaguely familiar passages in poet after poet, one marvelous writer after another. And of course, I was reading other books to fill the gaps: novels, history, philosophy, psychology. I made lists of the important books I had to read. I would be sleepless, sometimes humiliated, sometimes desperate, at the discovery of another great book I had not read or had just heard of. My wife, whom I met in the fall of 1947, tells me the iron stacks of the Carnegie Library are permanently embedded in her mind, that she remembers me reading nine to ten hours a day, that the first books she remembers under my arm were Herrick and Yeats and Joyce. I was in the 52/20 Club, a World War II G.I. benefit, twenty dollars a week for fifty-two weeks, a very tidy sum for those days. My dear President, the little scholar from Missouri, gave me twenty dollars a week to read old books and transform my life.

In the winter of 1948 I was reading *Poetry* and reading the thin volumes in the new-acquisitions shelf at the Pitt library. Sometimes, I quickly discovered, they were very thin. And I was piecing together the story of modern poetry—learning the language—and collecting my own library. I think Yeats and Pound were the two modern poets I cared for most then, though I began to know all the famous poems that were in the anthologies and all the names and dates and histories. I met Jack Gilbert and Richard Hazley that spring, or rather re-encountered them, since we all had been on the debate team together, and had indeed been the international champions, and they discovered, to their astonishment, that I was reading poetry and writing, and I discovered, to my delight, that they were too, although I recall that Gilbert's plan then was to become a novelist. We had to be the only people writing and reading poetry in Pittsburgh at the time. At least we never found any others. The peculiar thing about that period was that we didn't spend much time exchanging poems with each other but rather talked about the poets we were reading. It was as if poetry was a holy art, a religion, and we were not yet ordained. I know I was writing a great number of new poems, even if my friends weren't, but the idea was not the workshop idea—at least not then. We shared great poems, great lines, with each other, we talked about the mission of poetry, we developed our scorn. Pound was the poet we most admired, Pound of *Personae*. And after him the early Eliot, and MacLeish and Cummings, and Hart Crane. I was, as I recall, reading the late poems of Yeats and all of Auden and Marlowe. We didn't talk much about Frost and Stevens and Williams. Not then. I think our theme was "the poet in a hostile world." I don't mean to make fun of it. It's a real enough subject and as important today as ever. It has been the very *mythus* of poets, at least in Europe and America, since the beginning of the nineteenth century, in a way since Ovid, and it was the natural myth for three poets under siege in their real lives in inhospitable and merciless Pittsburgh. For us, poetry had to be serious and lyrical and personal and approach the sublime. The beautiful or moving line was the measure for us, even perhaps more than the whole poem. Thus some lines from Milton or a short speech from *Faustus* or a phrase from Yeats. Of the generation just preceding ours, we would become most interested in Thomas and then Roethke and Lowell, but not for a while. We were hardly interested in realists like the early Shapiro or the early Ciardi. Academicism was already in the air, but the cloud was slow in coming to Pittsburgh. I remember the horror with which I greeted Richard Wilbur's first book of poems. I literally tore it up on the steps of the Carnegie Library—for which crime I humbly ask mercy from the trustees, and sympathy from Dick himself. We had all gone our separate ways by the early and mid fifties, but in our periodic reunions we never failed to curse out the new academics, with their wit and elegance and politeness and forms, for their cowardice and bad faith, most of all for their disloyalty. To the Dream. Maybe, in some strange way, we were saved by our distance and our ignorance and our innocence. We didn't learn either the new style of writing or the new style of living. We had no insurance, no cars, no jobs. No wit. Maybe Carnegie's evil angel, which kept us blind and filthy and confused, should, after all, be thanked.

I spent most of the fifties in Europe or New York City, living on next to nothing—a stretch of G.I. Bill, an odd job here and there. I was rather vaguely working on a Ph.D. at Columbia University, but had no identity with the other students and seldom went to classes. I quit forever one warm beautiful spring night. I had written a long poem in 1950 called *Ishmael's Dream:* my first epic. I remember writing ten gorgeous lines a day, on schedule. I was living on Rue Boucherie, in Paris, a few blocks from Notre Dame. I prepared for the writing by reading from *The Bridge* and *Paradise Lost* and Isaiah out of a huge rotten Bible I had stolen from the American Center on the Boulevard Raspail. The subject, which I never consciously thought about, was the regeneration and transformation of the world, and myself as religio-politico-linguistic hero, a common enough theme for a first generation American Jew only son. I showed the poem to Auden, who was living on Cornelia Street at the time, in the Village. He made a rather vague comment about the ending, and that was that. It was my only attempt to make a connection. Of course, he was the last person I should have sent such a poem to, but I was a little dumb. I eventually did come to use Auden in my poetry, years later, and in an unforeseen way, but I never did see him face to face after that, although I always loved him, poor dead soul, writer of lovely songs. By the mid-fifties I was writing some good poems and publishing them. The underlying theme was still transformation and the hero's call, but I was now more coherent. I occasionally used rhyme and the stanza, but I had nothing to do with the polite domestic verse of the day. The poet I was most involved with then was Wallace Stevens. I had reduced the number of useful "older" poets to two, Lowell and Roethke. After a while I turned more toward Roethke because of Lowell's subject matter and his turgidity, as I saw it then. It was early

Roethke—the mystery, the strangeness, the loss, the love of small animals and plants, the sense of justice. I would return to Lowell again when *Life Studies* appeared. I was interested in Williams not so much for his language but for the way he combined health and madness, domesticity and wildness.

When I began teaching at Temple University in Philadelphia in the fall of 1956, I had a definite style. I read every poet and magazine I could bear, and I was totally unknown. I was in no community of poets, either in person or by mail or by phone, so I figured things out for myself, as I always did. When everything started to blow, West Coast vs. East, beat vs. feet, I took an independent stand, finding in the poetic left an approximation of my own view, yet hating what appeared to me then to be its lack of imagination and its anti-intellectualism. I disliked the academics, yet I was working for a university. But I was slave labor, a subversive, a hater of their tide. Unfortunately, my separateness and self-absorption not only prevented me from transcending the two extremes, but made me insensitive to what other younger poets were doing—to Creeley, say, or Bly, or Levertov—or made me judge them too quickly, and I was the loser for this.

In 1958 I began working on *The Pineys,* a long poem about the presidency. It was going to be my ticket. It was humorous, extravagant, mystical, buoyant, wordy, and very long. There were elements of the *Cantos* in it, and *Paterson* and *The Prelude* and *The Bridge* and *Song of Myself.* There was reconstituted prose and lists and lyrics. It was going to do everything. I was still an eternally old student and an eternally young instructor. I had a mustache and smoked cigars. I propped up the high chair with obscure dictionaries. I lived in a lovely timelessness. But one day, while rewriting the very last section, I realized the poem was a failure, that it was indulgent, that it was tedious, that it no longer interested me. It was 1964 or '65; I was going on forty, living in Indiana, Pa., and teaching at the state college there. I was devastated. I had been a practicing poet for almost two decades and I had nothing to show. I suddenly was nowhere; I had reached the bottom. I remember walking around for months in that dull little city, teaching my classes by rote, not sleeping at night. Certainly I was going through a tremendous change—and a crisis. Certainly it was ironic that that crisis should be right on target, a real *crise de quarante,* on my own fortieth. As far as the poetry went, it had to do with realizing that I was taking an easier way than I should, or could, or must, that I was not wrestling my own angel, that I had not arrived where I had to go. It also had to do with a realization that my protracted youth was over, that I wouldn't live forever, that death was not just a literary event but very real and very personal. It was a liberation though I looked upon it at the time as a horror. I was able to let go and finally become myself and lose my shame and my pride. It meant literally starting over, but I didn't care because I was alto-gether interested only in the work and not in the rewards the work might bring. Not then. And suddenly I had very little envy of other poets and almost no sense that I was competing with them—even if they were ten years younger than I and were winning all the prizes.

Maybe I'm not accounting for it enough. Was it because *The Pineys* was a failure that I fell apart? Why did I think it was a failure just then? A few years later, 1967, I had a chance to publish it, so in a few days I got rid of a lot of dead wood, did some rewriting, and sent it off. And it didn't look that bad. Wasn't it just the last stage of an endless series of rejections and abandonments that had plagued me since my early twenties? Why did I "come to" just then and start writing with authority and precision? Isn't that anyhow just what many other poets do, only they do it much earlier? Maybe if I had not got bogged down in such a long poem I could have made my move earlier—say when I was thirty-five. But then, the very occupation with that poem was a way of delaying or deferring the change I was going to make. I'm suddenly remembering now a visit to a doctor and his concern with my health—overweight and such. Did an ordinary event like that, producing a slight shift in my view, allow me to tap into material that was formerly warded off or ignored? Was it my lot to speak for the second half of life and not the first?

I think, when I look back now, that it was my own loss and my own failure that were my subject matter, as if I could only start building in the ruins. Or that loss and failure were a critical first issue in my finding a new subject matter, that they showed me the way. Or that my subject was the victory over loss and failure, or coming to grips with them. But I certainly started with loss and failure. Moreover, in a certain sense I always did start with these two and I was merely finally coming fully into my own, doing the thing more purely now that I had always done, more perfectly. It was as if I had been preparing for this all my life—certainly since my sister's death and my mother's sadness—and now I was ready. At any rate, after a little agony, the poems started to come easily and simply. The first group were written in the winter and spring of 1966, at the time of my forty-first birthday. Those poems are collected in *Rejoicings* (the name of the tractate on mourning in the Talmud), and there has been no letup in the writing from that day to this.

A couple of commentators have talked about the issue technically. Bly, for example, referred to my long lines. But I know that the issue is emotional and not technical and that it always is when a vital change is involved in art, although I recognize that the technical can stimulate, even make available, the emotional, that it can be a facilitator, that the challenge and demand of free verse in the sixties, for example, helped James Wright make the changes he did in *The Branch Will Not Break,* that Whitman's change was aided by form and Keats's also, in the Odes. When I look at the statement I made for *Contemporary Authors* a few years ago, I see I emphasized my attraction to weeds and waste places and lovely pockets and staking out a place that no one else wanted because it was abandoned or overlooked. Aside from my attraction to these places because they are a relief from civilization, I think I found in them a perfect location for my own emotions, although after a while I realized I had to be careful I didn't suffocate from too many weeds. At any rate, I could sink there as low as I wanted, I could be utterly alone, I could even be without hope, and I found a kind of support. Such abandoned and neglected places have been used by many other modern writers, and by all the Romantics, and they have become a familiar metaphor for our lost world and a familiar arena for our holocausts and our ruined dreams, but they were for me very personal. I think I valued as much as anything else the secret aspect of such places and I have always loved the secret places that were just beyond the reach of our penetrating minds, the tiny black locust woods of my childhood, the obscure reading rooms of my young manhood, the hidden studies I go to now.

The longer I live, the happier I get, and the more I write, the more I arrive at my own place—I almost said my own assigned place—and I am ready to let Sylvia's hand go and I am finally ready to accept my abandonment, although I doubt if that's what it is, and simply call it a blessing. What I don't understand is why I waited till my fortieth year, although I'm sure I waited so long because I had no critical guide and I'm sure I had no guide not only for the accidental reasons I have mentioned, living apart from the mainstream and such, but because I couldn't find a way to incorporate someone in an acceptable manner, given my own impulses and obsessions, including my obsession against the very idea of having someone as a teacher or guide. I could have sought Kunitz out, or Roethke, or Lowell, poets who were teaching and whom I admired, but already the pride and the secrecy had set in. It was truly as if I couldn't afford, and couldn't bear, any kind of accounting at the time, as if that would interfere with my destiny. I can't imagine myself, say, at thirty, sending a sheaf of poems off to one of the middle-aged masters. Part of it was just habit, and part of it was just insecurity, but some of it, most of it probably, was a lack of connectedness. As smart and verbal as I was, I was totally impractical and artistically crazy. I was living in a stubborn perverse proud dream place. I went where I did go because I didn't have a guide and I became what I am for that reason, although I am not recommending it to anyone. If I did have someone, if I had belonged somewhere, the poetry would have been different—and would have come sooner—but it's the life mainly that makes the poetry and I don't think I really had a choice. In the meantime, I've recently discovered that I must be on guard lest I am too impatient or too indifferent to the new poets looking for help, so I don't start mumbling in Hittite or arrogantly lecturing them on the self-made man, and so I don't lose the opportunity of making someone a little happier or a little less bewildered in the lovely and terrible struggle for beauty and understanding we call poetry.

Beginnings

C. K. WILLIAMS

C. K. Williams lives in Brooklyn and Paris. His books include *Lies, I Am the Bitter Name,* and *With Ignorance.* He has held a Guggenheim Fellowship. At present he is completing a new book of poems and finishing a translation, with William Arrowsmith, of *The Bacchae* for the New Greek Tragedy Series, Oxford University Press. He is a professor of English at George Mason University.

I

When I got out of college, I did what I imagine every would-be writer does: I sat down and tried to read everything I'd ever heard of. I read all of Homer, Shakespeare, Sophocles, and Aeschylus. Dante and Virgil, and of course *Paradise Lost,* which for one long week almost made a Christian of me. As much Blake as I could struggle through; some Chaucer; Whitman, who'd been the first poet I'd ever read voluntarily; Yeats, the poet I'd gone at most passionately while I was in school; Eliot, who was *the* poet then, especially in the academy, especially "The Waste Land," or its footnotes. A lot of Stevens, some William Carlos Williams, although I didn't quite understand him yet—mostly I read *Paterson;* some Auden, Keats, Coleridge, not much Wordsworth, whose clarities deceived me, not enough Shelley, who seemed so long-winded; Donne, Herbert, even Traherne; Wyatt and Sidney, Marlowe, Webster, no Spenser, who was a perfect soporific, not much eighteenth century, which was the moon. There were many others —Crabbe and Meredith for starters—and probably many I've forgotten. I was also going at the novelists—almost all of Dostoevski and Tolstoy, Melville, Hawthorne, Conrad; most of Laurence

Sterne, a lot of Faulkner, Hemingway; Joyce, except *Finnegan,* a little Dickens, who was so entertaining I found him suspect; less James, too stuffy; not many contemporaries, Bellow and Gaddis, and a little later and more thoroughly and gleefully Henry Miller. I struggled through what I could of the philosophers and social thinkers. Of the philosophers the Greeks mostly, mostly Plato; of the others a lot of Frazer and Jung, who were still having their vogue then. I once outlined, out of Lord knows what forgotten good intention, the entire Tibetan *Book of the Dead,* and copied out in its entirety the *Mystic Gloom* of the Pseudo-Dionysus. It was all more or less nonstop: I'd fall asleep every night over a book, dreaming in other people's voices. In the morning I'd wake up and try, mostly fruitlessly, to write acceptable poems.

In memory, those years seem so distended, so grotesquely swollen with frustration, uncertainty, and loneliness. It wasn't until I actually stopped to count that I realized there were only four or five years, and not the greater part of my adult life, of what could most benignly be called my apprenticeship. Just learning to be alone was such a Heraklean task. The world always offered so many enticements. And, at my desk, how my mind would drift, how I'd tear at myself with doubts, with self-accusations—I was surely indolent, probably spiritually inept, trivial, inconsequential, not cut out at all for this; no gift, no discipline. That fractured image of myself became myself: I was just as unhappy as you were supposed to be, as all the stories had you be, which may have been all that kept me going, because I was so lost by then; I had no idea anymore of what I was doing, I had no notion of what a poem even was.

I knew that I was deeply committed to poetry, but I wasn't quite sure why and was very uneasy about it. I hardly read any contemporary poets at first, I didn't know any other poets, had no idea of how to find any, and the poems I did come across I usually dismissed as either incomprehensible or trivial. It's remarkable how young artists always seem to make and feel perfectly comfortable with such outrageous exaggerations. Right along with a wracking lack of confidence, you can proclaim to yourself that there's nothing around of any real value, nothing in sight, and nobody but you who has any notion of what's really going on or needed. All you're really trying to do is clear the slate enough to get your own scrawl on it, but all this struggling can be very aggressive, maybe because you often have then so much the sense of being put upon, oppressed, by just about everything. Because I was so alone in it, I think I may have been even more impressionable than the young poets I've met since then. I was always coming to odd conclusions. Once I decided that the whole tradition of English poetry was useless to me, and for a few years I didn't read anything but translations. That was before the great age of translating that began in the middle sixties, and I must have inflicted an awful lot of wretched translationese on myself. I did, though, find Rilke and Baudelaire, who were terribly important to me, and Verlaine, Rimbaud, and Char; Montale and Seferis, the Haiku poets, and Rexroth's Chinese and Japanese, mostly Tu Fu and Li Po. Really, what I read seemed to have been determined mostly just by what had been done, what I could get my hands on.

Ransacking other traditions that way, though, still didn't help me much in my own work. I was still frustrated, still mostly at loose ends and without direction. Then somewhere around that time I came to another odd conclusion, and made what seems to me now, considering how confused I was about most things, a surprisingly concrete and purposeful decision. It mostly had to do with all the work in longer forms I was reading, with how comfortable I felt with Homer or Dostoevski, and how ill at ease with contemporary poetry. I began to feel that a great deal of human interaction, a large portion of real moral sensibility and concern, had somehow been usurped from the poets by the novel and drama, and that in the face of it there had even been a further kind of protective withdrawal and a tunneling of vision on the poets' part. It felt to me as though anything that was on a large emotional scale, anything truly passionate, absorbing, or crucial, had been forsaken by poetry. What the poets of our time seemed to be left with were subtleties, hair-splittings, minute recordings of a delicate atmosphere. Even in the poetry I could find to admire for one technical reason or another, there seemed to be a meagerness of theme and attempt compared to the works in longer forms. I think my ideal as a poet then was Homer: I was fascinated by the sheer weight of the data, in the *Iliad* particularly, the utter factness of its human experiences, its absolute commitment to the given.

Oddly enough, the conclusion I drew from these reflections

didn't send me to write novels or plays myself, certainly not epics. I was still, although I might have had a hard time saying why, absorbed in the lyric. I had, though, been writing some stories, I'd composed a play in college and assumed I would again, and had done some criticism—book reviews and reviews of art shows—for a local paper. Now I decided I wouldn't do any of that anymore. I resolved—the word applies; there was that much unexpected will to it—that anytime I had an idea for a story (I had notebooks of them) or for a dramatic sketch, or for anything resembling more purely intellectual activity—criticism, any sort of philosophizing—I'd try to find a way to get its matter into a poem.

It's hard to remember how long exactly it took me to come to what seemed like such an extreme notion; it's harder to remember what it felt like at the time. Surely all young poets flounder through similar crises, and make as unlikely fusses; fortunately, we don't have to know that everyone else is doing it too. However little my decision may have actually affected the evolution of my work (that kind of thing would be hard to know really), it was certainly very important, primarily because beyond the vague sense it gave me of having a purpose now, a sort of goal, I was paradoxically able for the first time to begin to study other people's poems in a genuinely useful way: I needed them now, I wanted to see how aspects of my project might be being handled.

This all happened sometime between 1960 and 1965, and it's impressive to consider the books that appeared during those years which were important in any regard, and were astonishingly what I had been looking for. (That they incidentally made a joke out of my idea of the limitations of poetry went by me with hardly a flicker.) William Carlos Williams's *Pictures from Brueghel* came out in '62 and was the key for me to the rest of his gigantic achievement. Then there were Lowell's *Life Studies,* Roethke's *Far Field,* Berryman's *77 Dream Songs,* Plath's *Ariel,* Ginsberg's *Kaddish,* Merwin's *Moving Target,* James Wright's *The Branch Will Not Break,* Kinnell's *Flower Herding . . . ,* Bly's *Silence in the Snowy Fields* and the remarkable series of translations that he did himself, or edited: Vallejo, Neruda, Hernández, Jiménez, Lorca, Trakl. . . . They were all books that became crucial to me as soon as I stumbled across them, or as soon as one of the poets I'd begun by now to meet would direct me to them.

Now that I did know some other poets, it probably goes without saying that my project, my resolve, became even more of a secret than it had been before. I wasn't about to call that much attention to myself. Although I'd begun to write some poems that I wasn't completely ashamed of, I was still terribly shy and excruciatingly diffident about my situation as a poet. I still felt sheepish, for one thing, even guilty, about how I'd arrived at poetry. I'd never had that blazing calling our teachers had always indicated was the primary credential for it. Poets, we were given to understand, know who they are in the cradle: the rest is just a dechrysalization.

Poetry didn't find me, in the cradle or anywhere near it: I found it. I realized at some point—very late, it's always seemed—that I needed it, that it served a function for me—or someday would—however unclear that function may have been at first. I seemed to have started writing poetry before I'd read any. Although why this should have seemed to have been so much of a sin eludes me now, it reinforced the uneasy feeling that I'd had to create the interest in myself rather than having it dawn on me in some splendid conflagration. I'd always read a lot, but I wasn't particularly compelled by words for their own sake, or by "literature," which had always repelled me with its auras of mustiness and reverence. I detested almost any book I had to read, hated English in school, and I must have been surprised, maybe even a little put off, to find myself, just as the dreary poetry survey courses ended, turning the stuff out myself. I started writing one day, for no real reason (I had a girl who liked poetry, or liked the idea of me writing it anyway: not much of a clue), but once I did, I knew, I can't remember exactly how, that the realities poetry offered me differed in essential and splendid ways from those of every day. My every days were all either tormented with confusions of one sort or another, or were intolerably humdrum. There was something about the way poetry isolated experience, its powers of demarcation, that promised a way to endow experience with forms that if nothing else would be at least more dramatically satisfying.

My first model as a poet wasn't even a poet, but an architect, Louis Kahn. I met Kahn just as he was becoming famous. My closest friend was a student of his and he brought me to Kahn's office, a marvelously strewn muddle of rooms over a luncheonette.

I liked Kahn and spent a few years at the edges of his circle. I think
he enjoyed having a young poet in his entourage; he may also have
liked having someone around who occasionally disagreed with him
—his disciples never did—but I can't say that I studied with Kahn
so much as that I studied *him*. I was fascinated to begin with by his
notoriety: architects and critics were making pilgrimages to Philadelphia to see his buildings and to meet him. More to my real
advantage, though, he thought aloud. He was a compulsive theo-
rizer and lecturer, and it was an unusual opportunity to see how
a mature artist approached his work. I'd had some inspiring teachers at Penn—Schuyler Cammann, the Orientalist, Maurice Johnson, my wry, wise adviser, and Morse Peckham, who to my great
good fortune was developing then his system of close reading—
but it was Kahn who without my quite remarking it formed most
of my attitudes about art and the artist's task. He worked constantly, day and night. I was awed by that. Even more than his
industry, though, it was what informed it that impressed me: the
astonishing patience he confronted his work with, the numbers of
attempts he demanded of himself before he found a solution he
would trust. He demanded a complexity in defining a problem, so
that its necessities would always be as demanding as possible; the
solution then was a purification, a refining to essentials, and his
work always achieved a simplicity which belied what had gone into
it.

It occurs to me that I've never really considered why, given
all my admiration for Kahn, I didn't simply try to become an
architect myself. It may have had to do with the fact that there
were architects in my life at all. In some ways, for whatever obscure reasons of rebellion or reaction, I seem to have been looking for a sort of negative identity. I'd never, as I've said, met a
poet, had no idea what one would be like, and I didn't particularly care. Not only was there no glamorous or heroic imagery to
being one, there wasn't any imagery at all, and there must have
been something about that lack of detail I found compelling. I'm
still not sure why, but it feels as though I wanted to be something
which *wasn't*. I wanted a way of being in the world without having
to admit it. I was after marginality: I wanted to be at the edges of
things, not quite really visible.

Such oblique needs. For a long time I fretted about it. Machado says somewhere that in order to write a poem you have to invent a poet to write it. You also, I think, have to invent a whole literature to receive it, and a whole community of poets who will have produced that literature. They'll all have biographies you've worked out for them, and I found after a while that my own biography had become as fluid as any of theirs. One's retrospective sensitivities and dramas can be absorbing—young poet being battered to splendid consciousness—but sooner or later reality recurs.

I think I had a normal enough childhood. Aside from the Depression miseries of never enough money, money battles at dinner, late at night when they thought you were asleep, it was mostly all right. My mother may have worried about us a bit more than most—her father and a sister had been killed in accidents—but she had, and still has, too much sheer joy in life to have let her cautiousness affect her much.

What I remember most from my childhood is how restless I always was, how hard it was to sit still. I always seemed to be trying to get away, out, from home, from school, from anywhere. I imagine I was just sharing in the general atmosphere of that war and postwar time. Things were moving fast then: it was the Boom, the "Rebirth of America." Coming out of those sad gray years of the war, there must have been so much promise in the air, so much hope.

It's odd. I realize I never heard during those years the word *hope* used in the sense I mean to give it here, not in our household anyway. Maybe because our hope, our ambition, our passion to advance, to move up, was so pervasive, so all-involving, that it never had to be mentioned, perhaps more urgently *couldn't* be mentioned, because expressing it might imply its opposites, doubt-in-hope and, unthinkable, loss of hope.

I didn't know at that age, naturally, how great a part of the population was rushing through those expansionist years with the same ambition, toward the same promise, and what an outlandish number of them were making it. Our fathers toiled their unbelievably long hours, drove themselves, worked like madmen. Our mothers abetted them, laboring themselves when they had to, at the store, on the kitchen table with the books. There was even something demanded of the children, something that, even if we didn't

quite understand it, we knew was our duty. We were to have an
awareness of it all, of our complicity in it. We were to be flexed,
somehow, before it. Concentration, what's what it was. We were
meant to *concentrate.* It was my father's favorite word in the little
pep talks he'd offer me. *Concentrate!* Sometimes I felt terribly inadequate because I had no idea of how to go about it. That didn't
matter, though. My father's lectures were very dear to me. What
I took from them had to do more than anything else with his
attentiveness, with how important he considered my outcomes to
be. The seriousness with which he regarded how I was to project
myself into my life probably was central to that general sense of
tension and responsibility that came so early, but if at times it was
inconvenient, I was mostly honored by it.

There were some kids, though, who amazingly didn't have it.
We weren't all on the same flight after all, apparently. My friend
Tommy's father was a fireman: Tommy was going to be one too.
How relaxed he looks. I can see him strolling home from school,
ambling, dawdling along. I never ambled: I ran, trotted, paced,
counted steps, got there fast, faster, first, even when I was by
myself.

Tommy was different in other ways too, it not so gradually
dawned on me. His mother, for one thing, never let me in their
house. A gang of us would be playing in back, the other kids would
trail in for lemonade or whatever, and I'd somehow be deftly
amputated from the group to wander off by myself. Richard's
mother did the same thing, and Michael, one of my best school
buddies, got me down one day and slapped my face until I'd admit
that I'd killed God.

Small stories. It doesn't at this late date bear constructing any
edifices on the relatively offhanded ethnic indignities of a Newark
boyhood. The Holocaust was happening somewhere, we'd know
about it soon enough (though much later than one would think:
it was for a long time a parents' secret), and we'd finally know, too,
something about what the Black experience in America really was.
Still, this business of being Jewish was complicated. The prejudice,
overt or otherwise, was easy enough to incorporate into a part of
one's personality where it wouldn't obtrude onto active reflection.
("Spit in my face, you Jewes," says Donne, me hardly blinking.)
What I did notice with something that must have approached

intellectual interest was that I seemed to have several histories.
Everyone else did too, of course—Tommy was Irish, Michael Italian; they were both pugnacious enough about it—but they participated in a way I never quite did in the official history, the one
we were taught at school, all those dates and names leading triumphantly to Christian Capitalist America. I don't know when I'd
have noticed that that history and the one I was getting at *shul* had
essentially nothing to do with each other. Very early, I know I'd
squirm when we'd be exhorted by the principal—you still were
then—to be "good Christians," but I already knew the advantages
of expressionlessness, mild interest, mild boredom. There was
such a discrepancy, though, between the two histories that I find
it striking I never had any inclination to put them together, to
collate them. They were perfectly distinct, and I left them that way:
having two histories was as unremarkable as having two parents.
I may even, on the imaginative level, have enjoyed it. Their narratives ran in opposite directions: the American one started in the
present and reeled out backward, ending with the cavemen, whom
I liked a lot, and the other one started at the beginning, which was
a garden this time, and came this way.

That there were several Gods, too, was beyond doubt. Michael, finally, after how many years of coyness, let me see his
catechism. (It was exactly the same handy pocket size as the even
more intriguing pornography he'd produce for me a few years
later. Speak of influence! Whenever did language offer so much
sheer glittering revelation as it did in that grubby, hand-typed
samizdat of erotica which resolved so many burning questions of
anatomy and mechanics?) The catechism, anyway, said, in cold
print—yes, there it was—that the Jews *had* killed Christ, God, *that*
God, a God I had to admit I found, despite the contentiousness of
his adherents, not all that unsympathetic. Later, when I came back
to it all, through Buber and Kierkegaard, and had my theodicy
arguments with the God I created out of I-Thou and my Sickness
Unto Death, probably much of the energy for it arose from the
possibility of there being a kind of Manichaean double to go along
with that self-absorbed Lord of rapture and good intention. It may
also have had to do with why in the poems I wrote for that theodicy,
I mustered all the insistent Baalshem childishness I could to inform my queries and consternations. God as the path of accusation

is famously self-limiting: that I kept it up as long as I did certainly had to do, too, with Michael's little book, the first one, that is.

II

Halfway exactly from when I began writing to here (again, another distortion: I'd never have believed it was that long ago), I stopped writing poetry, then started again. This time, though, there was no resolution or decision, however naive. All I knew at first was that something was wrong, that the poems I'd been writing no longer had any urgency or even interest at all for me, and that I had no idea of what kind of work I wanted to do next.

In the poems I had been working on, I'd been engrossed by varieties of disjunctive consciousness. I was trying to find ways to embody political and social realities by structuring and figuring poems in ways that went beyond apparent limits of logical connectiveness. Although I wouldn't use that nomenclature now, I was trying to bring the unconscious to bear on those issues. Among the poets who'd marked a direction that way, I was taken less by the Surrealists, who'd possibly gone farthest with it but who I felt were too playfully sure of themselves, than by those like Vallejo, Hernández, Mandelstam, and the anguished Rimbaud and Artaud, who were driven to the limits by their ethical sympathies. I'd also been quite involved with Freudian and the more eclectic psychoanalytic theories. I was particularly taken with what is called "primary process" language, the language of schizophrenia, a very concrete way of speaking which manifests an overriding absorption in the gross emotional charge of symbols, and little concern with logical coherence, or "meaning." (Vallejo's *Trilce* is probably what would come closest to it in poetry.)

Morally, this way of speaking, or of assembling reality, seemed to me to relate very closely to what I felt was the cardinal intellectual sin, that of coming to moral conclusions. The consciousness we call "logical" works with systems of grammar and symbolic structure which presuppose conceptual conclusiveness, but obviously our motivational apparatuses have little to do with the clarity those kinds of conclusiveness seemed to me to imply. The historical plague of conceptual fanaticism which drives humans to oppress or slaughter one another I believed had its roots in that kind of incomplete realization, and I had wanted to write poems and imply existences which subverted, or at least circumvented, it.

Why the poetry I'd evolved out of these issues should have suddenly become of such little interest to me is probably beyond recapturing; my life in general then was in disarray, but whatever the reasons, unlike ten years before, when I'd analyzed my situation and thought I'd found a way to act on it, this time I groped. When I began to compose the poems I'd been looking for, I didn't even realize it. I wrote drafts of several of them, put them in a notebook, and forgot them until I came on them later during a reading, read one, and knew I had what I'd been looking for.

Trying to speak now of how I arrived at those poems is of course reconstruction, but I went through a similar procedure at the time as well, because when I did realize that I was under way in a poetry that interested me, I had to examine it to find a way to ground more surely my so far intuitive notion of it. I had to describe to myself what I'd done, in order to be sure it was valid, and that I wanted to go on with it.

I'd been studying a lot of longer lyrics: Williams's "Asphodel," Whitman, Akhmatova's "Requiem," Apollinaire's "Zone," Rimbaud's "Season in Hell," and Artaud's "Van Gogh," and I realized that I needed before anything else more space to operate in. Secondly, and more importantly, I decided that the poems I'd been writing, and many of those I'd been reading, operated by using a sort of code, what I called a "rhetoric." Poets and sophisticated readers of poetry share a fluency in this rather arcane system. That lyric poetry is all but a cipher to those who aren't regular readers is a sometimes distressing given, but it bothered me that even those who could and did read poems, seemed to do so with a consciousness which was so aware of itself as being in a unique, literary mode that what could really happen to them was severely limited. The reader came to the poem, moved into that special space off in a corner of consciousness for a time, and then resumed real life. Although I had no interest in making any sort of democratically motivated "simplification" of the poem, in making it more "accessible"—poetry is, and should be, a passionately complex experience—I felt that the elements of that complexity could become less specialized, less "poetic," than we were accustomed to.

Williams writes:

> It is difficult
> to get the news from poems
>   yet men die miserably every day
>   for lack
> of what is found there.

I thought it might be possible to make the news Williams was
speaking of somehow less difficult to get. (Williams had obviously
thought the same thing.) Much poetry takes as its lyric stance a
rather passive position in the world. The poet in the poem is
primarily a perceiver, meditator, reflector, usually of sensations,
states of being, conventionalized slices of reality. Most of life,
though, happens to us in terms of events, or at least in anticipation
of events, or reflections on them. Couldn't there be a way to deal
more directly and intensely with genuine life stuff, with the crude,
turbulent emotional storms in which even the most trivial of our
experiences seem actually to be embedded? Not "narrative,"
which implies process, progress, denouement, possible release
from tensions of expectation: the universe I found more interesting would reflect more clearly in tragedy, which is always reaching
beyond its primary anecdotes toward the deterministic, even
mythic, consciousness that presumably precedes occurrence.

I wanted to continue to construct tight lyric poems, using the
complex structures and systems of logic I'd been interested in
before, but there was another problem here. That is, those "tight"
lyrics generally work by what we call compression. Compression
implies a rigorous and admirable elision of anything not essential
to the movement and resolution of the poem, but I felt that compression had in fact often become a convention which worked
primarily by hints, and by omission. Much of the material of normal emotional activity tended simply to be left out, or at best
implied. I felt that in order to begin to get some of that material
back into the poem, I'd have to make the surface of the poem more
flexible, and more immediately germane to our more pressing life
issues. What I came to feel was that I wanted the poem to happen
to the reader without the reader's at first quite realizing it; I wanted
it to become a part of the reader's felt life in a less willed way, and
in order to do that, I came to think that the workings of the poem,
its interior, all that offers us the purely aesthetic delights of poetry,

its music, its language tensions, the patterns of figurative association we might call the subconscious of the poem, would have to
happen in terms of that surface. A poem might be able to sacrifice
a possibly crippling terseness without having to lose any of the
nondecorative tensions and intensities which are primary defini-
tions of the lyric.

It seemed clear to me that the odd sort of motions my new
poems had were just what I needed to begin to handle all these
diverse necessities. I'd been experimenting with prose poetry, as
most of the poets I knew had, but I didn't feel much interest in a
non-verse poetry. The opacity of verse, what we call its musicality,
its tendency to call attention to language's potential as abstract
sound, as a music which indicates a matrix beyond, or previous to,
itself, was too compelling to me. At the same time, though, while
I wanted my verse to continue to be grounded in the language of
ordinary usage, or more precisely, ordinary usages, the rhythmical
units I was using were more and more extended. I pushed them
farther and after a while found that I was working in a much longer
line than I would have expected to. It was a line, though, that while
still asserting itself as a generative verse element, seemed to be
able to handle more comprehensively the sort of subjects I was
interested in getting into the poems.

What those subjects are to be once the space is cleared for
them is, needless to say, the most important question. Rather than
influences, it might be more useful here to speak of assumptions,
of what the historical, cultural, and spiritual axioms are that determine and define the poetic identity. Since the French and American revolutions, since Blake, Shelley, Goethe, Wordsworth, on
through Whitman, Baudelaire, Rimbaud, Nietzsche, Yeats, Mandelstam, Eliot, Williams, to mention those who have meant most
to me, the artist moves to the center of history, not as commentator
or moralist, but as lyric participant, as the most exactly self-conscious enactor of secular and usually democratic aspiration. Art
becomes not merely an instrument of ethical suasion or of delight,
but is a redemptive resource in and of itself. Whitman defines it
most self-consciously and perhaps with the greatest degree of
premeditation: through the poem, he says, the very substance of
our spiritual consciousness is to be redeemed; we are, finally, to
become utterers ourselves, intimate and active participants in the

universe of ecstatic awareness of "Leaves of Grass."

Whether, at the end of our wretched, murderous century, and stumbling moreover into the mean, vindictive future of Reaganism, there is still enough hope on the planet to sustain such apparently exalted ambition is a difficult, possibly depressing question. If, though, the artist has had to assume a more humble, or at least a more canny, stance, the absolute minimum demand we would still seem to have to make of ourselves is that we be what Eliot calls the "socially engaged personality." There are risks in this, the risks of hopelessness, of fanaticism, of despair, but beyond that, for the poet there is a special anxiety, that which has to do with what we could call the lyric gamble. Choosing to enact one's self in the first person implies a belief that the person so evoked will have a connection to reality in ways that are spiritually essential and productive, but in fact there is no way of knowing, no matter how scrupulously one tries to oversee one's solipsisms, that the matters one is struggling with aren't ultimately idiosyncratic, having little to do with issues of any moment. We have to presume that all poetry is written with great seriousness: there doesn't seem to be any way to *decide* to inform one's work with cultural or historical significance, and it doesn't take much in the face of all this to have the sense of one's own case, and sometimes even the case of poetry itself, being trivialized or deconsecrated by events.

More and more lately, although I still come across poets I didn't know, or didn't know well enough—Milosz, for example, or Ashbery or Seidel—and even some who for one reason or another I knew about but wasn't ready to hear—Elizabeth Bishop, most notably, who dawned late for me, but explosively—I find that influence mostly consists now of going back to those who have endured for me—Williams, Whitman, Donne, Yeats, Eliot, Rilke, Lowell, Homer, Shakespeare—and studying them again. What I want from them, and what I find, beyond the ever engrossing mysteries of technique, is a reinforcement of the faith that poetry continues to be essential to what is most precious in the human, and that the sometimes painful responsibilities the life of poetry demands are not only not specious, not a burden, but an opportunity.

A Voice Speaking
to No One

PAUL ZWEIG

Paul Zweig lives in New York City, and spends several months each year at his house in southwestern France. He teaches comparative literature at Queens College. His books of prose include *The Heresy of Self-Love, The Adventurer,* and *Three Journeys: An Automythology.* His books of poetry are: *Against Emptiness* and *The Dark Side of the Earth.* At present he is completing a book on Walt Whitman, and another volume of poems.

Poetry was part of my father's self-respect. In the series of dim apartments we lived in when I was a boy, or walking on Brighton Thirteenth Street, with its sagging three-family houses, or along the wet sand at the edge of the beach, he would recite to me from memory: Wordsworth, Milton, Shakespeare. He would be wistful and remote, his voice pinched, a little thin. Sometimes he would get me to recite some favorite passage of his. I remember standing in one of our living rooms holding a table knife: "Is this a dagger that I see before me, handle toward my hand?"

In those days, nobody spoke properly except my father. My grandparents hardly knew any English at all. They spoke Yiddish, but mostly they spoke with their hands and shoulders, a shrugging dance accompanied by mouthfuls and throatfuls that said everything, but weren't quite words. Voices, yes, caresses; but all wrong. The streets, too, were wrong, and that got my father mad. Language got all twisted out there, like the cracked sidewalks, and the boys who mumbled instead of talking.

When my father recited, his voice became strangely incommunicative. Pronunciation was important; you had to let your breath out in miserly pinches. It was a voice speaking to no one.

When I heard it, I squirmed, and wanted what was wrong: the broken language of the streets; my grandparents' rumbles and shrugs; Yiddish expressions like *oi* that made my father livid.

For a while we lived with my grandparents in a second-story apartment on Brighton Thirteenth Street. The building had a backyard with a wooden shed in it that smelled of urine and dry weeds; it had a tar-paper roof. The smells of that shed are with me still, voiceless, a smell of refuge. It troubles me that I remember so little of my childhood, as if I were a man without a true past. Yet I remember the shabby refuge of that shed, and I remember what my grandparents and I shared so profoundly: together we were condemned to a guilty silence; language was almost beyond us; we were inarticulate, not too smart.

Years later, in college, I took a course with Mark Van Doren, shortly before he retired. In the large classroom, I listened to this leathery old man talk about Kafka and Cervantes. His face was a mask of wrinkles, with a wide active mouth. But it is his voice I remember: understated and slow, expressing at all times a level kindness. Although he spoke with enormous clarity, there was a kind of whisper in his voice too, as if he were humbled by the greatness, not only of Kafka and Cervantes, but of life itself, and of all of us in the room. I listened, awake down to my bones, and yet somehow troubled. Something stirred me here. Then, one day, I knew what it was. Never before had I encountered an elderly person who spoke English so well. This stiff angular man, wise with the knowledge of centuries, combined qualities which, I now saw, had always been separate in my mind: on the one hand, the mysterious benevolence of the elderly, which I associated with my grandparents; on the other, the mastery of language and superior thought, which I associated with my father. I had known that kindness and love were unintelligent, wrong, inescapable. They were qualities of the flesh; of the face speaking no language; of the heavy body and wild wiry hair of my grandmother.

The old people I grew up with stumbled through English, or mashed it along with Yiddish into a gamy idiom that I understood, while observing it distantly as an intolerant spectator. In the warm weather, they sat on folding chairs in front of the apartment buildings, or lined up along the boardwalk facing the ocean, with silver reflectors held up to their faces. These old people disturbed me.

They seemed partly outside of life. Their black coats and somber dresses expressed a permanent sadness. This was, I know now, a shadow of the death camps. Unspoken horrors were hiding in their faces: unbelieving fear, rumors of a world destroyed. Now they lit candles on Friday nights for their myriad dead, and sat in the long sunlight on the boardwalk. Among them was my grandfather, tall, broodingly physical, a former teamster, a former plasterer and contractor, now a tireless player of pinochle. He rasped, scorched, and thundered; he complained and dreamed. He was a stubborn, solitary man. The bristling sandpaper of his beard hurt me when I kissed him.

My other grandparents—my father's parents—owned a laundry in the Williamsburg section of Brooklyn, and we visited them almost every week. Of my father's mother I remember a braided swirl of white hair, wire-rimmed glasses, the smell of hot soup mingled with hot starched sheets. Of my grandfather, I remember the watery light on his unshaven face, a week after my grandmother died. His socks were rolled down to his ankles. He sat heavily on a straight chair, half turned to the window. His grief frightened me, it was so unspeaking. His lips moved, and I could tell he was saying something in Yiddish, a low, confused murmur. Then he hugged me, almost absentmindedly. Soon after, he died of heart failure. His legs swelled, I overheard my parents say, and I thought of the fat rolls of socks around his ankles.

Before finishing college, I took several courses with Mark Van Doren. I remember thinking: if I had to be someone else, I would like to be this man. The idea startled me, yet I thought it often, like a repeating dream. Deceptively, casually, my life was changing, and this thought belonged to the change. I had begun to lose interest in my engineering studies, and to write poetry. Perhaps the wrenching changes in one's life are like that: not willed, or even conscious. Half a lifetime later, I don't know which is more mysterious to me: the piecemeal awakening of those years, or the somnambulism which preceded it.

Van Doren's voice, whispered, thrillingly clear, brought together parts of my life which had never been truly related. Was this the detonating mixture? The wearing away of inner walls, spilling together a power of blessing I had associated with the elderly, in all their speechless incorrectness, and the world of language, Milton, Shakespeare, Wordsworth, shadows ballooning above me in a heaven of pinched voices, speaking to no one: my father's voice.

Since then I have whored much after strange voices, and often it has seemed that I had no voice of my own: only precisions, a patchwork of echoes; words lifted beyond what I could know. For ten years I lived in France and spoke French, even wrote in French. Like an animal to whom smells are a kind of speech, I sniffed out voices, their Gallic vowels and pouting consonants; their sleeves of a purer sound. French, to me, was the language of the angels. It was cold and stratospheric, entirely meaningful, resistant to chaos, not hugging, rasping, and kind. It was language wholly clothed, and I lived with my clothes on.

Voices come from underneath the mind, produced by a spongy bellows attached to a distiller's tubing. Teeth, tongue, and throat tease the outrushing air into a variety of sounds which, like the face they emerge from, exist at the friable edge where matter becomes spirit. Like your face, your voice reveals you as you are, at ground level. Van Doren's whispered Protestant clarity, the wintery anti-Yiddish of the French: these were voices I lusted after, and impersonated.

In 1966 I returned to America, with a handful of poems under my arms, and the first draft of a treatise on the exhibitionistic coy soul of Western civilization, entitled *The Heresy of Self-Love*. This was my first attempt at autobiography, concealed and mediated by vast subject matter. I wrote about Gnostic fantasies and medieval mystics; Rousseau, Kierkegaard, and much in between, in order to expose a shipwrecked, insular soul: Narcissus peering into his pond, a self-ignoring, lone soul, not knowing what everyone else knows—the identity of the face in the water; not knowing himself.

I came back because, after a decade away, something had been lost: syntax, sentence structure. I could still discuss all the higher matters in English, but I ate, shit, fucked, and wept in French. The slaty drizzle of winter days; the soul-scorching of a dead marriage; the names and feel of ripe cheeses, coarse wines; the internalized neural map of the city's narrow streets, including one-way passages, unlikely shortcuts, and the timing of red lights: all in French.

Language, like Freud's diagram of the psyche, is a communicating vase of light and dark, high and low. You are boiling with love or rage when, suddenly, a blunt voice fights past your lips, as the Brooklyn of dull consonants and barked rhythms comes briefly alive, like the dormant monster in a Japanese horror film. This is necessary. Without it, you will turn into some bloodless and recessive Mallarmé, or worse: a mere homeless spreading of wings; a ghost of talk.

There is often an embarrassing side to influence. For a while, your personality seems ready to flow into a new mold. You are gripped by a mood of reckless, even indecent experiment. You begin to laugh like another person, and speak like him. You write spontaneously, and they are his images, his unmistakable turns of phrase. Such moments of influence are like gay little suicides, from which we recover, bearing permanent traces of another's life. We are a mosaic of vanished others who have blurred into our voices, and haunt our laughter. A population of ghosts speaks through us. This may be what the Sufis mean by "the friend": the layered otherness which inhabits us, and is ourselves.

A year or so before leaving Paris, I met the poet Robert Bly, in a bookstore across the river from Notre Dame. Robert was a big, very American man, from Minnesota, as far from the ocean as you could be, probably in the world. It was a country of flat fields, the houses shielded by patches of cottonwood from the winds that drove farmers wild in the pioneering days, not so long before. When I went out to visit with him, a year or two later, he seemed to be a man of that place: wintry and large, talkative as solitary men often are, yet curiously impersonal.

He seemed beyond embarrassment as he strode about Paris, taking up half the sidewalk. I had never been friends with a poet before, and there was so much to say. Above all, there was the awkward pleasure of speaking English again; of listening to Robert's Midwestern voice, a little nasal and brutal, almost a preacher's voice. Robert's poems surprised me, they seemed so flat, so minimal. Yet, as I saw much later, they stood for a forceful idea. Because America had become an imperial monster, the poet could save himself only by shrinking his focus to what is small and forgotten: shadows of fence posts, heaps of used tires in dumps, old cars, old horses. Because America spoke loud, the poet had to speak softly; his voice had to merge with the ordinary, become itself ordinary, almost unnoticeable. Robert's model was the classical

Chinese poets, especially Tu Fu and Li Po, who had also lived in an unimaginably vast empire, and written about the small perception, the uninjured detail.

Although I had reservations about Robert's poetry, I found it curiously inescapable. Its willed rhythms, even its clumsiness, seemed to me signs of a deeper seriousness, as if the poems originated in a layer of truth where even language couldn't be trusted. A poetry too serious even for language? I liked that idea. It stood for an adventure that transcended practical effort; something I could carry around with me, regardless of an audience, regardless even of actual poems. Was the idea Robert's or mine? Mine, probably. It reflects my tenuous anchoring in language at the time; my distance—by now a decade long—from the safekeeping of English; indeed, of any completely known language. When I wrote in English, my sentences tilted and went awry. Even speaking it required a pressure of thought to keep my words from sliding into dead ends. My French, too, was keyed up, tightened by an effort of will, like walking on a high wire. I did it well, but it wasn't the same as running free, unconscious of where the ground is. Normally human beings don't have to worry; no matter where they fall, it will be inside a voice. I found myself skirting ghostliness, a thin silence running alongside all my words.

Robert helped me make my first steps back toward America, toward the effortless language he imitated badly but understood well; a language close to the ground, close to the uninjured life of things.

Others, too, have imparted to me a voice, an idea, or more likely the form of an idea, a slope of the mind.

Lionel Trilling, whom I knew briefly when I taught at Columbia University in the late 1960s, was to me, above all, a strongly aged face. He was soft-spoken, with a hesitation in his voice, which I saw as his response to aging. In some way he felt diminished, and refused to hide this from himself. I loved his face, I think, even more than his writing. As he sat in his book-cluttered office, softened by a haze of cigarette smoke, he embodied a brink of darkness which, previously, had been unimaginable to me: an impersonal laboring of the flesh—old age, death—during which a man becomes sharpened with thought.

Among poets, there has been Galway Kinnell's unruly appetite for language, combined with a catlike tendency to approach rather than back away from what disturbs him most. C. K. Williams's obsession with language rhythms; his seemingly endless curiosity about poets who are often remarkably different from him, but whose work discloses some problem of craft importantly resolved. Czeslaw Milosz's understated voice, his slight physical clumsiness, a feeling of modest self-sufficiency, all focused into a style of writing I can almost hear: casual rhythms, a wiry clarity of line, as if the poems were structures of intellect that were poetic not because of language effects but because of their uncanny precision.

Half a dozen years ago, Czeslaw read some poems of mine, and told me he felt they lacked a calligraphic quality. Calligraphic suggested to me a pictorial effect associated with actual penmanship. It is characteristic of Czeslaw that he meant something less mysterious than this. The calligrapher, he told me a year or so later, creates a unified effect with apparently effortless strokes of the pen. Calligraphic referred to a craft so strenuously learned that it had become impulse.

Perhaps the most important influence of all, however, was of an entirely different sort. In 1974 I met a Shaivite spiritual master, Swami Muktananda, while he was visiting New York from his ashram near Bombay, in India. Muktananda didn't speak English, and his scorched, rasping voice, full of rolls and trills, fascinated me. I went to see him often during the months and years that followed. It was his voice that drew me: guttural and low, sometimes rising to a peak of anger, sometimes laughing or singing. When he came into a room, I often thought of my grandmother. He even had a large belly, and curiously feminine breasts, like a Buddha; or rather he was loving and harsh, inarticulate yet thrillingly clear, like my grandfather, grandmother, and father, all made right, and making me right.

As a child, I was most alert and happy when I was alone. Probably because of this, my earliest memories are a chaplet of solitary moments, as I walked along the wide empty beach toward Coney Island, or clambered over a concrete esplanade that a hurricane had broken into slabs, with bent steel rods poking out of them, like the legs of crawlers. I remember the mica gleams of the rocks, and the hard glaring track of sunlight over the water; here and there, the white chips of sailboats; a low line of houses across the bay on a spit of land which my friends thought was Europe, and I knew (curiously ashamed of my certainty) was Rockaway. I myself was absent from these moments. There was only the ocean, or else a grove of tall pine trees laddered with horizontal branches, on a farm my grandparents had bought in upstate New York; later, the Paris streets which my aloneness had transformed into a kind of script, so vivid and tangible I could almost read it.

With the passage of time, these moments have become like seeds scattered over a gray ground. At times, they seem almost supernatural: the light inhabiting them is not ordinary; their details seem etched with a fine tool. There are times when I wonder why I didn't become a painter instead of a writer. Yet these wrenching miniatures are creations of memory, spiritualized by repetition. They are framed by voices which unaccountably have fallen still for a moment, but are about to begin again. I am one of the voices, jostling, running on, curious about the lighthearted durability of these intervals when, in my own absence, a whole perception sprang awake, like a work of art.

As a boy I had a passion for stories about desert islands. On Saturday afternoons, my father and I would visit the used-book stores on Fourth Avenue, below Fourteenth Street, and I would comb through the bins of old books, looking for tales of castaways: *Robinson Crusoe, Swiss Family Robinson,* and a series of sequels to it written by Jules Verne. Captain Nemo almost qualified, as did Huck Finn hiding out on an island in the Mississippi, and a handful of other titles I can no longer remember. It is not an especially rich genre, yet it thrilled me with feelings of intense longing. No doubt my seeds of memory were the model: there, no voices were necessary, or even possible; they were the opposite of language, yet a source of language too, for all of meaning was wrapped up in them. The monologue that accompanied them as if offstage, in a gray margin, was Robinson Crusoe's diary.

Sitting with Swami Muktananda, I have often been alert and happy in just the same way. His rumbling grandmotherly voice has made me feel like a child again, curiously alone, but speaking now, possessing a voice.

In the eight years that have passed since I met Muktananda,

I have visited him twice in India. I have meditated sporadically, and chanted Sanskrit hymns. More often, I have done neither. Yet something has changed. A layer of imperceptible fright has begun to thaw. I had never known it was there, curiously dimming and gray: a hood of anxiety, of self-judgment; it is going. Call it courage, a greater willingness to let feelings take their course; meaning, I suppose, a willingness to take the consequence of those feelings. My enemy voices have begun to converge: father and grandparents; glistering vocabularies, and scuffed cries. Muktananda has taught me the value of a persistent, uneventful labor: to bring language and feeling together; to surrender to that sliding adventure of the voice, which speaks because it is not complete; because Robinson Crusoe's "silent life" is a philosophical joke, the fantasy of a loveless man.

A man's life cannot be silent; living is speaking, dying too is speaking. My voice calls other voices, creates weavings that are not so much exchanges of sense as they are a form of touch. We make love with our voices. As a writer, I have sought this quality of touch. I have sought to make my words and their inarticulate shadow partners, their gestures of feeling and knowledge, dance together in one gliding hug, neither leaving the other behind.

Walt Whitman wrote about following the human voice as irresistibly as the tide follows the moon. Whitman's image is true. In the life of feelings, the voice is like the force of gravity: it acts from afar; it is irresistible; it holds everything human together. Because of it, we see the unfolding of laws. Because of it, all the paradoxes of intimacy in distance, love in separateness, are possible. This is elementary, yet I never noticed it was true. I notice it now, with the embarrassed delight of belated knowledge.